ANNE CARSON

UNDER DISCUSSION
Marilyn Hacker amd Kazim Ali, General Editors
Donald Hall, Founding Editor

Volumes in the Under Discussion series collect reviews and essays about individual poets. The series is concerned with contemporary American and English poets about whom the consensus has not yet been formed and the final vote has not been taken. Titles in the series include:

Anne Carson

Ecstatic Lyre

Joshua Marie Wilkinson, editor

UNIVERSITY OF MICHIGAN PRESS

Ann Arbor

Published in the United States of America by the
University of Michigan Press
Manufactured in the United States of America
⊗ Printed on acid-free paper

2018   2017   2016   2015   4   3   2   1

A CIP catalog record for this book is available from the British Library.

ISBN 978–0-472–07253–8 (hardcover)
ISBN 978-0-472-05253-0 (paper)
ISBN 978–0-472–12090–1 (e-book)

for Sri Wilson

Contents

Acknowledgments

I'd like to express my gratitude to University of Michigan Press staff and editors: Aaron McCollough, Susan Cronin, Marcia LaBrenz, and Kazim Ali among others who shepherded this book, along with the copyeditor, Richard Isomaki. I thank all the contributors for their essays. Many conversations helped guide me toward what this book was to become, and I thank Marjorie Perloff and Stephen Burt for their encouragement from the beginning. I'd like to thank all the poets (friends and strangers alike) who attempted a contribution; I now understand that difficulty, and I'm grateful to you. Elizabeth Willis's excellent anthology *Radical Vernacular: Lorine Niedecker and the Poetics of Place* was a model for this book, and I thank her for editing it. I thank the University of Arizona (and support of my amazing colleagues) for giving me time to work on this book. To Solan Jensen, David Rubin, Noah Eli Gordon, and Jessica Langan-Peck: all love.

Joshua Marie Wilkinson
Tucson, Arizona

JOSHUA MARIE WILKINSON

Introduction

Most writers fit neatly into a genre or two; a few writers seem to
exemplify the genres they work in; a small number really bend or
blend genres in order to create new kinds of texts and performances;
and still fewer seem to obliterate genre itself, from the inside out. I
would place Anne Carson's work in that latter, freakish category, for
what it's worth. In terms of content, rarely has an author so re-
thought gender, marriage, sexuality, family, love, death, religion, and
divorce from the fragment through the drama and all the way out
to comics, dance, video, performance, and back to the materiality of
the codex itself with *Nox*. In fact, "rethought" does not begin to
describe what "The Glass Essay" does to relationships; what *Autobi-
ography of Red* has to say about coming of age, abuse, and falling in
love; or what Carson's work on Sappho's fragments has done for
desire and textuality. Carson's concept of *being* itself is transformed
into something much more radically animal, other, peculiar, and in
perpetual flux.

Perhaps one of the salient things about genre is that a work of
literature *itself* cannot tell you which genre it belongs to. If some-
thing that looks and sounds like a poem calls itself a play or a novel,
we think we know better than to be fooled. Genre is always some-
thing added after the fact—a category, a likeness, a way of branding,
a way of indicating which shelf to put the book on, even a hybrid
label to argue about.

Let's take one of Anne Carson's best-known works: "My first
book of poems, *Short Talks*, was initially a set of drawings with just
titles. Then I expanded the titles a bit and then gradually realized
nobody was interested in the drawings, so I just took the titles off
and then they were pellets of a lecture."[1] Note that it is Carson
herself who calls them "poems" as well as "pellets of a lecture." In-
deed they are "talks" in all that word implies: concise, written to be
spoken, informal. You probably know that they also appear in *Plain-
water: Essays and Poetry* in 1995 (and that book does not indicate
which camp they fit). Curiously, they also appear in *The Anchor*

Book of New American Short Stories edited by Ben Marcus as well as in *Best American Essays,* edited by Susan Sontag. It's hard to imagine another first book of *poems* doing so much cross-genre pollinating. But it's even harder to imagine another debut collection of poetry selected to *exemplify* other genres like short stories and essays. An auspicious beginning, at age forty-two, does not begin to describe what would follow.

I'm not a scholar of Anne Carson's books or translations, and I am nothing approaching an expert on Carson's oeuvre. I came to Anne Carson's work rather typically: I was an undergraduate student in my home state of Washington when my English professor, Bruce Beasley, invited me into a graduate poetry course where, among other books, we read *Autobiography of Red.* If you are reading this introduction, it's an experience you might have had with "The Glass Essay" or *Short Talks* or "The Anthropology of Water." It was charged, yes. It blew me away, yes. But it had an exacting cost: every other thing I was reading at the time seemed sallow in its wake. Nothing seemed as precise, on the one hand, or as crazed, on the other.

Discovering Anne Carson's books also made me do another good thing: destroy the poems I was working on. Her work made me a better critic and reader, but her books—and by then I was devouring *Plainwater, Men in the Off Hours,* and *Eros the Bittersweet* simultaneously—seemed to suggest that criticism, reading, writing, visual art, philosophy, drama, poetry, and prose all seemed *of a piece.* And further: her work seemed to say we are fools to put all these banal categories on the work itself.

In a way, Carson's work is a model for revisiting what's long gone: Sappho, Simonides, Sophokles, Euripides, Gertrude Stein, Catullus, Kafka, the Brontës, and so on. What's particular about her approach—whether in *If Not, Winter: Fragments of Sappho* or *Economy of the Unlost* or *The Beauty of the Husband*—is that her writing doesn't seem like a greatest hits distillation of "Here's what I learned as a scholar of Celan or Keats or Weil." Nor does her criticism ever seem bent on creating a newfangled category for one of the old masters. Instead, Carson adumbrates hundreds of new entry points to the past by getting disarmingly close to the language at hand: etymologies, contexts, myriad meanings, and implications radiating out. Further, each new ingress seems well lit, alive, pulsing with mystery and curiosity. Not just *refreshed,* but simply back from the dead and breathing.

cross and genre

In my first or second year as an English professor in Chicago, I was given the charge of teaching a course called Literature from a Writer's Perspective. In my MLA interview in a Philadelphia hotel room, I asked: "What sort of course is it?" "Well, it's designed for English majors with an interest in creative writing; and you can teach whatever you like. The enrollment is capped at thirty-five." Now, thirty-five is an awkward number of persons: too big to be a workshop or intimate seminar, but a little small to be a straight-up lecture. The goal was to try to orient all these English majors with different approaches to genre. A lightbulb went off, and I decided I'd run it as a course on Anne Carson's works, and taught eight of her books. Why?

With Anne Carson, you get just about every genre imaginable—and then some: her work covers lyric, epic, and dramatic poetry; the fragment, epitaph, and elegy; her translations cover ancient comedy and tragic drama; and her essays are revelatory in their capaciousness and brevity from the scholarly to the short talks to her leaping criticism (like her essay on sleep) to her "fictional essay in 29 tangos," the subtitle to *The Beauty of the Husband*. In short, Anne Carson seems to invent a form for each of her works. Yet, however oddly, her apparent *freedom* to create, fuse, and otherwise repurpose extant genres seems to have everything to do with her *fidelity* to texts ancient and modern.

What Carson says about her translation work is telling about the kind of creator she is:

> A translation usually has a specific purpose. If it is a commission for a certain theatre director or company, the translator will be given parameters as to what kind of translation is required. If it's a free adventure of creativity, the translator will have their own attitude to that. I generally try to work first and most attentively out of the grammar, syntax, allusions of the original while keeping the language alive in a way that interests me, then later crazy it up if that seems appropriate. I put Hegel and Brecht into *Antigonick* because those readings of her are part of how she lives in our minds. I put Beckett in because Antigone would have liked him.[2]

One gets the sense from her work that there is a copious loyalty to the text: its materials, its language, its contexts, its critical histories, its available meanings. But counter to that, her work to keep "the language alive in a way that interests me, then later crazy it up" seems to belie the very fidelity she seems to exact on herself: I'd say that that contradiction is at the heart of all Carson's work.

Yet, as tempting as it is to find some through line from *Eros the Bittersweet* to *Red Doc >*, she is keen to warn us off that trail. When Will Aitken asks her, at an interview's close in *The Paris Review*, if Carson would like to add anything else, she replies: "I'd like to add a piece of wisdom from Gertrude Stein: 'Act so there is no use in a center.' That's what I try to teach my students."[3]

That sentence haunted me as I began to think about a collection of essays on Carson's work. Carson told Aitken: "I write to find out what I think about something."[4] In that spirit, I asked some writers whom I admire to write on things I love in order to find out what else we might see and learn from Anne Carson. And I began to gather pieces from a number of dissimilar writers who all recognized the influence and import of Carson's work on their own. Like Peter Gizzi and Bradford Morrow's terrific "John Ashbery Tribute," in an issue of *Conjunctions*, where each contributing writer tackled a single book of Ashbery's, I sought essays reflecting the value of a Carson's books to these writers. Jessica Fisher's broader essay opening this collection is the welcome exception here. And, of course, there is overlap, digression, and strangeness—as you might expect in a book about Anne Carson.

It should come as no surprise that the kinds of writers who responded to my call for essays on Carson's works have a thing or two in common: many of them are juggernauts of productivity, in multigenre writing, editing, translation, teaching, scholarship, and endeavors beyond. Perhaps it's now the norm to see a poet like Ander Monson also publishing fiction, nonfiction, unusual objects, and editing journals and anthologies. Graham Foust is also a translator of French and German poetry, and has published essays on topics ranging from Emily Dickinson to Willie Nelson lyrics. Dan Beachy-Quick is quickly becoming as known for his lyric essays, a recent novel, and collaborations with artists as he is for his poetry. Besides Julie Carr's five or six books of poetry—all authored after she retired from a decade of being a dancer in New York—she's published a recent study of Victorian poets, and created a bookshop/art space in Denver with Tim Roberts called Counterpath, where they run their poetry press, raise three children, and . . . you get the picture.

I suppose that one can take a cynical view of this: to survive in academia (just about all of us here teach to make rent), many of us have to manage many skill sets. But, honestly, I've never met any-

4

body who edited an anthology, published in three genres, or translated a dead poet's work because their department chair was hassling them to do so. Perhaps it happens, but I seriously doubt it. I'm given to think that we're editors, publishers, writers, teachers, and translators out of love for the work. And I add all this to say that—beyond her genre-bending and genre-obliterating books—Anne Carson, to my mind, is the model for this Venn diagram type of engagement. Nothing seems out of keeping with Carson's interests. For us, she's been more than an author to emulate, but a writer whose boundless activities and interests inspired us to develop *all* of the types of work we love—in the literary arts and beyond.

From these disparate writers, I hoped that myriad approaches to thinking about Carson's work would arrive, from critical and scholarly to personal and lyrical. They did. And as I could see how different they were one from the other I became gradually more nervous, if more excited. But a coherent, overly similar set of approaches to Anne Carson of all writers would have been as banal as it sounds. And I began to trust that this book would form a constellation of approaches to Carson's books, in the form of appreciations, readings, investigations, experiments, and performances themselves. There is at least one essay here on every book by Anne Carson to date. It will hardly surprise her closest readers that both *Nay Rather* (her rendering of Ibykos and meditation on translation) as well as *The Albertine Workout* (a reading Proust, among others) have appeared since these essays have been finalized. Indeed, there is no catching up to Anne Carson's voluminousness.

Rather than attempt to re-characterize each piece in a thesis sentence or three, I'll draw on the essays themselves to give a sense of the variety and intelligence from phrases and questions that appear in the essays that follow. That it's difficult to fathom how all these excerpts could be discussing the same author is, I hope, a credit to the contributors' unique reverence for Anne Carson's protean writings:

Survival is not what we think.—Brian Teare on "The Glass Essay"

What is this monster the poem creates?—Dan Beachy-Quick on *Eros, The Bittersweet*

Desire here is robust, brutal, and addictive.—Andrea Rexilius on *The Beauty of the Husband*

To talk about Anne Carson is to talk about myth.—Lily Hoang on *Red Doc>*

Carson herself, not Stesichoros, is the "reticent volcano" . . . who seethes, with buckled lips.—Bruce Beasley on *Autobiography of Red*

. . . to find the dry horror in the everyday, the nearly funny in the dreadful.—Kazim Ali on *Grief Lessons*

We are to blame for this suffering; however, it began at the beginning of us: at the beginning of creation itself.—J. Michael Martinez on *Wonderwater*

Carson locates an empathy/yearning we did not know we possess, by inventing it.—Harmony Holiday on *Autobiography of Red*

Reading, like loving, is a bittersweet endeavor.—Martin Corless-Smith on *Eros, The Bittersweet*

How can one tarry with the contested term *lyric* without also turning in earnest to its earliest variations?—Angela Hume on *An Oresteia*

Her brilliance as a writer is to show us the simultaneous proximity and distance between things, and in this sense she is always a translator—that is, one who carries something across a distance.—Jessica Fisher on Carson generally

I read, tasting that curious blend of pathos and sardonicism that marks so much of Carson's work.—Julie Carr on *Glass, Irony and God*

I was ill and could not attend, so I stayed home and YouTubed Anne's reading while Prokofiev went on making a racket.—Timothy Liu on *Short Talks*

Carson holds open textual space to the praise of thought and song that otherwise might be lost.—Karla Kelsey on *Economy of the Unlost*

There is tension between knowing and thinking.—Kristi Maxwell on *Plainwater*

In this sense, every translation has the quality of ventriloquoy.—John Melillo on *If Not, Winter: Fragments of Sappho*

Is a question a question or just an opening for your consideration? Is it us opening and considering . . . ?—Ander Monson on *Nox*

As with any good joke, the punch line holds: from time immemorial to time memorialized, we *enjoy* being little tin gods.—Vanessa Place on *Antigonick*

The lovers and soldiers are blind with the rigor of their collective desire.—Christine Hume on *Plainwater*

Surely this word [lyre], too, fits with the pattern that could be ascribed to the others: a vehicle for song; music as elixir of desire.—Elizabeth Robinson on *If Not, Winter: Fragments of Sappho*

Anne Carson is a poet familiar with language rot and its tragic effects.—Erika L. Weiberg on *Grief Lessons*

Overriding the normative terminal mark, a mute temporal mutant stays onstage, restless and recalcitrant, as formal convention collapses beneath a phenomenon that cannot state its name.—Andrew Zawacki on *Antigonick*

What are the limits of the human "creature" itself? Carson asks. Is it possible to confront those limits, or even move beyond them?—Johanna Skibsrud on *Decreation*

Anne Carson's *Men in the Off Hours* always suggests the limits and destructive agenda of patriarchal time.—Richard Greenfield on *Men in the Off Hours*

By setting her discussion of the radical self-externalization of these three women as an opera, Carson explains the wealthy surface that inner poverty causes.—Cole Swensen on *Decreation*

Her verisimilitude is shot through, however, with a postmodern despair over capturing the "essence" of truth in words.—Virginia Konchan on *Plainwater*

There a note on the wall was her handwriting tacked by his desk—desire, a spindle, if I remember correctly.—Douglas A. Martin on *Men in the Off Hours*

What matters is remembering to pause and examine the invention in your hands. To stand very close and then at a greater distance.—Bianca Stone on *Antigonick*

I'm also tempted to say that it leaves me wanting, but what I mean is that one of its pleasures is its lack of delusions of completeness.—Graham Foust on *Economy of the Unlost*

I first saw Anne Carson read in Seattle, in the late 1990s. I was a college student, and it was one of the very few readings I've attended with my mother. I think *The Beauty of the Husband* had just come out, and Carson wasn't quite as poetry famous as she is now. Her easy quiet at the podium—and her signature laconic, dry humor and wit—drew the audience in. It wasn't that she had us all eating out of her hand (though she did), it was that the audience seemed simultaneously stupefied and exuberant to hear somebody say a bunch of words. Now it seems I have corralled a group of writers together to produce a bunch of words—on Carson. Reluctantly, I wrote to Carson recently to let her know of this collection, and thereby implicitly request her blessing on it. She responded: "JMW / thank you for warning me. / I am indeed overwhelmed." In the intervening months, Peter Streckfus wrote to say that he had conducted an interview with Carson herself some years back that never saw the light of day. The two of them revisited it together, and I'm grateful to include it here as a kind of coda to the book.

And, now that I've read these essays, I am overwhelmed as well. What Carson says of reading, I hope to be true of these essays also: "if you read Virginia Woolf or George Eliot, there's a fragrance of understanding you come away with—this smell in your head of having gone through something that you understood with the people in the story."[5] I hope you, too, will get a little overwhelmed by that "fragrance of understanding."

Works Cited

Carson, Anne. "Unwriting the Books of the Dead: Anne Carson and Robert Currie on Translation, Collaboration, and History." Interview by Andrew David King. *Kenyon Review*, October 6, 2012. <http://www.kenyonreview.org/2012/10/anne-carson-robert-currie-interview/>.

Carson, Anne. "The Art of Poetry, No. 88." Interview by Will Aitken. *Paris Review*, No. 171, Fall 2004. <http://www.theparisreview.org/interviews/5420/the-art-of-poetry-no-88-anne-carson7gt.

Notes

1. Anne Carson, "The Art of Poetry, No. 88," interview by Will Aitken, Paris Review, Fall 2004, 204, http://www.theparisreview.org/interviews/5420/the-art-of-poetry-no-88-anne-carson7gt.

2. Anne Carson, "Unwriting the Books of the Dead: Anne Carson and Robert Currie on Translation, Collaboration, and History," interview by Andrew David King, Kenyon Review, October 6, 2012, http://www.kenyonreview.org/2012/10/anne-carson-robert-currie-interview/.

3. Carson, "Art of Poetry," 226.

4. Ibid., 205.

5. Ibid., 194.

JESSICA FISHER

Anne Carson's Stereoscopic Poetics

Of all the boundaries Anne Carson works to dissolve in her allusive, intergeneric work, the most trenchant is that of the self. A strong line of philosophical inquiry runs through her writing, which frequently addresses the startling question she poses in *Glass, Irony and God*: "I wonder," she asks, "if there might not be . . . another kind of human self than one based on dissociation of inside and outside. Or, indeed, another human essence than self."[1] Carson explores the problems with the self most deeply in *Decreation*, a term she borrows from Simone Weil to indicate "an undoing of the creature in us—that creature enclosed in self and defined by self."[2] While the mystics Carson describes find themselves in the painful position of being "at the crossing-point of a contradiction" and literalize the deprivation of the self in choosing death, Carson prefers a dialectical approach: she argues instead that "to undo the self one must move through the self, to the very inside of its definition."[3] Carson's writing therefore privileges moments like ecstasy, a state of "decreation" that she describes as resulting from "being up against something so other that it bounces you out of yourself to a place where, nonetheless, you are still in yourself; there's a connection to yourself as another."[4]

Carson has long maintained that desire is that very human essence that might supplant *self*. And yet desire is an odd sort of *essence*, since this "foundation of being" (*OED*) neither stems from nor is confined within the individual, although it "presume[s] to exist in human forms." Instead, Carson figures desire as a "vast, absolute and oddly *general* . . . liquid washing through the universe, filling puny vessels here and there."[5] She frequently imagines the erotic charge between people as water being poured between vessels: when Geryon meets Herakles in *Autobiography of Red*, for example, she writes, "The world poured back and forth between their eyes once or twice."[6] Or, in "On the Mona Lisa," she imagines that when Leonardo painted his model "he poured his question into her, as you pour water from one vessel into another, and it poured back."[7] That Carson figures Leonardo's desire as his question is not accidental. Indeed, to *want* and to *wonder* are parallel actions for her, as she makes clear in *Eros the Bittersweet*, where she posits a "resemblance between the way Eros acts in the mind of a lover and the way knowing acts in the mind of a thinker."[8] And yet imagination, and not possession, is the end point of desire—like one of Zeno's "famous paradoxes," desire is "a reach that never quite arrives," since it "folds the beloved object out of sight into a mystery, into a blind point where it can float known and unknown, actual and possible, near and far."[9]

Carson's understanding of desire is fundamentally Lacanian—she describes it as "organized around a radiant absence" and as having lack as "its animating, fundamental constituent."[10] Crucially, the blindness desire inscribes is not only at the point of the occluded object, but also within the subject, since the act of "reaching for an object that proves to be outside and beyond himself" shows the lover or thinker the limits of self: "From a new vantage point, which we might call self-consciousness," she writes, "he looks back and sees a hole."[11] The "experience of the self as self" is therefore not, as one might assume, an experience of self-presence.[12] Rather, Carson writes, "When we try to think about our own thinking, as when we try to feel our own desire, we find ourselves located at a blind point." This is, as she explains, a reiteration of Michel Foucault's argument about the Velasquez painting *Las Meninas*: "he calls the blind point 'that essential hiding place into which our gaze disappears from ourselves.'" Because "the vacancy recorded by the mirror . . . is our own," the act of seeking our self-recognition—whether through reflection in the mirror or by the other, or through the attempt to "think thought or desire desire"—therefore only inscribes *within* us the central absence that is the cause of desire's unceasing circuit.[13]

Carson's reenactment of the drama of the vanishing point is only one of the visual metaphors she uses to describe the split subject. Throughout her work, Carson adopts a related aesthetics of disjunction, which above all serves to show the fundamentally disruptive "underside of consciousness" that overturns theories of psychic and narrative unity.[14] Indeed, Carson has been continually obsessed with forms of blocked visual perception, primarily with stereoscopy, which serves as a figure for desire's triangulated structure: "The difference between what is and what could be is visible," she writes. "The ideal is projected upon a screen of the actual, in a kind of stereoscopy."[15] Although stereoscopy, like binocular vision itself, is meant to ensure the perception of three-dimensional reality through what is usually an occluded optical illusion, Carson instead trains our focus on the "edge between two images that cannot merge in a single focus because they do not derive from the same level of reality." The aim of the imagination, as she writes in this fascinating passage, is "to know both, keeping the difference visible," thereby providing "the reader that moment of emotional and cognitive stereoscopy which is also the experience of the desiring lover."

Carson's expressed desire for "sustained incongruence"[16] helps to explain her predilection for intergeneric works, her commitment to translation and philosophical speculation, her love of figurative language, her penchant for yoking together an immense range of sources, and her tendency to "crash" her subjects "into other lives."[17] Her brilliance as a writer is to show us the simultaneous proximity and distance between things, and in this sense she is always a translator—that is, one who carries something across a distance. Indeed, in a passage where she considers the "similes of the *Iliad*," she argues that poetry's task is "to translate our mind" by drawing the lineaments of "a likeness" between incommensurate things. Here, Carson is clearly drawing on the fact that etymologically speaking, *translation* and *metaphor* share the same root (from *ferre*, "to bear"). Homer's comparisons, she suggests, "build a parallel world," a contraption for sight not unlike the stereoscope, "with eyeholes through the war to gaze at it. You can look away from Troy, from the heap of broken toys, the soiled bandages and smell of cordite, to a woman staining ivory in a workroom." Carson is not only interested in creating the conditions whereby we might account for the "strange similar things [that] go on all at one time" within the material world;[18] she also "likes to finger the border between nothing and something," between "the realms of sleep and waking, life and death."[19] In an astounding passage, she describes the poet's role in figuring this relation of the physical to the metaphysical, once again defining poetry according to its function, rather than its form:

> "*If to you the invisible were visible*," says Simonides to his audience, "you would see God." But we do not see God and a different kind of visibility has to be created by the watchful poet. The poet's metaphorical activity puts him in a contrafactual relation to the world of other people and ordinary speech. He does not

seek to refute or replace that world but merely to indicate its lacunae, by positioning alongside the world of things that we see an uncanny protasis of things invisible, though no less real. Without poetry these two worlds would remain unconscious of one another.[20]

While poetry cannot show the invisible, it can suggest its existence by drawing our attention to the holes in being, thereby further revealing "the absent presence of desire."[21] In a recent essay, Carson describes finding such lacunae in the metaphysical silence of an untranslatable word, in the Rembrandt self-portrait where the eyes have no sockets, and in the haunting line from Hölderlin, "Often enough I tried language, often enough I tried song, but they didn't hear you." "Something about the way the pronouns in this sentence come face to face with themselves reminds me of Rembrandt's eyes," Carson explains. "Those socketless eyes are certainly not blind." Instead, "seeing is entering Rembrandt's eyes from the back. What his look sends forward, in our direction, is deep silence."[22]

The struggle to find aesthetic forms equal to the task of figuring absence animates all of Carson's work, and is particularly charged when she turns her attention to death. In "Appendix to Ordinary Time," for example, she describes her fascination with the deletions in Virginia Woolf's journals and manuscripts, choosing one of them for her mother's epitaph. "Crossouts," Carson explains, "are like death: by a simple stroke—all is lost, yet still there. For death *although utterly unlike life* shares a skin with it. Death lines every moment of ordinary time." Weaving absence into the web of presence does not erase the differences between the two, but rather shows us again the movement of desire, which reaches across insurmountable distances. In the same way that a double negative makes a positive, the deleted assertion Carson quotes as part of her mother's epitaph, "~~Obviously it is impossible . . . to compare the living with the dead~~," affirms not the impossibility of the task, but rather its necessity.[23] Just as "people who experience total eclipse are moved to such strong descriptions of its vacancy and void that this itself begins to take on colour," so too is death transformed into something like "a double negative of light."[24]

In *Nox*, Carson radically extends the logic of the crossout, further undoing the opposition between presence and absence. The book functions stereoscopically: Carson's elegy for her brother— told through a mash-up of text, illustration, letters, and photos—

unfolds in tandem with her word-by-word translation of Catullus's #101, in which he offers to his late brother "the last gift owed to death." In the unfurling pages of this accordioned, handmade, multimedia book, photographed for publication, she documents what one might call *remains*, recording on successive pages the everfainter imprint of writing, the ghosted reflection of image and type, the bleeding through of marker. "It may be I'll never again think of sentences unshadowed," Carson wrote in the piece for her mother, and indeed the sentences here are shadowy—soaked in tea, scumbled with charcoal, darkened through an overlay of transparent film.[25] Both in content and in presentation, *Nox* maintains an atmosphere of incongruence, wherein no claim to coherence is left unchallenged, no lacuna unfingered; rather, the "stops and silence of various kinds" that punctuate Carson's text "defeat narrative wherever it seeks to arise, which," she explains, "is pretty much everywhere."[26]

Although we "want other people to have a centre, a history, an account that makes sense," thinking that it might "form a lock against oblivion," we know from the beginning that there is no safe house.[27] "To Death we are all debts owed"—this is a favorite line of Carson's, who uses it in an essay on poetry's economy, in a poem on her mother's death, and in *Nox*, where it hides under the lexical definition of the word "perpetuum"—but there is, she argues, "an endless space and time on the far side of restitution."[28] Our death pays our debt, but, Carson writes, "in that silence, one has the feeling that something has passed us and kept going, that some possibility has got free." Although most of us see the play of absence and presence "as a zero sum game," Carson argues that "the benevolence of translation . . . . give[s] us a third place to be." Because desire does not emanate from the individual, and was never wholly contained in the "puny vessels" it filled, its movement is unhalting, as Carson describes in this mysterious and compelling passage:

> I was trained to strive for exactness and to believe that rigorous knowledge of the world without any residue is possible for us. This residue, which does not exist—just to think of it refreshes me. To think of its position, how it shares its position with drenched layers of nothing, to think of its motion, how it can never stop moving because I am in motion with it, . . . to think of its shadow, which is cast by nothing and so has no death in it (or very little)—to think of these things is like a crack of light

showing under the door of a room where I've been locked for years.[29]

What is this residue? Just to think of it refreshes me. *Desire*, Carson might call it, which strips us of self and leaves us in the shimmering silence.

Works Cited

Carson, Anne. *Answer Scars*. In *Wonderwater (Alice Offshore), by Roni Horn, Louise Bourgeois, Anne Carson, Hélène Cixous, and John Waters*. Göttingen, Germany: Steidl Verlag, 2004.

Carson, Anne. "The Art of Poetry, No. 88." Interview by Will Aitken. *Paris Review* 171 (Fall 2004): 190–226.

Carson, Anne. *Autobiography of Red: A Novel in Verse*. 1998. New York: Vintage-Random, 1999.

Carson, Anne. *Decreation: Poetry, Essays, Opera*. New York: Knopf- Random, 2005.

Carson, Anne. "Economy, Its Fragrance." *Threepenny Review* 69 (Spring 1997): 14–17.

Carson, Anne. *Economy of the Unlost*. Princeton, NJ: Princeton University Press, 1999.

Carson, Anne. *Eros the Bittersweet*. 1986. Normal, IL: Dalkey Archive Press, 1998.

Carson, Anne. *Glass, Irony and God*. 1992. New York: New Directions, 1995.

Carson, Anne. *Men in the Off Hours*. 2000. New York: Vintage-Random, 2001.

Carson, Anne. *Nox*. New York: New Directions, 2010.

Carson, Anne. *Plainwater: Essays and Poetry*. 1995. New York: Vintage-Random, 2000.

Carson, Anne. "Variations on the Right to Remain Silent." *A Public Space* 7 (2008): http://www.apublicspace.org/back_issues/issue_7/.

Carson, Anne, trans. Euripides. *Grief Lessons: Four Plays by Euripides*. New York: New York Review of Books, 2008.

Lacan, Jacques. *The Seminar of Jacques Lacan. Book XI: The Four Fundamental Concepts of Psychoanalysis*. 1978. Trans. Alan Sheridan. New York: Norton, 1998.

Notes

1. Anne Carson, *Glass, Irony and God* (New York: New Directions, 1995), 136–37.

2. Anne Carson, *Decreation: Poetry, Essays, Opera* (New York: Knopf-Random, 2005), 179.

3. Ibid., 175, 179.

4. Anne Carson, "The Art of Poetry #88: Anne Carson," interview by Will Aitken, *Paris Review* 171 (Fall 2004): 200.

5. Anne Carson, *Grief Lessons: Four Plays by Euripides.* (New York: New York Review of Books, 2008), 311.

6. Anne Carson, *Autobiography of Red: A Novel in Verse* (New York: Vintage-Random, 1999), 39.

7. Anne Carson, *Plainwater: Essays and Poetry* (New York: Vintage-Random, 2000), 37.

8. Anne Carson, *Eros the Bittersweet* (Normal, IL: Dalkey Archive Press, 1998), 70.

9. Ibid., 166, 110.

10. Ibid., 18, 63.

11. Ibid., 33.

12. Anne Carson, *Economy of the Unlost* (Princeton, NJ: Princeton University Press, 1999), vii.

13. Carson, *Eros the Bittersweet*, 71–72.

14. Jacques Lacan, *The Seminar of Jacques Lacan, Book XI: The Four Fundamental Concepts of Psychoanalysis* (1978), trans. Alan Sheridan (New York: Norton, 1998), 83.

15. Carson, *Eros the Bittersweet*, 17.

16. Ibid., 69, 85.

17. Carson, *Grief Lessons*, 8–9.

18. Anne Carson, *Wonderwater: Alice Offshore* (Göttingen, Germany: Steidl Verlag, 2004), 143.

19. Carson, *Decreation,* 24, 26.

20. Carson, *Economy of the Unlost*, 58–9.

21. Carson, *Eros the Bittersweet*, 30.

22. Anne Carson, "Variations on the Right to Remain Silent," *A Public Space* 7 (2008): http://www.apublicspace.org/back_issues/issue_7/.

23. Anne Carson, *Men in the Off Hours* (New York: Vintage-Random, 2001), 166.

24. Carson, *Decreation,* 149.

25. Carson, *Men*, 166.

26. Carson, "Variations."

27. Anne Carson, *Nox* (New York: New Directions, 2010).

28. Anne Carson, "Economy, Its Fragrance," *Threepenny Review* 69 (Spring 1997): 15.

29. Carson, "Variations."

DAN BEACHY-QUICK

What Kind of Monster Am I?

I imagine the heat of the day is building and puts a fever in the air. Cicadas sing from the trees beside the river in whose cool waters they walk, Sokrates and Phaedrus. They are there with a third, though he cannot feel the current. He is rolled up and hidden in Phaedrus's sleeve, Lysias, speech-maker, who gave Phaedrus, beautiful young man, a speech. The speech says one should give oneself to a nonlover and not a lover, for the nonlover will bring no harm to the beloved. Lysias is there with them, all rolled up, text replacing body, word containing breath but not breathing in the blood-hot air. Sokrates follows those words; he wants to hear them read, he is "a lover of speeches." As they walk down the river to a place he knows, where the grass is long and the flowering trees bloom, where a plane tree offers its shade, he keeps asking Phaedrus a curious question, interrupting the conversation: "Do I seem inspired?" The question thrills because it doubts where doubt cannot be felt. It insists something as divine as inspiration can be but an appearance, even to the one feeling inspired. Sokrates admits to a glorious confusion, one that is self-mocking and mocking of other at once. Just before they stop, just before the day has reached its noontime heat, Sokrates admits the depth of his own ignorance—an ignorance excited into near-bliss by the words soon to be read, that speech Lysias wrote down, anticipation nearly sexual. He says:

> I am still unable to fulfill the command of the Delphian inscription and "Know myself. . . ." Am I monster more complicated and swollen with passion than Typho, or a creature of a gentler sort, naturally a part of some divine, and not monstrous, dispensation?[1]

Sokrates's genius resides in him in such a way that it damages the solidity of the self. He feels his ignorance as a lover feels desire, and like a lover, his desire worries him, frets and frays self into selvage. He wants to know what kind of monster he is. Like Typhon, is he

17

hundred-headed and from every mouth can he speak in every voice, using words to convince, to beguile, to seduce? Can he speak so as to mask his ignorance with knowing? Can he appear inspired? Or is he a monster of a gentler sort, a monster I might call a lover?

Anne Carson's *Eros the Bittersweet* ends as a loving consideration of the *Phaedrus*, this book that, as does her own, insists that writing and desire must be intimately interconnected, nearly one, if a reader is to become a lover. It is only on returning to her book that I realize its fundamental importance to me, though I long had felt its influence, the way one remembers encountering the necessity of something that cannot be wholly grasped, say the scent in the air only after the flowers have been walked past. But returning I find this book has been for me the guide into how it is I want to read, a little lover's manual on the erotics of the page. How does the lover begin? The lover begins by breathing in.

Carson suggests a lovely mystery: how is it the poets who introduced their audience to Eros were also the first to write down their verse in letters? The fact beneath the subtle suggestion that lyric poetry helps create the desire it both invokes and suffers involves the nature of the Greek alphabet. Greek introduced vowels into the Phoenician system of writing, creating a method to record the nuances of sound in unprecedented ways. "A script that furnishes a true alphabet for a language is one able to symbolize the phonemes of the language exhaustively, unambiguously, and economically."[2] The written page could suddenly mimic the intimacy of the human voice, not only by offering phonemic clues to the words as they would be said, but by marking in them a figure of utmost intimacy, those vowels that contain the breath they are uttered by. A living principle of speech embedded itself in the written word: breath, *pneuma*, genius, soul. The written word has become a place of indwelling. The word, like the beloved, excites desire because, like the beloved, the word is ensouled.

Lyric epistemology creates desire. Carson writes, "There would seem to be some resemblance between the way Eros acts in the mind of a lover and the way knowing acts in the mind of a thinker."[3] Eros acts, as Carson notes, in paradox, that devastation of contradiction which is also a form of bliss. Desire seeks out the lack that births it, this need for the other that supersedes and overwhelms the need for the self to remain inviolate. Desire finds in the mind of the lover a resource of lack, a space of wanting that makes desire desirous; when knowing acts in erotic ways it discovers in the mind a similar insufficiency. It discovers an ignorance it deepens. The poem offers to one who reads it by its own paradoxical terms an unexpected difficulty: not acquiring knowledge, but reaching into ignorance as the mind's primary resource; and by that reach which, by going so far into the self it inverts and reaches out, one becomes that figure with outstretched hands, that figure of longing, the lover. The poem places itself between poet and reader as the world into which both must reach to become real. Just as Carson describes the source of the *symbolon* as "one half of a knucklebone carried as a token of identity to someone who has the other half,"[4] it feels that the poem is the place in which the half that is a reader meets the half that is a poet and on the page they consummate a wholeness. But as with love, there are consequences. Each half of a symbol reaches through a distance it also gathers into itself—a coiled spring of nothingness—so that the formation of the symbol includes within it a source of absence. The symbol contains in it the very force that will ruin it: the erotic distance of the lover's reach. It contains that distance as the vowel contains breath. To read is in part the lover's dream: that no breath save what the beloved breathes out is needed to breathe in. To read also confronts the lover's great fear: that when the wholeness is done, when the poem has been read, when the mind steps out of the nuptial bed and over the threshold back into knowing, that the distance crossed expands, and one must learn to desire more fully to experience again that pleasure within the written sheets.

What is this monster the poem creates? A hybrid one that in saying "I" means "we"? Aristophanes's myth of the lover's lack, where we want so heedlessly the love of another because we two were once one—two-headed and eight-limbed—an erotic whole so powerful it seemed within our reach to challenge the gods. Zeus took the threat seriously enough to sever each in half, and so now I pick up the poem with two hands, and cross one leg over the other, and must begin love's work alone. Or are we Typhonic, as Sokrates feared of himself? Each poem allowing us to alter our voice, to speak as anyone, to mimic the already-loved voices and so seduce by a heartless trick the one we desire? Or might my disposition be gentler? Might I need to become, brief as the time may be in which it occurs, this lover in the sense Carson offers—this *symbolic* creature, birthed only in the poem being read as it's being read, in which the opposition of reader and writer ceases as does the division keeping lovers apart? I'd like to think so. I do think so when I think *as* I desire; that is, when my thinking *is* desire.

The honest lover departs. He must do so to learn to desire again, to desire more fully, more truly. Carson makes us remarkably aware of edges in relation to eros. She writes, "The self forms at the edge of desire."[5] If we read as lovers, if the poem opens within itself a place for that consummation called reading to occur, then when reading stops, only then, do we become that thing in which our ethical and our erotic lives are one. Only then am I me. The poem has granted me myself in giving me that lack by which I not only desire, but find in myself "desire for *desire*."[6] Such wanting reorients the reader to the world in that most remarkable of ways; it does so by introducing us to it and telling us, as does the beloved to the lover, that "sometimes I am permitted to return." A poem places a seed in unexpected ground. Not soil, not earth. It grows in nothing, takes root in nothing—that nothing desire deepens in us, that lovely emptiness of wanting. Right there it takes root. We find the startle of our moral life when we feel it begins within our erotic one: that the care of what *is* depends upon the longing that springs from what *isn't*.

> As Sokrates tells it, your story begins the moment Eros enters you. That incursion is the biggest risk of your life. How you handle it is the index of the quality, wisdom and decorum of the things inside you. As you handle it you come in contact with what is inside you, in a sudden and startling way. You perceive what you are, what you lack, what you could be. What is this mode of perception, so different from ordinary perception that it is well described as madness? How is it that when you fall in love you feel as if suddenly you are seeing the world as it really is? A mood of knowledge floats out over your life. You seem to know what is real and what is not. Something is lifting you toward an understanding so complete and clear it makes you a jubilant. This mood is no delusion, in Sokrates' belief. It is a glance down into time, at realities you once knew, as staggering beautiful as the glance of your beloved.[7]

Suffer beauty, says the poem to the one that loves it. Bear its thrill. Endure longing longer. What we could be may be perceived only by feeling what we most truly lack. Such is desire's bittersweet gift. Anne Carson encourages us into Sokrates's belief because it feels to us who read her words that she is herself such a believer. We must learn to want if we wish to live fully, and our teacher in this is the words themselves, not the lesson they may impart, but the fact of the breath in the vowel, that "mood of knowledge" which drifts upon us like an erotic reverie in which the soul seems larger than the body that contains it, and the eyes, when they open, open on desire itself, word and world, beloved's eyes, poet's mouth open in invocation, that one letter which contains the breath of the mouth that holds the shape of its last utterance: O—

Notes

1. Plato, *Selected Dialogues of Plato: The Benjamin Jowett Translation*, trans. Benjamin Jowett (New York: Modern Library, 2000), 118.
2. Anne Carson, *Eros the Bittersweet* (Champaign, IL: Dalkey Archive Press, 1998), 53.
3. Carson, *Eros the Bittersweet*, 70.
4. Carson, *Eros the Bittersweet*, 75.
5. Carson, *Eros the Bittersweet*, 39.
6. Carson, *Eros the Bittersweet*, 109.
7. Carson, *Eros the Bittersweet*, 152–53.

MARTIN CORLESS-SMITH

Living on the Edge
The Bittersweet Place of Poetry

When I was offered the chance to write on Carson's *Eros the Bittersweet* I worried that I had read it insufficiently, that my relationship with it was at best tangential—in fact I worried that the whole scape of my reading was entirely too unruly and determined by extraneous factors and extravagant detours that had no true bearing on the text being offered. My reading dilemma was not particular to Carson's text of course, but in the end it did seem a problem the book itself might acknowledge to some degree (even if in the end the book does try to settle into a conclusive shape). Reading any book entails much of the erotic reaching that forms the central concern of Carson's volume.

Reading, like loving, is a bittersweet endeavor.

Eros the Bittersweet is a book of readings, of links between disparate texts that tries to perpetuate and support a developing theme. It examines the erotic crisis as exemplified by Sappho's neologism *glukupikron*,[1] the *bittersweet* of the title. It becomes apparent that the term's affective tension comes from the inherent paradox of its juxtaposing simultaneous opposing feelings (sensations, or tastes), and that it is the frisson of the simultaneity of these dissonant counterparts that is Carson's essential investigation.

In his book *Erotism* Georges Bataille describes the Erotic crisis as the defining instance of selfhood (which Carson endorses: "As Sokrates tells it, your story begins the moment Eros enters you").[2] Bataille describes the state of the self-conscious individual as "discontinuous," that is, separate from everything else, from the "continuity."

> We are discontinuous beings, individuals who perish in isolation in the midst of an incomprehensible adventure, but we yearn for our lost continuity.[3]

That continuity is the ground from which our individuality is rent. Returning to that continuity spells an end to selfhood:

> Continuity is what we are after, but generally only if that continuity which the death of discontinuous beings can also establish is not the victor in the long run. What we desire is to bring into a world founded on discontinuity all the continuity such a world can sustain. . . . For the man in love . . . love may be felt violently. . . . We ought never forget that in spite of the bliss love promises its first effect is one of turmoil and distress. . . . Its essence is to substitute for the persistent discontinuity a miraculous continuity between two beings.[4]

Entering or reentering this continuity would require a fusion with otherness that would end our individuality. We could never experience continuity as our selves.

Hence love spells suffering for us in so far as it is a quest for the impossible.[5]

The structure of Erotic crisis is not limited to the model of the frustrated desires of a lover (although this is the preeminent example in Carson). It is the crisis of being in general.[6] According to Bataille:

> Man achieves his inner experience at the instant when bursting out of the chrysalis he feels that he is tearing himself, not tearing something outside that resists him.[7]

Carson describes this as "the moment the soul parts on itself."[8] Man is not an object ripped from the mold of nature, man's consciousness is the rip. Man stands abashed before Love and Death, those catastrophic events that offer to heal the wound of his isolation, yet simultaneously to overwhelm and annihilate. This is the erotic crisis housed in Sappho's neologism, the bittersweet paradox of Carson's title.

The event of this crisis is also where we might find Heidegger's description of the Poet lurking. Bataille's *continuity* is markedly similar to Heidegger's *Open* (which he himself finds in Rilke). The term denotes all that which is beyond the limits of the discontinuous self. It is the task of the Poet to push into the Open.

The higher its consciousness, the more the conscious being is excluded from the world. This is why man, in the words of Rilke's letter, is "before the world." He is not admitted into the Open. Man stands over against the world.[9]

Plants and animals "do not will because, muted in their desire, they never bring the Open before themselves as an object."[10] Thus it is man alone whose "desire" places him before the Open. Heidegger names this willing *venturesomeness*. The poet is that being who ventures, turning toward the Open. The poet's being is directed toward the continuity, in the same way a lover's is toward the beloved. The poet's "being" is marked by the word:

> Language is the precinct (templum), that is, the house of Being . . . [poets] dare the precinct of Being. They dare language.[11]

Or as Carson puts it: "Eros is the ground where logos takes root between two people."[12] Much of her book examines edges and borders, and that uncanny space between self and other, whether that be between lovers or between reader and writer. Both lovers and readers and writers are motivated by erotic desire. What seems different though is the presence of the text.

When I started to read Carson I was disturbed by a strange but increasingly dwelt-upon metaphorical slip, as I saw it. A movement from a split to a triangulation.

In describing the action of metaphor, that which like *bittersweet* itself, brings "two heterogeneous things close to reveal their closeness,"[13] Carson enumerates the effects as "triangulates, haunts, splits, wrenches and delights." Notice two making three. So let us look at the metaphors Carson uses to illuminate the instant of the erotic split.

> Sweetbitter eros is what hits the raw film of the lover's mind. Paradox is what takes shape on the sensitized plate of the poem, a negative image from which positive pictures can be created.[14]

Here we have the rip of consciousness described as film. One sees the rupture of consciousness, if you like, in the act of peeling the Polaroid negative off its positive, so that we have both sides of a desired union reft in the forging of the image of that desire. But it seems a step removed somehow to have this rupture projected upon the raw film of the lover's mind. Somehow the rupture has produced an image that is now projected. The Polaroid is immediate, the film projection requires a secondary step.

If the erotic act of desiring is itself the act that causes the consciousness of the rupture. The ego's arousal marks the division of self and other by its very action. What happens next is the ongoing project of the ego. In short, the split becomes itself a realm of investment. Someone looks at the Polaroid (someone took it).

The schism between lover and beloved or the *discontinuous* and the *continuity*, a whole broken into two, now becomes three. It is the worrying of two into three that plays throughout Carson's book.

In his critique of Heidegger's portrayal of Hölderlin, Hans-Jost Frey[15] looks at exactly this worrying of a duality into a triangulation. In particular Frey is concerned about Heidegger dragging the semantic meaning of the poem onto the event of its making.

> The general essence of poetry . . . is equally valid for all poetry [not just work such as Hölderlin's which chooses as its subject the writing of poetry]. . . . Writing the essence of poetry does not mean expressing it.[16]

If for Heidegger "the word is the occurrence of the sacred,"[17] Frey wants to make sure we realize that the "sacred does not exist in the word by being named but by happening with it."[18] For Heidegger "song is not just mankind's work." Something is also not the work of God, who is dependent on mankind. Song therefore testifies neither to mankind nor to God but to their inseparability. In this case the song (or poem) is the ground upon which the erotic catastrophe is enacted. But this is (if we choose to agree) song's ontology, not its semantics. "The word that names the sacred is not itself sacred."[19] It is, however, the occurrence of the sacred.

> If the poem is not what it expresses insofar as it expresses what it is, then this does not mean that it can't be what it expresses. It only means that it is not by making itself the object of its own discourse that the poem is what it expresses.[20]

Frey argues that Heidegger conflates these two states, "the expressed event for the event of expression," whereas Hölderlin is careful to distinguish them:

The immediate ubiquity is the mediation for everything conveyed, that is for the mediate. The immediate is itself never a mediate, although the immediate is strictly speaking, the mediation, that is, the mediateness of the mediate, because it enables it with its own essence.[21]

The poem is the event of the reach from the discontinuous poet toward continuity. According to Frey the proposition of a poem is a mediation that might discuss its mediation, but the discussion as such neither helps nor hinders its task. But this does not seem to allow the poem to function as anything more than an instant of language. Frey sees the poem as a significant event but importantly not as an event of signification. It seems in separating the two events he believes Heidegger conflates, he has not kept the two as necessary counterparts in the poetic act. The poem in its mediation marks the realm of the necessary link between self and other. Nature (for Hölderlin), the Open (for Rilke or Heidegger), or the continuity (for Bataille) is the realm within which the poem articulates its separation from Nature et al.: "as the unmediated enabling of all mediation, nature is the immediate."[22] Or as Carson puts it: "Eros is the ground where logos takes root between two people."[23] But why should a poem be important for this job, more so than a simple sentence?

In discussing Sappho's most enduring lyric, Fragment 31, Carson discovers a "ruse" whereby Sappho interposes a male viewer for her beloved. This "triangulation" offers an allegorical model of the structure "for, where is eros is lack, its activation calls for three structural components—lover, beloved and that which comes between them."[24] Continuing her film metaphor, Carson imagines: "the ideal is projected on a screen of the actual, in a kind of stereoscopy."[25] This layering of the structure of the erotic split with the observation of its enactment is exactly the conflation Frey points out in Heidegger. But Carson does not conflate, she understands the necessity of the "ruse":[26]

> A space must be maintained or desire ends. Sappho reconstructs the space of desire in a poem that is like a small, perfect photograph of the erotic dilemma.[27]

This is a significant space, for it marks the arena where self comes into being. According to Bruno Snell, Sappho's split adjective *gluku-*

pikron is the actual historical instant where the Greeks invent self-consciousness. It is the instant of the maintained schism that produces the ground upon which consciousness can be projected. Metaphor and thinking work "by projecting sameness upon difference." Bittersweet manages the deliberate ruse of meaning two incompatibilities. We read it as an intentional impossibility. It itself describes *and* enacts the erotic dilemma. It maintains the space of desire (albeit a small space between syllables). In a way we could describe this one word as a poem of sorts. This task is particular to poetry in that it houses blatant paradoxes that are both read and resist reading. Poetry revels in such frissons.

The self forms at the edge of desire.[28] The task of the poem is to perform these edges that signify their reaching out into the Open.

The poet, in reveling at (or in) the edge between self and other (in using language), in enacting a mediation, cannot rest in this mediation, as if now unified with otherness, she can only offer the instant up as one of reaching. The poem is an indication of the event of self-consciousness that enacts the occurrence of self in relation to otherness.

The semantic meaning of the poem is not identical to the ontological event of the poem, but it does seem that some special frisson, or *mise en abyme* occurs if the subject matter interacts with the functional event of the writing. If poetic language leans toward presence, if this is the open topic of its articulation, we gain as a reader both the mediation that is the house of self consciousness, and the drama of that self-consciousness, the signification of which seems significant.

Carson's *Eros the Bittersweet* reads the event of the poetic metaphor as the realm of the imagination:

> The innovation of metaphor occurs in . . . [its] shift of distance from far to near, and it is effected by imagination. A virtuoso act of imagination [such as Sappho's neologism *bittersweet*] brings the two things together, sees their incongruence, then sees also a new congruence, meanwhile continuing to recognize the previous incongruence through the new congruence.[29]

Carson argues that metaphor is the shape of thinking, the consciousness of being. The unprecedented effect of language is to provide a provisional realm where consciousness enacts its awareness, along with its desire to house that consciousness more permanently in the world. The drama of being is to come into the joy of acknowledging selfhood by an event that causes that self to be held adrift. Poems seem to be then, both the event, and the drama of that event acknowledged:

> The construction of poems becomes the record of a series of individual thresholds of the experience of being conscious; they form the definitions, in time and in language, of human identity.[30]

The significance of Sappho's poem is not merely that it provides an historical marker as perhaps the first acknowledgment of the ontological structure of poetry; it is simultaneously the event of consciousness opening the fragile arena where we might observe selfhood (and otherness) performing and performed. As Carson exquisitely reveals, Poetry is the self-conscious event of human consciousness par excellence.

Works Cited

Bataille, Georges. *Erotism: Death and Sensuality.* Trans. Mary Dalwood. San Francisco: City Lights Books, 1986.

Carson, Anne. *Eros the Bittersweet.* New York: Dalkey Archive Press, 1998.

Forrest-Thomson, Veronica. *Collected Poems and Translations.* London: Allardyce Barnett, 1990.

Frey, Hans-Jost. *Studies in Poetic Discourse: Mallarmé, Baudelaire, Rimbaud, Hölderlin.* Trans. William Whobrey, translations from the French and Latin by Bridget McDonald. Stanford: Stanford University Press, 1996.

Heidegger, Martin. *Poetry, Language, Thought.* Trans. Albert Hofstadter. New York: HarperCollins, 1971.

Notes

1. The word is originally translated by Carson as *sweetbitter* in an attempt to mimic the progression from sweetness to bitterness in the Greek original.

2. Anne Carson, *Eros the Bittersweet* (New York: Dalkey Archive Press, 1998), 152.

3. Georges Bataille, *Erotism: Death and Sensuality*, trans. Mary Dalwood (San Francisco: City Lights Books, 1986), 15.

4. Bataille, *Erotism*, 18–19.

5. Bataille, *Erotism*, 20.

6. The structure of this schism as the foundational event of consciousness bears a striking resemblance to Lacan's mirror stage, and to Freudian models of the birth of identity that Carson refers to later in her book.

7. Bataille, *Erotism*, 39.

8. Carson, *Eros the Bittersweet*, 7.

9. Martin Heidegger, "What Are Poets for," *Poetry, Language, Thought*, trans. *Albert Hofstadter* (New York: HarperCollins, 1971), 106.

10. Heidegger, *Poetry, Language, Thought*, 108.

11. Heidegger, *Poetry, Language, Thought*, 129.

12. Heidegger, *Poetry, Language, Thought*, 145.

13. Heidegger, *Poetry, Language, Thought*, 73.

14. Heidegger, *Poetry, Language, Thought*, 9.

15. Hans-Jost Frey, *Studies in Poetic Discourse: Mallarmé, Baudelaire, Rimbaud, Hölderlin*, trans. William Whobrey, translations from the French and Latin by Bridget McDonald (Stanford: Stanford University Press, 1996).

16. Frey, *Studies in Poetic Discourse*, 178.

17. Frey, *Studies in Poetic Discourse*, 180.

18. Frey, *Studies in Poetic Discourse*, 180.

19. Frey, *Studies in Poetic Discourse*, 183.

20. Frey, *Studies in Poetic Discourse*, 184.

21. Frey, *Studies in Poetic Discourse*, 188.

22. Frey, *Studies in Poetic Discourse*, 189.

23. Carson, *Eros the Bittersweet*, 145.

24. Carson, *Eros the Bittersweet*, 16.

25. Carson, *Eros the Bittersweet*, 16.

26. "To know both, keeping the difference visible is the subterfuge called eros." Carson, *Eros the Bittersweet*, 69.

27. Carson, *Eros the Bittersweet*, 26.

28. Carson, *Eros the Bittersweet*, 39.

29. Carson, *Eros the Bittersweet*, 73.

30. Veronica Forrest-Thomson, *Collected Poems and Translations* (London: Allardyce Barnett, 1990), 263.

BRIAN TEARE

Reading Carson Reading Brontë RE
The Soul's Difficult Sexual Destiny

From *Eros the Bittersweet* (1986) to *Nox* (2010), Anne Carson's body
of work insists upon reading as formative of selfhood and thus fun-
damental to being human, integral to everything from erotic love to
mourning. Indeed, reading overtly or implicitly plots many of Car-
son's most compelling texts, those in which her protagonists pursue
reading as alternative to heroic actions. In the same way she con-
trasts Herakles's extroverted epic hero with Geryon's introverted
lyric hero in *The Autobiography of Red*, Carson in *Eros the Bittersweet*
contrasts oral and literate cultures, and claims the shift from the
former to the latter radically changed Greek poets and their sense
of self:

> As an individual reads and writes he gradually learns to close or
> inhibit the input of his senses, to inhibit or control the responses
> of his body, so as to train energy and thought upon the written
> words. He resists the environment outside him by distinguishing
> and controlling the one inside him. (44)

Thus her heroes and heroines—introspective, thoughtful, melan-
cholic—tend to attempt to organize their overwhelming interior
lives through reading, interpreting, or translating texts. In doing so
they resemble the Greek poets who first wrote down their lyrics, a
process Carson describes as a "struggle from within a consciousness—
perhaps new in the world—of the body as a unity of limbs, senses
and self, amazed at its own vulnerability" (45). Because the Greeks
conceived of erotic love as a force that entered the individual from
without, Carson argues, the experience of subjective unity created
by literacy left poets like Sappho particularly, peculiarly vulnerable
to the rending effects of eros. As sensitive to lived experience as the
Greek poets she describes in *Eros the Bittersweet*, Carson's typical
protagonist turns to reading to recuperate a sense of self disturbed

in the wake of upset, the apprehended word acting as temporarily ordering border between a wounded psyche and a world ruled by uncertainty.

"The Glass Essay," among the earliest of Carson's poems to figure reading as a form of recuperative self-fashioning, is fittingly a poem about reading poetry in a time of erotic and existential crisis. Couched within a frame story in which the protagonist returns home to visit her mother, the poem tells of a love affair's difficult aftermath, and it also essays about the life and work of the protagonist's favorite author, poet and novelist Emily Brontë. Her readings of Brontë are informed as much by her identification with the writer as her anxiety over their similarities, the fear that she's "turning into" Brontë, her "lonely life around [her] like a moor" (2). A poem at once about "love and its necessities" and an autobiography of the soul (10), "The Glass Essay" is also is an essay about vocation, gender, and "the terrible sex price" women pay to men (32). Taken as a whole, it reads as a highly compressed feminist *bildungsgedicht*, a narrative of the protagonist's "jerky passage from girl to woman to who I am now" (35).

And though her reading of Brontë plays a crucial role in that passage, Carson's protagonist is not a Greek newly born to literacy. Informed by psychoanalytic theories of subject formation as well as by feminist analyses of familial life, her protagonist admits to formative influences aside from the ones in books. If Brontë serves as interlocutor for the protagonist's vocational questions about poetry and the soul in solitude, it's the protagonist's mother who serves as interlocutor for the no less pressing questions of sex and romantic love. A taut triangle drawn between protagonist, mother, and Brontë unifies the poem. All of them are effectively single women: the protagonist alone in the wake of her abandonment by her lover Law; her mother alone while her husband, suffering from advanced Alzheimer's, lives in an assisted care facility; Brontë surrounded by family but preferring discourse with the moor and with the Thou of her poems. "The question I am left with," Carson writes late in the poem of her reading of Brontë, "is the question of her loneliness" (31). The question we are left with: whose loneliness does she mean? It seems that into her own solitary nature she has gathered the sexual solitude of her mother and the spiritual solitude of Brontë. "It is who I am," the protagonist asserts, "this soul trapped in glass" (34).

Like its prose cousin the *bildungsroman*, the *bildungsgedicht* generally treats its protagonist like a question to which their destiny is the answer, and "The Glass Essay" is no exception. The protagonist insists throughout that, for Brontë as for herself, gender crucially shapes destiny, vocation, and the dynamics between body, mind, and soul. This insistence imbues the protagonist's metaphysical and existential crisis with a feminist analytic that complicates the usual questions about self and self-worth that arise during major transitional moments in our lives. To ask these questions as an adult, as the protagonist does, is not only to recall all the uncertainties produced by prior life changes, it is also to recall all the answers once fabricated in the attempt to produce a functional self-image, hopefully as bearable to ourselves as it is loveable to others. If the erotic rejection by her lover creates in the protagonist, as it did in the Greek lyric poets, "a personal struggle of will" against a negative force "that assaults or invades the body," it is during such a struggle that the functional, bearable, lovable, hard-won self-image falls away (*Eros the Bittersweet*, 45). In its place she confronts "a nude glimpse of [her] lone soul" (*Glass, Irony, and God*, 17), a series of glimpses that also reveal her "difficult sexual destiny" (35). She calls these visions Nudes.

The Nudes most explicitly link "The Glass Essay" to Brontë's own poetry, particularly "'the cardboard sublime' of her caught world" in which personal agency is often reduced to pure capture (19). As gruesome as they are melodramatic, the Nudes stage mind-body dualism as a feminist drama, compressing the *bildungsgedicht*'s narrative of destiny and maturation into a series of literally visceral symbolic tableaus. But if these visions are so awful, the protagonist's therapist asks, "Why keep watching? Why not / go away? (18). It is through the protagonist's relationship to her Nudes that she most resembles Brontë, who, like her, was a *whacher*. A nonce word of Brontë's that the protagonist assumes denotes a vocation, to *whach* is both a form of labor and a subject position. And in describing Brontë, she describes herself:

Whacher is what she was.
She whached God and humans and moor wind and open
    night . . .

To be a whacher is not a choice.
There is nowhere to get away from it,
    no ledge to climb up to . . . (4–5)

While the narrator would "like to believe that for [Brontë] the act of watching provided a shelter," she is very clear that the stakes of being a whacher are not the same for her, that in whaching "I find no shelter" (35). Nonetheless, it is their ability to endure the inability to look away that links the protagonist and Brontë; it is also the shared source of their great strength of character and their acceptance of and participation in the more violent aspects of metaphysics. Carson teases from *whacher* both *watch* and *whack*, a physically passive action and a physically active one, a duality that characterizes both women in whom agency and apparent passivity were at war. In the course of the poem the protagonist shows herself to be, like Brontë, one of those who "whached eyes, stars, inside, outside, actual weather," but who also "whached the poor core of the world, / wide open" (8). How did she get so strong?

Through her readings of Brontë's life and writing, the protagonist does a marvelous job of making a mirror in which she ultimately sees herself not as unlovable but as unbreakable, but she would not have the strength to do so without the support of her mother. If her lover's rejection triggers the fear that she is essentially unlovable, and if Brontë in her solitary ruthlessness comes first to embody and then counter that fear, then her mother counters both rejection and ruthlessness with a strangely grudging, sincere loving-kindness. She's a marvelously drawn character, like all the mothers in Carson's oeuvre, lovable because she's at once transparent and opaque, surface and depth, typical and unpredictable. The relationship she has to her daughter is ambivalent yet supportive, tonally subtle in its mix of opposite qualities. And in ways weirdly crucial to the reconciliation of the protagonist to her destiny, the mother's loving antagonism is analogous to the narrative tone that has become Carson's signature.

A distinctive mix of logos and pathos, it's ruefully confessional, personably impersonal. "It pains me to record this," the protagonist admits regarding one of her Nudes, "I am not a melodramatic person" (9). Such statements seem to literalize a subtle split between a protagonist-who-feels and a narrator-who-thinks, both of whom of course coexist within an "I" as likely to express herself as to turn against her own feelings: "When Law left I felt so bad I thought I would die. / This is not uncommon" (8). Following the protagonist's heartfelt confession with her own ruthless assessments, the narrator knows better than to be impressed by such suffering. She knows there is agon in a protagonist; it's a universal principle. But not all protagonists are narrators, and while a third-person narrative might be content to recount events that illustrate such a principle in action, a narrator is moved—and then moved to tell. At root, the telling of *narrate* is related through *gnarus* to *knowing*; it's the narrator's job to transform agony into knowledge. In this way, the narrator is as much a mother to the protagonist as her mother is, both of them offering a critical distance that crucially transforms difficult experience:

> My mother speaks suddenly.
> That psychotherapy's not doing you much good is it?
> You aren't getting over him . . .
>
> It isn't like taking an aspirin you know, I answer feebly,
> Dr. Haw says grief is a long process.
> She frowns. What does it accomplish
>
> all that raking up of the past?
> Oh—I spread my hands—
> I prevail! I look her in the eye.
> She grins. Yes you do. (3–4)

It is traditional that the protagonist of a *bildungsroman* or *-gedicht* overcome her *agon* and prevail, but it is not a given. Think of Goethe's Young Werther putting a bullet through his head to end his erotic suffering. Though her soul is alien to this world, though it is locked in antagonism with both mind and flesh, though it is trapped in glass, the protagonist nonetheless prevails, doggedly sheltering her soul despite visions of its being roughly divested of flesh or run through with thorns. Though born a *whacher*, her resilience in the face of a difficult sexual and metaphysical destiny has everything to do with the advocacy of a mother for her daughter. As Carson says of her own mother,

> I think it was hard for her to be on my side but that she thought it through and decided to be. But it wasn't natural. . . . She had to make that choice. I was who I was and she would never understand it, but she was going to support it. It's unconditional. (*Paris Review*)

If Brontë's fierce and uncompromising vocation of anger, though powerful as a literary model, fails to offer a viable, survivable response to a bad fit between the soul and the world, Carson's mother models a more loving response to a bad fit between daughter and mother. "The Glass Essay" in fact suggests such an analogy: as the self to the soul, so the mother to her daughter. Carson's protagonist prevails because unconditional maternal support supplies her with the strength not only to endure her solitary visions, but also to accept them despite their disturbing nature. By loving her angry alien soul the way her mother loves her, she accepts a difficult sexual destiny. It isn't that the soul is relieved of the burden of embodiment; it isn't that the soul comes to feel at home. The point is that the protagonist continues to suffer, moving "from fire to shelter to fire," and prevails anyway (35). Survival is not what we think.

Works Cited

Carson, Anne. "The Art of Poetry, No. 88." Interview by Will Aitken. *Paris Review* 171 (Fall 2004): unpaginated. Accessed March 16, 2013. http://www.theparisreview.org/interviews/5420/the-art-of-poetry-no-88-anne-carson.

Carson, Anne. *Eros the Bittersweet*. Normal, IL: Dalkey Archive Press, 1998.

Carson, Anne. *Glass, Irony, and God*. New York: New Directions, 1995.

VIRGINIA KONCHAN

The Gender of Sound
No Witness, No Words (or Song)?

Every sound we make is a little bit of autobiography.
—ANNE CARSON

Mere speech, if not designated as meaningful discourse by the polis, did not guarantee recognition in ancient Greece, nor does it, today, wherein minority and majority representations, despite the rhetoric of neoliberal identity politics, are still scripted by those in power. Recognition is granted legally, to those considered citizen-subjects, and, along with interpretative validity (if seen and heard, considered to be signifying or "making sense"), symbolically, in social contextures. The stakes of being ignored or acknowledged based on a subject being too "unlike" dominant representations (or resisting gender norms) are those of reified social presence or death, in a framework wherein a constitutive identity is not a priori established (legally or symbolically) to women, as described in in Anne Carson's essay "The Gender of Sound."

It is the sole essay in *Glass, Irony, and God* whose provenance is the gendered politics of the aural senses; elsewhere in this collection, the optic reigns, such as passages in "The Glass Essay" exploring Emily Brontë's habitual misspelling of "watch" ("Whaching a north wind grind the moor / that surrounded her father's house on every side, / formed of a kind of rock called millstone grit"). As Carson says, "to be a watcher is not in itself sad or happy." One wonders, though, particularly in light of this essay: might it not be tragic, if not sovereign biopower, but mutual recognition, constitutes presence in the world?

Carson's eighteen books have established her as a critically acclaimed postmodernist *avant la lettre*. *Nox,* a text-object elegizing her brother's death, attenuates the mourning process as a problem of duration and form; in *Decreation,* she deploys oratorio and opera libretto to explore the antimonies of what Heidegger warned against:

the will not to de(con)struct, but to destroy self, other, or world. In *Eros the Bittersweet*, and *The Beauty of the Husband*, Carson navigates personal territories: the latter is a text whose formal constraint is the tango, whose twenty-nine moves must be danced, Scheherazade-style, to the end. Throughout her creative and critical writing, and many works of translation (Euripides, Sophocles), Carson's lyrical investigations of gender, desire, anger, self, and language foreground Greco-Roman logos, while invoking classical topoi and epistemes: a subtext absent from American academe's praxes of pragmatism, structuralism, and now neoliberal, poststructuralist critical theory.

Bringing Romantic tropes (eros, truth, beauty) and high aesthetics (opera, Greek drama) to bear on modernity's ghostly tropes (impersonality, collectivist identity, self-consciousness, the loss of tradition and grand narratives, and the death of authority) and forms (metonymy, parataxis), Carson's neoformalist texts seek to incorporate rather than excise the layered epistemologies of metaphysics, phenomenology, philology, and theology, privileging moments of verité (the erotic text's sine qua non) over an empirical account thereof, in an effort to "make sense," through "construct[ing] a convincing surface of what life feels like." Her verisimilitude is shot through, however, with a postmodern despair over capturing the "essence" of truth in words: "If I read Virginia Woolf or George Eliot describing emotional facts of people, it seems there's a fragrance of understanding you come away with—this smell in your head of having gone through something that you understood with people in the story. When I think about my writing, I don't feel that."[1]

Rejecting euphonic closure and formal closure, Carson describes her work as "an irritant," just as, in "The Gender of Sound," she describes the female voice as interpreted by the Greek polis, as an excrescence not able to be assimilated or heard.

The aversion of the semiotic as excess was inscribed by Plato, whose character Timaeus describes the chora as a receptacle anterior to paternal nomination meriting "not even the rank of syllable."[2] The vaunting of self-discipline (strict policing of inside and outside, body and soul) is a Grecian art, *sophrosyne*. Distinctions between noise and music, and glossolalia and speech, have historically served the perceptual biases (and rigid censorings) of male interlocutors, rather than biology or culture: vowely, affective tones or texts of excess (rich in semiotic rather than semantic content) "sound" distasteful, threatening to transfer the Freudian economy of lack ascribed to women (sans phallus) onto men. Carson locates the "sites" of women's locutionary power in Baubo, who in a fourth century BC statue from the Asian Minor has no distinguishing features except a mouth and genitals: "The doubling and interchangability of mouth engenders a creature in whom sex is cancelled out by sound and sound is cancelled out by sex."[3] The threatening fecundity of women's speech, and multiple erogenous zones, is easily "solved" in patriarchal representations wherein the sexual "mouth" appropriates a communicative mouth, in an economy where women are reduced to objects, rather than speaking subjects, for the scopophiliac and sexual pleasure of men. Irigaray: "Women's jouissance is more multiple than men's unitary, phallic pleasure, because a woman has sex organs just about everywhere . . . [her] 'masculine counterpart' . . . is unable to discern the coherence [of her language]."[4] A woman speaking authoritatively in Western culture is met with terror, according to Alice Jardine, citing female *penseurs* from the French intellectual tradition (Christine de Pisan, Marguerite de Navarre, Flora Tristan) as well as Anne-Marie Dardigna, who offers two representational extremes of female textual and sexual possession of knowledge (both "improper") in *Les chateaux d'eros*: the "phallic shrew" and "S & M mistress." As we examine history, "it becomes evident man's response to a woman who knows (anything) has been one of paranoia."[5]

The historic silencing of female knowledge (what Carson calls the "somatic compliance of women's prophetic body") is also psycholinguistic. Gendered sound production has been a focus of sociolinguistic research for nearly a century: descriptions of women's speech as inherently deficient began in 1922 with Otto Jespersen's "The Woman," a chapter in his book *Language: Its Nature and Development*. In literature, Cassandra's mourning sounds, and Ophelia's heteroglossia are full of sound and fury, yet signify nothing, to a male or female other, who hear merely "sounds of nature": not a human speaker compelling reciprocity or acknowledgment.[6]

The delegitimization of women as signifiers echoes the conflicted relationship Western culture has to the semiotic language of poetry, bridging the gap between affective sound and conceptual "meaning," also dating back to Plato's jettisoning of poets from the Republic, as inferior statesmen: Marina Tsvetayeva declared the poetic language to "express the sigh a-a-a- with words."[7] Lyric poetry's sonic effects make the relation between sound and meaning particularly complex (such features of sound manipulation in poetry include counterpoising, tagging, echo effects, diagramming, and the ornamental devices of rubrication and embellishment).

Reading and listening are considered passive activities of reflection rather than creation: what if the stakes of listening, in a poem, are the stakes of the authenticated "reality" (rather than performative hijinks) of the speaker herself? Language games are speech acts with transferential implications: "I am listening," also means "Listen to me." Or, as Jonathan Culler notes, a "work has structure and meaning because it is read in a particular way, because . . . properties, latent in the object itself, are actualized by the theory of discourse applied to the latent act of reading."[8]

While postlanguage poetry tends to be defeatist about the power of language to signify or communicate, premodern forms of poetry, from Hesiod to Swinburne, were invested in language's incantatory powers (apotropaic utterances), and the trance-effects of metrical rhythm. The giving of face and voice to create a textual interlocutor, and the establishment of the lyric structure as a formal site of mourning, play, or erotic relations with existent others conjures the I/Thou tropes of apostrophe (address to a nonhuman listener) and prosopopoeia: both tropes seek to animate the inanimate, calling forth, Susan Stewart says, that which has not yet been named.

> Poetry speaks to self, other, apostrophe to dead, or nature, or a crowd. . . . Through lyric we return literally to the breath and pulse of speech rhythm in tension with those formal structures . . . for making time manifest . . . lyric expresses "the good faith in intelligibility" by means of which we recognize each other as speaking persons. The object of that recognition is a sound that becomes a human voice.[9]

The stakes of the intersubjective encounter (in lyric and diachronic time), in Carson's oeuvre, are fraught with mutual vulnerabilities: in love stories by Greek poet Stesichorus, imaginary interviews, and anthropological accounts of travel (her *Plainwater* essays) Carson documents the technics of attraction, power, and love through the double lens of scholarship and verse. This translingual vulnerability is the ground of ethics, as well as aesthetics: recognition-based increased tolerance for sounds, appearances, and communicated experiences of difference.

As with satire and self-irony, repressed during totalitarian regimes, or punning and laughter (the "ah-ha" moment of *fort-da* or the mirror stage), moments of self- and other-recognition widen our perspective and enrich our humanity. Throughout *Glass, Irony, and God* (a punctum or counterpoint to the other-making, and desiring, work of *Autobiography of Red*) Carson creates spaces for *ostranie* through the sensory appearances of persons and concepts (monsters, gods, lovers, and history) wholly different from the unsolved quanta of "ourselves."

Works Cited

Carson, Anne. "The Art of Poetry, No. 88." Interview by Will Aitken. *Paris Review* 171 (Fall 2004): 190–226.

Carson, Anne. "The Gender of Sound." In *Glass, Irony and God*. New York: New Directions, 1995.

Cixous, Hélène, and Catherine Clement. *The Newly Born Woman*. Trans. Betsy Wing. Minneapolis: University of Minnesota Press, 1986.

Culler, Jonathan. *Structuralist Poetics: Structuralism, Linguistics and the Study of Literature*. New York: Routledge, 2002.

DuPlessis, Rachel Blau. *The Pink Guitar: Writing as Feminist Practice*. Tuscaloosa: University of Alabama Press, 2006.

Irigaray, Luce. *This Sex Which Is Not One*. Trans. Catherine Porter. Ithaca: Cornell University Press, 1985.

Jardine, Alice. *Gynesis: Configurations of Women and Modernity*. Ithaca: Cornell University Press, 1985.

Stewart, Susan. *The Fate of the Senses*. Chicago: University of Chicago Press, 2002.

Thorne, Barrie, and Nancy Henley. "Difference and Dominance: An Overview of Language, Gender, and Society." In *Language and Sex: Difference and Dominance*, ed. Barrie Thorne and Nancy Henley. Rowley, MA: Newbury House, 1975.

Notes

1. Anne Carson, "The Art of Poetry No. 88," interview by Will Aitken, *Paris Review* 171 (Fall 2004): 171.

2. Rachel Blau DuPlessis, *The Pink Guitar: Writing as Feminist Practice* (Tuscaloosa: University of Alabama Press, 2006), 84.

3. Anne Carson, "The Gender of Sound," in *Glass, Irony and God* (New York: New Directions, 1995), 12.

4. Luce Irigaray, *This Sex Which Is Not One*, trans. Catherine Porter (Ithaca: Cornell University Press, 1985), 103.

5. Alice Jardine, *Gynesis: Configurations of Woman and Modernity* (Ithaca: Cornell University Press, 1986), 101.

6. Carson, "The Gender of Sound," 103.

7. DuPlessis, *The Pink Guitar*, 38.

8. Jonathan Culler, *Structuralist Poetics: Structuralism, Linguistics and the Study of Literature* (New York: Routledge, 2002), 113.

9. Susan Stewart, *The Fate of the Senses* (Chicago: University of Chicago Press, 2002), 105.

TIMOTHY LIU

On Anne Carson's *Short Talks*

On "Introduction"

Everything that happens is pushed by something else. I emphasize this. Audacity. I copy out everything that was said, anything to avoid boredom. Anne, I said, it is the task of a lifetime.

On "On *Homo Sapiens*"

In every short talk comes a point where we see her face in a pan of water. I hate that point. That moment when she reaches out and things get taken apart.

On "On Chromoluminism"

Essays and poems slow down Americans. Look at all those dots plastered on her softee cone as Anne strolls through the park on a Sunday rather than a Saturday afternoon, "lost in thought." Looks almost like a fucking Seurat stuck to her tongue—a new lingua franca opening and closing her stone lips.

On "On Gertrude Stein About 9:30"

How curious: I had no idea today has already ended! T. S. Eliot: "Poetry is punctuation."

On "On Disappointments in Music"

I was ill and could not attend, so I stayed home and YouTubed Anne's reading while Prokofiev went on making a racket.

On "On Trout"

Worn out, completely exhausted, the haiku are floating out to sea in origami boats. Swedish fish. Oriental massage. Occasionally spent in deep winter pools, these were called "bottom feeders."

On "On Ovid"

I see him there on a night like this, but what about Montaigne and his *Essais* published in 1580? Attempts. Trials. Now Ovid is weeping but goes on writing, teaching himself the local language (Getic) in his spare time. So wipe that shit-eating grin off your face, Mr. Montaigne—we're all anachronisms.

On "On Parmenides"

What if the names for things were utterly different? Canada, for example. I have a friend "who lives in Canada," as the back-flap copy on her book jacket states. What if Anne continues to publish and never tells us more about her lonesome? The avant-garde is irked. Lang-Po. We pride ourselves on civilized forms—poems more sturdy than cities fashioned by Calvino. A grandeur of delusions.

On "On Defloration"

Anne's poetics can accommodate a moist pussy. Sigh. Let's go in, cross that Bridge of Sighs. Her vagina a Venetian birth canal that can cause her vocal chords to swell. Pronoun slippage. First you. Then a brother who says, "What's wrong with your voice?" Poor Anne. Now we see it, now you don't.

On "On Major and Minor"

I think of you reading this, Anne, and damn, it's like knowing what I wrote on your Facebook wall will have to be taken down immediately when the restraining order goes through. Sorry! My inexhaustible love for you, separated by a wire mesh lined with glass from your life itself. But Salome, not Elektra. You got the opera wrong.

On "On the Rules of Perspective"

When asked to teach at the University of Michigan in the spring of 2002, I was given your old office in the Rackham Building. Why? When I touched the same keyboard your fingers had touched, I knew. Why? I even rechristened the town *Anne* Arbor! Got down on all fours to sniff the cushion on that swivel chair left behind your desk, its drawers emptied out.

On "On *Le Bonheur d'Etre Bien Aimée*"

Day after day I think of you as soon as I wake up. Anne. Is it true that your lover in "The Anthropology of Water" from *Plainwater* was in fact Asian, and I don't mean in your book but in your actual life?

On "On Rectification"

Someone told me you were a *visual* artist long before you became a *verbal* artist. Is it true *Short Talks* started out as a collection of drawings accompanied by titles that you then "expanded" only later to drop the titles and then the drawings themselves? Who has access now to the originals, I wonder. Would that be an argument for or against marriage? Forgive me for saying it. All desires are purloined.

On "On Sleep Stones"

Come visit me, she says. Boing! My hands grow huger and huger like two parts of someone else loaded onto her knees. We could snuggle up on that pull-out couch your MacArthur "genius" grant paid for, watch *Camille Claudel*, the whole house filled with the scent of microwave popcorn, extra movie butter. Finger-lickin' good times, Anne, before I put out your lights.

On "On Walking Backwards"

The first "Short Talk" I ever read, which, if memory serves, appeared in *Best American Essays* that Susan Sontag edited, was it 1992? Maybe that in part explains your subtitle "Essays and Poems" for *Plainwater*. Two years before that, "Kinds of Water" appeared in *Best American Poetry*. Go girl! you *Canadian*, you.

On "On the Mona Lisa"

She sits behind bulletproof glass. A copy. One from an edition of nine, or twelve, depending on whom you ask, the original stored in an underground vault. Don't tell me Leonardo was painting his mother, lust, et cetera. Who knew she would end up like this.

On "On Waterproofing"

The original needs no gloss.

On "On the End"

We had such a good time, hey! why didn't you call me? I thought I'd see you again. In the Frick Museum, there's a late Rembrandt self-portrait that looks a lot like Macy Gray when I saw her open for David Bowie at the Garden where I sat up in the nose-bleeders, utterly buzzed and high.

On "On Sylvia Plath"

Look at her, masturbating a glitter while the peanut-crunching crowd shoves in to see her striptease. Puh-leaze! Somebody give it a rest. You did *not* just say "jungle hatred wild jungle weeping chop it back chop it," did you? only to wake up with Ted's face.

On "On Reading"

Some children hate trips but love to read interviews from the *Paris Review* you can now find online for free on your smartphone while riding in the back of your dad's Chevy. Take issue number 171. The cover image looks a lot like the face of a tenement building in the L.E.S. after a car bomb has gone off. Drive, Daddy, drive! Are we there yet?

On "On Rain"

Slippery When Wet is a road sign I've never actually encountered in "real life," only on the cover of a Bon Jovi album. I wonder if Anne has the wherewithal to "lip-sync for her life" to the song "You Give Love a Bad Name" if an AR-15 (the one used in the Newtown shooting) were pointed at her head in a dream from which we cannot wake.

On "On the Total Collection"

When I first asked her to sign my cloth first-edition copy of *Plainwater*, she simply wrote: "Timothy a c 1996 Iowa" which seemed to confirm what I suspected all along, that indeed there was a spark between us, wouldn't you say? The next time I heard her read, she wrote the exact same thing, only this time, we were in New York City right after the Twin Towers "pancaked" to the floor. Damn. She *remembered* me! She said, "You're the guy who always sits somewhere in the back, marking the differences between what I read aloud versus what's there on the page, aren't you?" Anne, I said, aren't we nothing if not works in progress? From childhood on, I've only dreamed of being able to keep with me all the objects in the world lined up on my bookshelves.

On "On Charlotte"

It's still a hub for US Air, isn't it, unless it has merged with another carrier? How my heart aches to hear Miss Carson walking, walking on alone.

On "On Sunday Dinner with Father"

My father smokes a brand of cigar called Mona Lisa Lewinsky. (Don't take that dress to the cleaners, honey, not so fast!) We were drawing Dalí moustaches on busts all over town till things went south, till we went back over our work with Hitler moustaches only this time in permanent marker. (The Prize song from *Die Meistersinger* blaring out from an ice-cream truck whizzing past.) Or was that you crooning in my ear like another daddy's girl? (She wore blue velvet . . .)

On "On the Youth at Night"

Like an Amish quilt with an intentional mistake sewn into the fabric as a means to show humility to our Maker.

On "On *The Anatomy Lesson of Dr. Deyman*"

It was the hunger winter of 1656 when Black Jan took up with a whore named Elsje Ottje and for a time they prospered. This is the second time she's name-dropped Rembrandt into her magnum opus. The only other figure featured more than once is Kafka (first in "On Rectification" and later in "On Waterproofing" which, IMHO, may well be the pick of the litter). No women are ever mentioned in more than one poem at a time which makes me wonder if there's not something male-identified about her classicist ass? And what is Dr. *Joan* Deyman's gender anyway, pray tell? One wonders if Elsje ever saw Rembrandt's painting, which shows her love thief in violent frontal foreshortening, so that his pure soles seem almost to touch the chopped-open cerebrum.

On "On Orchids"

The fragrance is undying. Asia. Vermont. Ground Zero. A Little Boy has run away where people are buried alive.

On "On Penal Servitude"

"In the Penal Colony" (German: "*In der Strafkolonie*") (also translated as "In the Penal Settlement") is a short story written by Franz Kafka in German in October 1914, revised in November 1918, and first published in October 1919, not by Dostoevski! (also spelled Dostoyevsky) nor to be confused with the BDSM porn flick *In the Penile Colony* which my friend Hildebrand von Furstenberg both directed and produced in the late nineties which you can fact-check for yourself on wiki anytime you want.

On "On Hölderlin's World Night Wound"

King Oedipus may have had an eye too many between his legs.

On "On Hedonism"

When I look at the city of Hoboken, I want to wrap my legs around it, Anne said, on the rooftop of a condo on West Twenty-Second overlooking the Hudson. I asked her if she knew about Snug Harbor just a ferry ride away, and she said, Come again? So I asked if skyscrapers made her keen on Skype sex, if that were up her alley. Yes, she said, I've heard about that Chinese Philosopher's Garden shipped to Staten Island piece by piece from another continent! My darling, I said, there's a Moon Gate made of stone in that garden that is perfectly round; walking through it gives one a sense of complete serenity. Timothy! she said, how open you are to the power of suggestion!

On "On the King and His Courage"

He looked out at the world, the most famous experimental prison of its time. That was years before Brick Books brought out the first edition of *Short Talks* in 1992. How quiet the world seemed then, how calm and still, when his hard-on had yet to seek pardon.

On "On Shelter"

I am writing this to be as wrong as possible to you! Jacques Lacan: "The reason we go to poetry is not for wisdom, but for the dismantling of wisdom." Who never cared much for my Beloved in the way that I do: "Made wise though compassion, a pure fool."

Work Cited

Carson, Anne. *Plainwater: Essays and Poetry*. New York: Knopf, 1995.

CHRISTINE HUME

How Is a Pilgrim Like a Soldier?

Anne Carson's "Kinds of Water: An Essay on the Road to Compostela"

> They say that the Tehuelches hunted the ñandu by physically
> exhausting the animal. The entire tribe would walk for
> weeks chasing the flock until the ñandu would give up or
> die of exhaustion. We, of our time, must chase mirages.
> —FRANCIS ALŸS, "A STORY OF DECEPTION"

> My mother forbade us to walk backwards. That is how the
> dead walk, she would say. Where did she get this idea? Per-
> haps from a bad translation. The dead, after all, do not walk
> backwards but they do walk behind us. They have no lungs
> and cannot call out but would love for us to turn around.
> They are victims of love, many of them.
> —ANNE CARSON, "ON WALKING BACKWARDS"

Francis Alÿs's *Guards* (London 2004–5) is a thirty-minute video
documenting a loosely scripted narrative of sixty-four Coldstream
Guards, the oldest regiment in the British Army. By different streets,
unaware of one another's route, the uniformed guards wander
through London looking for one another. When they meet, they
fall into step, picking up members of their regiment as they go.
When a lost solider hears the percussive marching, his legs seem
activated by the sound. One by one, as if blindly drawn by martial
history, each Coldstreamer falls into formation. The sound of
marching spreads like a rumor, building a powerful narrative by col-
lectivizing. As a social allegory on esprit de corps, the piece reveals
the human inclination to seek identity in group formations. When
the soliders are alone, their walk is a casual *dérive*, marked by idio-
syncrasy, but as soon as they meet with others, it becomes rigidly
mechanical, a perfect machine of synchronization. Alÿs's guards vi-
sually represent lost individuals finding their way, finding the path
to their own completion. As a parable of the return of the prodigal
son, the piece reveals the seductive power and moral righteousness
of organized collectivity at the same time it exposes its necessary

temporality. The center cannot hold. Once the guards are assembled in an eight-by-eight square, they march toward the closest bridge. As they step onto the bridge, the guards break step and disperse haphazardly.

Introducing isolated characters through a drama of division, the piece accumulates into a climactic reunification that finally breaks back down into the chaos of individuality. The work's chiastic structure points to a terrain of instability, in which seeming oppositions overlap and trigger one another. The guards loudly and confidently become a unified "we," but this resolution is flanked by candid views of the guards as individuals. We glimpse a subjective intimacy of the many anonymous individuals that the "we" holds within it. Anne Carson's "Kinds of Water: An Essay on the Road to Compostela" insists on this same sense of fluid identity, which is highly relational and easily displaced. "A bridge," in Carson's work, "is a meeting point, where those who started out—how many now how many nights ago—come together" (132); though a symbolic image of connection, the bridge in both works acts paradoxically to dissolve a sense of communality. Both Carson and Alÿs employ the conceptual system of fable whose conflict relies on the tensions between self and union. Carson's narrator—"a young, strong, stingy person of no particular gender" (123)—sets off on a pilgrimage, hoping to walk her identity into more knowable ground.

Carson's pilgrim's diary plots a contemporary couple trudging together through many layers of literary and walking traditions as they traverse the medieval route, the *Camino de Santiago*. The narrator nicknames her paramour My Cid after El Cid—a medieval, Castilian military hero and the subject of an early epic—in order to condense the storytelling. Each chapter or diary entry begins with an epigraph from the Japanese literary walking tradition, the haiku or *halibun*. Carson and Alÿs evoke and trouble multiple pedestrian modes, but the pilgrimage and the military march by their very nature eschew more exploratory walking strategies—the contemplative perambulations of the *flaneur* (defined by Baudelaire, Benjamin) and the psychogeographic *dèrive* (practiced by Situationists)—in favor of ancient forms. Both Carson and Alÿs research and amplify the effect of these structures' regimentation on the individual. The forms these walks take seek to control the characters who take them, yet their walkers implicitly question the homogeneous, synchronic, universal, and classified notion of the traditions they are participating in. As the guards make their way through a modern city, they are marked by their Old World uniforms—red jackets, bearskin hats, gold buttons—whereas the modern lovers in Carson's work navigate an ancient rural route marked by history. Both parties come laden with anachronistic weapons—the guards carry bayonets; the pilgrims carry knives. The figurative language of the latter is often fraught with shooting, guns, lances, bullets as well as knives and stabbing. These weapons—hardly threats—act like the literary and historic references that bend the narrative by grafting one reality over another. Carson's militaristic language suggests her lovers hold onto a conflictual way of understanding love that makes juxtaposition leap into metaphor. Drawing startling significance out of odd pairings and paradox engines both works. By juxtaposing historic and contemporary realities, Carson and Alÿs suggest the ways we all walk in ideologically complex worlds of multiple authorities and temporal paradoxes.

As they participate in historic forms of walking, we come to understand these routes as scripted and their narratives, overdetermined. The ceremonial nature of love and war dramatizes the will of the individual. The lovers and soldiers are blind with the rigor of their collective desire. As viewers/readers we *see* this blindness through photography, both as a trope and a physical artifact. Each work is framed in multiple shots that never allow us to absorb into a cinematic moment. In both, the camera documents at the same time it self-consciously distorts and obscures visual memory by drawing our attention to structural repetition and reflection rather than scenic moments. The flags of courtship and war share the same colors: black, red, and gold. These colors repeat with talismanic fury throughout both pieces, offering the feeling of backtracking and of being lost as well as a characterization of the indistinct vision of both the soldiers and the pilgrims. Color becomes the object of our gaze and even as it shifts onto surfaces, color never relinquishes its subject position. The red, black, and gold British military uniform rhymes visually with much the guards pass in the video, including pedestrian clothing and architectural features. Color patterns reinforce the rhythm of inevitability carried through the sound of marching. Carson uses the colors to suggest the limits of her characters' perception, though as with Alÿs's piece, the characters seem to infect their environments with red, black, and gold, as markers of themselves—marks of their presence—on their route. Carson's visual descriptions are indistinct and deceiving, dwelling on light, color, or atmospherics rather than concrete detail. Her scenes are out of focus, figure and ground suppressed, over- or underexposed to light, and too close or too far away to see. Linguistic descriptions of photographs often direct narrative attention. Photographs set the narrator where she wants to be, a witness to her own story, allowing her to embed a third-person perspective in a first-person voice. Perhaps this is something akin to Maurice Blanchot's concept of a narrative governed by the neuter; she is after all a person "of no particular gender" who needs photographs to be able to view anything at all. But even clear photographs here do not offer common ground or a shared set of eyes. They become mirrors to her internal confusions: "Love is the mystery inside this walking. It runs ahead of us on the road like a dog, out of the photograph" (145). As the narrator describes photographs, they regularly offer more ambiguity than clarity: "Look at this one, for instance—it could be a drowned dog floating in bits of stone. Can you make it out. The picture has been taken looking directly into the light, a fundamental error" (165). This narrative voice, as Blanchot theorizes, rattles the "circumspect consciousness." According to Blanchot, "From now on, it is no longer a question of vision. Narration ceases to be what is presented to be seen" (139). Though insistent, Carson's visual gestures are always either obscured by the wrong distance, frame, or light, coming through photographs, or else they are entirely imagined, coming through historic reference, metaphor, and dream, thus reinforcing sight as a means of reflection rather than perceptual information.

Visual logic destabilized, both pieces suggest that a walkers' most acute sense is hearing. Potent sonic memories and futurities load each step. Note the elision of tense in Carson's essay, which interlocks living and thinking: "Your voice I know. It had me terrified. When I hear it in dreams, from time to time all my life, it sounds like a taunt—" (175). Sounds come out of the fog—voices, foghorns, bells—as signals to the pilgrims. Carson's walkers tell stories as they amble along, they understand travel by conversational mythmaking. "My Cid's" stories "make people seem real" (151) the narrator relates, reiterating the way she makes him into a historical and literary character by renaming him. He assumes a third-person position with occasional bursts into second-person address: Carson's narrator talks to and about him, attempting to tell multiple stories simultaneously. She claims, "My Cid tells these stories wonderfully well" (137) but later confesses to "contradict everything he says" (159). Carson's lovers exhaust themselves conversationally by shifting positions dialectically in relation to the other. As they listen to one another, they look ahead at the same thing or not, but they do not look at one another. The narrator muses, "A voice coming from behind your back is different. Animals who ride on top of one another do not have to see one another's face. Sometimes that is better" (150). But what is not seeing one another's face better for? An answer may be found in Francis Alÿs's *Guards*, where structure organizes through sound. The guards' marching rhythm resonates through the city's narrow and mostly deserted streets; its percussion calls in its own. As the guards navigate by an unseen system, the acoustics of hiding and seeking play out amid reflective and repetitive surfaces. Carson's characters also seem to fall into place—obedient to couple formation and to gender structures—as inevitably as the guards. Their storytelling "entangles"—one of the words the narrative hangs on—them both. Sounds, particularly voices, engulf, like the titular "water," but optics lock us in frontally, offering orientation and perspective. Without a clear visual framing—historical long shots mix with extreme close-ups of private moments—we listen out for a middle ground. "Listen, footsteps go fading down the street" (162). Step by step, each sentence moves the narrative into greater emotional distance. We hear identities being swept along into fables, riddles, history, and unbearable silence. The road is a voice behind them, pushing like a ninth-century wind at their backs, leading them into predictable narratives. Though their course was set long ago, and well traveled, it is not without surprises: "You get almost no warning. Something is coming along the edge of the wheat, dumming the plain like a horseman, you stop, listen, begin to turn—don't!" (155). Fractured myths recombine and reassemble, but the sociohistorical structures of their journey trap the characters in performances of conventional gender roles and dynamics. Readers aren't surprised by the couple's increasing alienation, loneliness, rage, and resentment because we understand this development as historically inevitable.

Another way of thinking of this state of affairs is that Carson's narrator performs bad translations of her roles (see "On Walking Backwards"). As a pilgrim seeking answers, she generates too many contradictory answers, and thus more questions. As a woman in love, she is a figure at a distance who often mistakes herself for a trapped animal. In the end, as in the beginning, Carson's narrator identifies with a drowned dog, an image which haunts her walk and makes her question herself as a walker, or even as a human, at all.

What is abandoned in Carson's narrator? At most everything, she keeps moving. When the narrator and her companion reach the end of the road, instead of backtracking or walking backward, they assume a static tableau that shifts the story's perspective. As the narrator lies in the sea, she recalls: "You take hold of my paws and cross them on my breast: as a sign that I am one who has been to the holy city and tasted its waters, its kinds" (187). The narrator leaps into fable by transforming into a dead dog, an act that reinforces the radical instability of her identity and our sense of her as an object. Just as the narrator slips out of humanity, she addresses an indeterminate someone (the watchers? the reader? My Cid?) directly— "you take hold of my paws"—with the necessary intimacy of love story.

How is a pilgrim like a soldier? They are victims of their mission.

How is a pilgrim like a soldier? They accept the partial truth of the moment, which necessarily includes an acceptance of death, which in turn allows an escape from the ancient coordinates of narrative space.

Works Cited

Alÿs, Francis. *Guards*. With Rafael Ortega and Artangel, 2005. Viewed November 20, 2012, and March 31, 2013, at University of Michigan Art Museum.

Alÿs, Francis. *Le temps du sommeil*. Ed. Sean Kissane and Catherine Lampert. New York City: Charta Books, 2010.

Blanchot, Maurice. *The Gaze of Orpheus*. Trans. Lydia Davis. Barrytown, NY: Station Hill Press, 1981.

Carson, Anne. *Plainwater: Essays and Poetry*. New York: Knopf, 1995.

The Unbearable Withness of Being
On *Anne Carson's* Plainwater

Anne Carson's *Plainwater* studies companionship, or, perhaps more accurately, *Plainwater* is a study of *being with*—being *with* others, *with* oneself, *with* texts, *with* language, *with* bodies of water, *with* bodies of land. In the face of all this *withness*, unsurprisingly, given all that Carson has reinforced for us (and all we know) about desire, lack and longing still emerge; *withness* is not a synonym for completeness. *Withness* has a relationship to mobility (another keyword for Carson's *Plainwater*, invested as it is in how we move toward and away from people, places, things, and ideas). *Plainwater* might be retitled or titled again *The Unbearable Withness of Being*. The title *Plainwater* itself—a portmanteau, a term recalling the baggage language can be, burdened by each of our own contexts, a term that denotes the adjoining of words—suggests an interest in being *alongside*. Here, the union is clarifying: "Plain" makes the water both more itself (giving it a distinct characteristic that sets it apart from other water, if we read *plain* as an adjective, or locating it, if we read *plain* as a noun) and more than itself (*both* plain *and* water). One might think of Carson writing on adjectives in the poem-essay that opens *Autobiography of Red*: "Adjectives seem fairly innocent additions but look again. These small imported mechanisms are in charge of attaching everything in the world to its place in particularity. They are latches of being."[1] How does a latch differ from a tether? If an adjective is a latch, perhaps a preposition is a tether, "governing nouns and pronouns and expressing a relation to another word or thing." What thoughts are we tied to? Where are our ties? When might they loosen, and when might they strangle? We are caught up—

If we read *Plainwater* as having a consistent speaker, versions of that speaker abound: she is scholar, daughter, translator, pilgrim, sibling, interviewer, hotel occupant, one who records, one who wonders and wanders, a lover who partakes in sexual role-playing, a woman, an androgyne. As Carson writes, "The joy of living is to alter it."[2] These myriad roles suggest that identity exists in meaningful ways only in relational contexts. The very autobiographical feel of the text plays on autobiography as an invention and investigation of selfhood: the autobiographical subject is always already counterfeit, its success or failure is how authentically it passes for human; there is a joy in counterfeiting, in passing, in getting one over (a crossing)—the joke is on one's sense of boundedness and of boundaries. The premise is the possibility of successful recognition. Much of *Plainwater*'s investigation of being highlights the simultaneous richness and limitations of empirical observation: a brother is one who swims and does not swim. A dog is one that floats when dead. A city is a place in which one stops and starts and stops and starts again. A painting is one that becomes an Anna.

Building on the combinatory gesture of the title, the subtitle, "Essays and Poetry," which may at first give the impression that the book consists of interspersed essays and poetry, comes to suggest that each piece is both essay and poem, both of which are accommodating to exploratory gestures. Carson's poems privilege inquiry, highlighting the processes of knowing over the objects of knowledge. Carson knows that knowing changes us; in *Plainwater*, she asks, "Who would you be if you knew the answer?"[3] To launch into Carson's writing, I want first to think about the work of one of her kin, Emily Dickinson, a writer who has become emblematic of the unconventional woman poet and whose own investments align with many of Carson's.

In the final stanza of "[I felt a Funeral, in my Brain]," Dickinson writes,

And then a Plank in Reason, broke,
And I dropped down, and down,
And hit a World at every plunge,
And Finished knowing—then—

The speaker seems neither panicked nor surprised. In fact, what may at first seem like uncontrollable falling ("And I dropped down, and down") shifts into participatory descent: the speaker *plunges*, which denotes jumping and diving—she shifts from being *in for* it to being *into* it—and why not, what with the numbness of mind threatening her in the earlier stanzas and mourners already writing her off as done.

We can, of course, read finality in Dickinson's last line, interpreting "then" as a marker of a discrete moment in time (e.g., it happened right *then* and there). However, the repetition of "And" at the beginning of each of the final lines and the em-dash at the end of the stanza highlight continuation and support a reading of the final "then" as pointing to what's next (e.g., and *then* what happened?): what happens after we've used up what we know or hit an impasse? Ideally, we seek a different route, propelled by the very drive to know, despite the fallibility in knowing. As Carson writes, "Speaking as someone who is as much in love with knowledge as My Cid is in love with the light on the plain of León, I would say that knowing is a road. The metaphor is unoriginal but now you may set it beside the photographs of the pit in the wall and see what it signifies to me."[4] Intellect, as Dickinson's first line and Carson's knowing-as-road metaphor suggest, is not stable—the mind changes, moves; from what angle do we capture this slice of road? Carson uses language to construct artifacts of knowing in its various manifestations (to record our encounters with various worlds).

In Dickinson's poem, the descent from reason occasions journeying through various systems of knowing, represented by innumerable worlds: the speaker accrues experience, "hit[ting] a World at every plunge." Thank goodness, it seems, that reason is only so sturdy! The emphasis in the last line (via capitalization) is on the verb "Finished," and we might imagine that the poem's speaker has not simply stopped knowing, but has, somewhat ravenously, *finished* it off. There is plausibly more knowing to be had, should one get over the initial disorientation of being removed from a seemingly stable environment—should one commit herself to the descent, to exploring the worlds one does not yet know. The descent revives and opens up the possibilities for exploration. The plunge here is permission—permission to reengage without (already) knowing, permission to go (quite literally) *through* the world(s). Carson seems to ask: how do we make ourselves ready for knowing? How do we prepare to travel knowing's roads? What truth-statements will we test first? Given that Dickinson's poem suggests reason (and thus the intellect) can only support so much, the challenge, it seems, is to know differently (and with methods other than purely intellectual ones—imaginative? emotional?). This aligns with one of Carson's claims that may at first seem paradoxical: "You can never know enough, [you can] never leave the mind quickly enough."[5] The mind is unhinged from its figurative relationship to knowing; the body is sent out, dropped down. The mandate is *to seek*. Anne Carson is a poet up to the task.

In *Plainwater*, Carson's speaker (or speakers) is certainly a world-traveler, one who loves entering. This maps onto Carson's love of documents: a lover of documents is a lover of entering. We enter conversations when we enter texts. As in our conversations with acquaintances and friends, we encounter and develop kinship terms, ways of being *with*. In "Short Talks," Carson ties the landscape of the page to the landscape off the page: "I glimpsed the stupendous clear-cut shoulders of the Rockies from between paragraphs of *Madame Bovary*. Cloud shadows roved languidly across her huge rock throat, traced her fir flanks"[6]—the written text infuses and makes sensual the natural landscape. The point of view is inseparable from the view itself: perhaps this is an early lesson on the value of taking up a position, of role-playing, of what the role (or the view taken up) brings, of how it brightens or darkens, obscures or uncovers. Those who critique Carson's writing as off-putting because of its erudition perhaps undermine the role of performance in her texts (perceiving that scholar displaces poet rather than that poet performs scholar): the scholar, as one who is curious, is simply one of many vehicles for enacting the desire to know. The scholar values writing as a means to thinking and knowing; the poet performing scholar can thus be unburdened from the conventional conception of poetry writing as personal expression that conveys an epiphany (an answer) and can instead use the space of the poem to question and to form ideas.

There is tension between knowing and thinking. Perhaps the surety of knowing is distrusted: Carson's ambivalence toward the aphorism supports this; she undermines the authority of truth-statements throughout the text. Take for instance the shifts from aphorism to riddle in "Kinds of Water: An Essay on the Road to Compostela" (with aphorisms privileged on the early leg of the documented pilgrimage and riddles privileged on the latter leg of it): "Well, a pilgrim is like a No play. Each one has the same structure, a question mark,"[7] "Pilgrims were people glad to take off their clothing, which was on fire,"[8] "Pilgrims were people to whom things happened that happen only once,"[9] "When is a pilgrim like a photograph? When the blend of acids and sentiment is just right,"[10] "How is a pilgrim like a blacksmith? He bends iron. Love bends him,"[11] "When is a pilgrim like the middle of the night? When he burns?"[12] and "How is a pilgrim like a No play? His end is not the point. And yet it is indispensable, to the honor and to the shame."[13] This list is not exhaustive. The journey undoes certainty rather than brings clarity. If aphorisms represent unquestionable knowledge ("facts"), riddles represent knowledge-generating questions.

As water parts, *Plainwater* parts. Part 1, "Mimnermos: The Brainsex Paintings," iterates translations as companion pieces (rather than representations of) originals, suggesting translation is primarily an act of *being with*. The section also consists of transtemporal interviews, enabling conversation between an ancient Greek poet and a twentieth-century interviewer. Part 2, "Short Talks," revolves around topical vignettes. Each of the titles begins with the preposition "on," establishing what subject the body of the mind lies over or moves on top of at the moment—what subject the mind gets to knowing (there is an erotics of scholarship that emerges throughout the book): "On Gertrude Stein About 9:30," "On Defloration," "On Major and Minor," "On Sylvia Plath," "On Penal Servitude," and so on. In the third part, "Canicula di Anna," the objet d'art becomes the darting subject: one who moves the painter (and then, ideally, the viewer) becomes one who moves through the landscape of the page—a play on "living art," on audience and interpretation as an extension of creating/writing, on the interpretive processes that make the "work" distinct from the "text." Anna (the name given to the painter Pietro Vannucci's painted woman) is given mobility; however, "Let us make no mistake / about the freedom."[14] Anna's animation still relies on collaboration rather than self-actualization, though she herself is suspicious of reliance: "'Do not hinge on me,' Anna says. / 'If you want my advice, / do not hinge at all.' One of our many discussions of freedom."[15] Freedom is a fiction that sustains the notion of the individual; Carson's poems seem more invested in models of dependence (being *with*) that lead to autonomy, in the self-governing sense.[16] Part 4, "The Life of Towns," reminds us that each town has its own shape, and, thus, we exist in each town differently. Space shapes our thinking, and our thinking manifests spatially. A town is a description of its citizens, and vice versa. Sentences are a series of pathways that connect and lead to meaning; an idea is a town of partial and full sentences. Here is "Town of the Sound of a Twig Breaking":

Their faces I thought were knives.
The way they pointed them at me.

And waited.
A hunter is someone who listens.
So hard to his prey it pulls the weapon.
Out of his hand and impales.
Itself.

Part 5, "The Anthropology of Water," is the most substantial por-
tion of the book, length-wise, totaling more pages than the other
four sections combined and charting the effects of time and space
on the movement or stagnancy of relationships (between lovers,
between colleagues, between siblings, between different expressions
of gender). Position determines relation: how one is positioned in
relation to water determines whether one drowns or swims. Water's
identities circulate as if in a fish tank. The water's kindness is dis-
cerned by its relation to the body that enters it—there are *kinds* of
water whose differences are activated by verbs: the kind that drowns,
the kind that hydrates, the kind that enables swimming, the kind
that cleans, the kind that is read. Is it none of it or all of it that is
Plainwater?

Carson's lends us perceptions. As she writes at the end of "Ca-
nicula di Anna":

Having held you in my company so long, I find I do have some-
thing to give you. Not the mysterious, intimate and consoling
data you would have wished, but something to go on with, and
in all likelihood the best I can do. It is simply the fact, as you go
down the stairs and walk in dark streets, as you see forms, as you
marry or speak sharply or wait for a train, as you begin imagina-
tion, as you look at every mark, simply the fact of my eyes in
your back.[17]

To decide to write is to decide to create *withness*. It's a big commit-
ment, to become an enduring companion: the eyes in our paper-
backs we open and close with each return and departure. Perhaps
writing helps us figure out how to enact the *withness* living requires.
Carson's writing creates spaces for experiments in being, without
letting us forget that being *with* is upheaval; it's the best and the
worst thing—because the face of *withness* is always changing. As
soon as we've memorized the edge of its face, the edges shift. We
have such limited control, yet we decide again and again to commit.
A commitment we make ultimately without knowing (how it will

end, how it will change us, etc.). Like "the soul of the cat [which] is mortal" and "does its best,"[18] we are called to live our lives—all of them. Carson shows us the possibilities and impossibilities between which each existence is tethered.

Works Cited

Carson, Anne. *Autobiography of Red*. New York: Vintage, 1999.
Carson, Anne. *Plainwater: Essays and Poetry*. New York: Vintage, 2000.
Spahr, Juliana. *Everybody's Autonomy: Connective Reading and Collective Identity*. Tucsaloosa: University of Alabama Press, 2001.

Notes

1. Anne Carson, *Autobiography of Red* (New York: Vintage, 1999), 4.
2. Anne Carson, *Plainwater: Essays and Poetry* (New York: Vintage, 2000), 75.
   3. Ibid., 239.
   4. Ibid., 165.
   5. Ibid., 29.
   6. Ibid., 39.
   7. Ibid., 148.
   8. Ibid., 154.
   9. Ibid., 167.
   10. Ibid., 170.
   11. Ibid., 176.
   12. Ibid., 180.
   13. Ibid., 184.
   14. Ibid., 69.
   15. Ibid., 74.
16. Juliana Spahr discusses poetry and models of autonomy in *Everybody's Autonomy: Connective Reading and Collective Identity* (Tucsaloosa: U Alabama, 2001), and I refer interested readers to her text.
   17. Carson, *Plainwater*, 90.
   18. Ibid., 260.

JENNIFER K. DICK

The Pilgrim and the Anthropologist

"When is a pilgrim like a letter of the alphabet? When he cries out."[1] I read in Anne Carson's *Kinds of Water*, and think a letter cries out for a word, to be connected, made into meaning. A sense sought: to be, being. A reader and a writer—a connection like two points at the ends of a line bent into a parabola. Where shall we meet? I wonder, sitting in a café on the French-Swiss-German border reading Anne Carson's *Anthropology of Water*. It has been twenty-three years since I first read Carson's poetic essay. I've since read every other text by her and have myself walked over 1,080 kilometers to Compostela—not because "Something had to break" (122) but because the question of possible recovery, change, recuperation, rejuvenation, visitation (of/by past or future ghosts), and meditation infused me with the same question she asks at the end of section 1, on the eve of the summer solstice as she is about to embark on her own walk: "What is it others know?" (125) because "Pilgrims were people who loved a good riddle" (125).

Between les Vosges and the Black Forest not far from the snow-capped Swiss Alps, I'm thinking about how one reads, is a reader of Carson, asking—can the study of the other be a lament? Isn't the word "study" opposed to the emotional implication of the scientific self in the reaction to and relationship with the society, object, person, thing, and/or concept being examined? Setting up such a paradox (science/lament) is how Anne Carson's writing in this, one of her earliest recognized texts, reveals itself as being as fluid as its title. For how might one study water as if it were of man (from *anthrop* and *ology*), or observe water, that which is "something you cannot hold" (117) but which also does not lend itself to consistent observation—altered so radically by wind, light, or reflection? In the end, this is the study of something running away, mourned, sought, ungraspable slipping off through the fingers, touched, perhaps seen or seen through or which has only a projected reflection on its surface. As the text begins:

Water is something you cannot hold. Like men. I have tried. Father, brother, lover, true friends, hungry ghosts and God, one by one all took themselves out of my hands. Maybe this is the way it should be—what anthropologists call "normal danger" in the encounter with alien cultures. (117)

For the reader, the question is how or where to position yourself. Who is a member of the "alien culture"? Is plunging into Carson's book like being "condemned to spend eternity gathering water in a sieve" (118) like Danaos's forty-nine killing daughters described at the start, or is it like diving into deep water to locate the story of the fiftieth daughter, the one who let her husband live, the one who escaped her societally predetermined destiny? The questions the reader and author-narrator ask, as the "I" speaker of Carson's text tells us, are "as obvious as a door in water" (119).

But where is that door? If we pass through it, are we submerged, unable to breathe, seeing through eyes whose view is skewed, seeking clarity and the oxygen which will allow us to live? Or are we at the start underwater and the door is the opening back out, the text is the oxygen, and life above us, beyond the surface? In the end, this book is anthropology, a "science of mutual surprise" (117) where little is certain but the unexpected and where reading is an "encounter rather than (say) discovery" (117). Here, an observer begins as an "I" heading off on various pilgrimages, road trips, and reflections on the increasingly serious nature of the erasure of her father as his dementia grows, to shift in the end section to an "I" become "the Swimmer," a "he" potentially the brother of Carson, or a version of her lost brother, who "imagines himself dropping into the silent black water of that primitive lake. Shocks of fire flash and die above his head. The cold paints him. All at once he realizes it is not up to him, whether he drowns. Or why" (255).

Carson's reader simply must let go, flow under, breathe in the aquatic literary shifts, the pain of inhaling the impossible, of reaching across it into whatever connections emerge. As the "I" become "he," the swimmer "stands for a moment, then drops, down, through the dark mirror of the lake, to search for red legs and balancings and memories of the way people use love" (256). In the end, like at the beginning of the book, there will be a reflection on loss and mortality and the role of both the author-narrator-anthropologist and the reader-anthropologist who will learn by observing—"'For some must watch,' he [the swimmer] whispers . . . 'And some must sleep'" (260).

How to read such a layered text? How to read a person? The parallel is real. It is anthropological. The study of the other does lend itself to observation, but can it be unbiased, uninvasive? One of the main flaws of cultural anthropology is the impossibility of being a totally passive observer who does not activate any change in the observed subject. The observer, like the reader, changes things automatically: "Shapes of life change as we look at them, change us for looking" (173). The reader decides to see, examine, recall, think about specific moments they observe that are perhaps all their own. I am struck by one line. You are struck by another. These lines speak to us of something outside ourselves, but of ourselves as well. We wade into the waters, and perhaps drown.

A reader submerged, I begin to see more clearly that, among the issues which problematize the positioning of the reader are the fluidity of genre, narrative position, subject gender, and themes. Everything is multiple, inconsistent. For example, *The Anthropology of Water* is comprised of seven titled and subtitled sections. Three of the titles are not explicitly on water ("Very Narrow," "Just for the Thrill," and "The Wishing Jewel"), while the other four are water-specific ("Diving," "Thirst," "Kinds of Water," and "Water Margins"). Each section also has a subtitle, four of which are "Introduction to . . ." (sections 1, 2, 4, and 6), while the other three are called "An Essay on . . ." Yet most of these texts have been published as poetry, just as the book gets shelved in the poetry sections of bookstores.

As concerns the narrative position and subject, in the subtitled introductions 1–3 the main topic is Carson's autobiographically based writing on her own father's dementia. In the final introduction, the focus is on her brother. However, within those sections, there are layerings of critical references, from Kafka to Greek mythology, St. James, Helen Keller, Pindar, Aristotle, and Athena, to which one can add, when adding the three essay sections, allusions to Freud, Socrates, Bashō, Zeami, Machado, *The Poem of the Cid*, Noh plays, *Moby Dick*, civil war ballads, tales of wolves, Modigliani, da Vinci, Chinese history and phrases of wisdom, Nam June Paik, Ray Charles, and more.

In addition to allusions and titling, the gender and characters in these texts are various. The men (real and fictional) in Carson's life overlap—father, brother, lover, men read about, men in the past, the men who are arriving, the men quoted, studied, read, and perhaps also speaking in parts of this book. Carson herself fluctuates, blends into these men, as she observes: "I am astonished to hear my father's voice coming out of my mouth" (230) or "I glance down. Hands on the steering wheel, tough skin pulling across the knuckles, are my father's hands" (209). In "Thirst" Carson writes, "I was a young, strong, stringy person of no particular gender" (123). This said, in "Just For the Thrill" the speaker self-identifies as a woman who is many women, perhaps even all women in one, as Carson writes: "Think of all the women I am" (206). Here, the speaker's uncomfortable situation traveling from Quebec to Los Angeles, the terminus of a relationship with a slightly misogynist partner and lover, parallels the concubines and wives of old Chinese emperors on their 1553 excursion across China. This nonfixity in time, geography, and traditional human gender positions extends to open forms of sexuality in this book, where her lover, the emperor, "likes the idea of making love to women fitted with false penises" (203) or, upon meeting this man who will become her lover, she feels liberated from the complexity of sexual attraction, thinking (erroneously), "Good he is homosexual" (224).

One of the dominant themes in *The Anthropology of Water* is circularity: "We circle, circle, circle again. Around each bend of the road, another, bending back" (167). Yet this wending road carries one only forward, since "Pilgrims were people to whom things happened that happen only once" (167). This collection advances in a kind of mutation-progression where the repetitions of words such as gold, water, loneliness, love, light, wolves, penance, God, the road, fire, blood, fish, bread, stone, heart, red, moon, and drown vary because their meanings and contexts mutate. In cases of lexical repetitions, some emerge as themes which the reader might chase. "Photo" appears at first to indicate real photos the speaker had intended to include alongside the text or which had accompanied it but are not part of the current version. Yet when a "you" enters as the one seeing, being shown, or having been shown photos, the unseen pictures become increasingly part of what's unable to be grasped. The photos themselves "are not helpful" (156) because they have "a certain absence of scale clues" (159). This photo inaccuracy participates in "facts form[ing] themselves this way and that" where something "we find" is rather something we "insist on" (174). The question which plagues the narrator, all scientists, and the reader, returns: "What is knowing?" (175) And what is it I—the reader—know?

Perhaps not adrift, the reader is instead a pilgrim on a quest, seeking to encounter answers. "Since ancient times pilgrimages have been conducted from place to place in the belief that a question can travel into an answer as water into thirst" (122). Yet finding an answer is like "Enlightenment [which] is not a place, no use rushing to get there" (202). This highlights Carson's focus on the voyage, implying that being on the road is, as some belief systems say, the real destination. Carson's speaker repeats, "Remember that enlightenment is useless, that life is an action and its end is a mode of action" (207). This sense of passage, of voyage toward, is the one solid consistency—the announcement that things are mobile.

The largest sections in this book are therefore journeys and/or travel journals organized in poetic essays whose regular form propels the reader along with a secure sense of ordered progression. The prose section titles provide a temporal-chronological pattern. "Kinds of Water" (124–87) includes forty subsections all of which are titled by the stops along the trek to Compostela. These titles are paired with the dates of the stops (beginning with the trek from France into Spain at "St Jean Pied de Port" dated June 20 and ending "To Finisterre" dated July 26).[2] These sections are one to three paragraphs long and preceded by a haiku or other epigraph. "Just For the Thrill" (192–244) includes sixty-seven one- to two-paragraph-long sections with place-name titles like road signs, followed by an "Appendix on Lady Cheng," and a list of sixty-seven "Maps (Ta'o Trek) 1553" ending with "67. Great Wall" (242–44). These sixty-seven maps mirror the sixty-seven segments along the North American trek and the dead end: the lover's move, leaving Carson's speaker for Los Angeles, a city by the sea, a wall. The final essay section, "Water Margins" (248–60), is twenty-eight sections long, one line to two short paragraphs each, titled by the day of the week (i.e., "Sunday"), a time (i.e., "9:00 a.m.") and the declaration "Swimming" or "Not Swimming."

Perhaps, I say to myself, closing the book, this is not a lament after all, nor an anthropological study, but rather a love story, as Carson states: "It would be an almost perfect love affair, wouldn't it? That between the pilgrim and the road" (154). After all:

Love is a story that tells itself—fortunately. I don't like romance and have no talent for lyrical outpourings—yet I found myself during the days of my love affair filling many notebooks with data. There was something I had to explain to myself. I traveled into it like a foreign country, noted its behaviors, transcribed its idioms, prowled like an anthropologist for the rare and unwary use of a kinship term. But kinship itself jumped like a frog leg, then lay silent. (190)

Note

1. Anne Carson, "Part V: The Anthropology of Water," in *Plainwater: Essays and Poetry* (New York: Vintage, 1995 and 2000), 143. All future citations are from this source with their page numbers in parentheses.
2. One exception is the untitled, undated section following Astorga and preceding Molinaseca, corresponding to the missing date of the of July 15.

HARMONY HOLIDAY

Masters of the Open Secret
Meditations on Anne Carson's Autobiography of Red

Rebellion and Contingency

Red, shorthand for *Geryon*, is a tender-hearted monster, let's say, slave to his own tenderness and so born inevitable and poignant like an open secret that always tells itself right on the border between intrigue and *just say it*. Red is a genius, a genesis, an alchemist who manipulates substances through the charges that comprise them— elements like silence, complicity, sex, exceptionalism, sandwiches, smugness, Muhammad Ali—the surreal, the sublime, and the mundane combine in Red and make it plain and happening and habitable for a double, autistic-seeming, instant of omnidirectional reckoning. The reckoning is now in mythological, not earthly terms. Eternity is Red. Memory. Mercy. Rhetoric. Chaos. Disaster. Healing. Lurking. Quickening. Egypt. Greece. Heracles. Refuge. Pride. Blasphemy. *The freed shadow.* The captive showmanship. The Misfit. The popularity. The homo. The hetero. Eros. The unknown. The eyes plunging or seeping into sun. Everybody wants to be this Red and redeemed for something and in her *Autobiography of Red* Anne Carson locates an empathy/yearning we did not know we possess, by inventing it.

Some Say Wings

Some say wings are a winning vestige. If only we humans had some wings, we could fly and span spacetime, instead of mumble along with grounded limbs, conditioned by gravity to act linear and suffocated with nearness to ourselves. And if we had wings, those universal/magnetic dreams about flight would turn untragic and bask in the seductive elastic they conjure, soaring would prove mundane and not a risk reserved for science fiction and the *White Diamond*. Tragedy would no longer be the highest form of art in the West or in the heart, for we would not have to lament attainment of the heights as a dizzying and isolating, yogic, monastic, decadent, grandiose, condition, instead delight would come of it, and justice rather than limbo. Everyone would know the peaks of the Oversoul and the vocabulary of that easy brand of excess would be perceived as redundant and recoil onto a wide open serenity like it is.

But for Geryon, the hero in *Autobiography of Red*, wings are his, and they are anathema, a curse, a hidden place so much a part of him he rarely visits it, they are the seat of his subconscious and since he's a Western hero, that means they're haunted and underexplored. At an early age he's told they are off-limits and they become a liability and a lie and an ever-present loss or denial. Every trauma from his brother's typical and atypical bullying to his mother's addiction to cigarettes and worrying and acting casual, to his own glorious Scotophilia, they all preoccupy this gift of his, they enlist the gift in neurosis so that he fears and conceals his own transcendent ability, his own true and innate thrill, in the petty decorum of the everyday. And for his secrecy he is rewarded with a kind of intimacy he can neither escape nor embrace. The people around him, his favorite people, his heroes, they covet his aura, adore it, but undermine it by considering it implausible, dangerous, awkward. Nothing can be suave, his own ability to expand is limited by the value he places on the imaginations and judgments of others, because he loves them. So he forgets his wings, his spine shudders and shatters moment after moment you can feel him ready to either fly away or fall away and wondering the difference, he's a new nuance in the sequence of motion we think we know. He's normal by feigning so. He's disappearing. He has no wings. His wings are a lie he tells his mind at it agrees. Other people's eyes reflect his edgeless wish for a secret so deep it devours all the others. Which is it? Can he fly or not? If you can't be free, be a mystery.

It's Like Eating the Sun

And you realize you're full mid-swallow and the swallow becomes a gulp and the gulp a globe of loss you thought would be love. Erupting, you arrow out to the whole village the radioactive accident, your miscraved heat, your sudden blackness, the drag from fast to festering. What you really wanted was the color of heat, the sound of it, the vibration, the love in there, the red of it, to tell itself to you, mineral after mineral like a soul on *yes*. The volcanoes in Geryon's tale are of this gold rushing manner of ambivalence. They mirror and shadow his misused wings with their frenzied containment, at any moment they'll stretch out leisurely and eat the sun. There is a latent energy so patient that when it readily succumbs to itself eternity is made. That's what eternity is made of, heretics and heroes alternately erupting, crossing the bridge of their open secrets, switching places, changing their minds, changing their mines, andthenagain.

Not Some Wounded Angel After All, but a Magnetic Person

If at the beginning of the tale of Geryon/Red (as elliptical as he is), we're skeptical, wondering where the common and the clandestine will coalesce and yield the cathartic hero we all want to identify with; that skepticism doesn't last. Red grows up, evolves, transforms in front us from obliging child to moody, verging on sultry, teenager with the kind of reckless restraint we all fall in love with, in others, and in ourselves. We're told we're being introduced to a monster and then we're seduced by him, and realize we're encountering a figure who is more god than monster, and this flatters us because we get to partake in the fruits of the paradox and shake a modern myth out of the psyche with him. Somewhere in the middle of the story the wings (seem to) disappear (again and again like being everywhere), or hide, play a trick on the ego, jive the hero into acting natural, and so wings become allegory for the ghost of memory. And when they return they seem denser and less willing to compromise, less like friendly spirits and more like inevitabilities not hostile but assertive aspects of Geryon's personality which will cause him suffering if they go unacknowledged. A kind of catatonia enters the atmosphere of the *Autobiography* as we feel our hero going from pitiful to proud but lacking the ideal mode of expression for his emergent self-confidence, for it emerges into the grammar of what should be flight and has to walk around hiding its rise. Charisma is displaced by reticence but we can feel the world become hinged and our hero's ability to unveil himself to the world, the remove the mask of freedom before it crushes him.

Glowing Like a Dogma

What's more, time doesn't speed up in *Autobiography* but serendipity teaches it to trust its staggered velocities. The story shifts to Argentina and somehow that makes it all more honest, for the hero finally acknowledges the rut of cloning day after day in the same tepid shame of phantom wings, by going to a place where he can reimagine himself. We hear less and less about the mother. Reunion becomes a theme before it occurs. We get the sense, finally, that Geryon, our yawning wingèd hero being, is being propelled toward his original premises, toward his soul's mystery, which will surely blind him to his form and rescue him from its misfitting with a lesson in its justice, that he will feel as beautiful as he is, or be as beautiful as he feels, just as soon as he recognizes why he is a destiny and rejects it, and accepts it at the same time. His subconscious, however, still seems to flare with angst over the lie on his spine. We wonder how emblems of liberation become so unfortunate and disconsolate in Geryon's world, we learn a lesson in how the way we see things determines the way they behave. Loved wings will save a man; shamed, nervous wings will kill a man. Fear of one's own power will surely only turn the power into a pernicious energy, it won't go away, but it will alter, change forms, turn on itself and glow like a dogma in the neon fog of regret as it atrophies. How does a dogma glow? Like a volcano about to erupt but afraid of the thrill so waiting, waiting . . . And when it finally does no one believes it.

There's Some Ancient People Here, and Some Modern People Here

How do we be, or at least populate, the difference, undo the desolation in the gulf between then and *nownow*. Geryon enters that impossible question as the limbo itself, the go-between, the portal. Our hero is trapped in an idea of himself, like all grand heroes, and loyalty to the idea causes him to betray himself. We witness that betrayal as *Autobiography of Red*. He is one who gives himself away as a matter of concealment. We know so much about Geryon, and even as we feel his very nerves strike and quiver in the presence of lovers or memories or fantasies, we cannot estimate the scale of his senses because his pleasure is of several worlds and psychologies simultaneously, some of those worlds within him and some outside of him, some archaic, some ahead, but all subject to the limits of his perception. The collective obsession we presently have, with pawning the more maudlin aspects of our nostalgia off on futurisms, is relieved in Geryon, for he seems to exist outside of time in such a way that he reconfigures it, like a hallucination. We cannot be sure if the volcano engulfs him at the end, just as we cannot be sure if his love and his lust are one and the same, just as we cannot differentiate between his wings and his more banal delusions of escape and resurfacing. Geryon is a topography for the yet-to-be realized mutations our spirits are currently undergoing, an experiment in forcing the subconscious to gain some integrity by making its musings and musics, come true, materialize. What if all that we imagined came into being, *Autobiography* suggests we prepare for such an occasion by learning how to imagine only what we want and need. Geryon needs the quiet and sustained heights and it hardly matters whether or not his wings are real or drastic energetic manifestations of that need, but either way, the make for a story that must be told, that needs to tell itself to survive itself.

Immortality

Survival is Red/ready/red again. Geryon survives his color and his wingspan/gled banner of will. And we know it's not a political thing; not about race or class or clinging to an attitude for the sake of contriving an identity, or reinvigorating an elite, it's more of a forever element that *Autobiography* is keen on and that Geryon conveniently represents without pupating or pulpiting. Once we feel the roots of ambition take hold of Geryon as his desire to travel and take photographs and make love to other men, we can predict that he's stuck here forever, wings or no wings, he's reached this planet to satisfy and augment and maybe someday transmute those modest cravings. Ache is red, and so is its alleviation. Geryon rests somewhere between ache/longing and self-realization in the final moments of his autobiography, a lot like a martyr who knows he'll be rescued by the great unknown he rescues us from, and *that's not freedom, that's indifference* and he's there for an eternity in this cycle, the god who doesn't believe in god willing to test his faith on the fire right before it blinds him we begin to witness his light. *We are amazing beings.* We are—all so Red and invisible by the end / in the beginning, there was *Red*.

BRUCE BEASLEY

Who *Can* a Monster Blame
for Being Red?

*Three Fragments on the Academic and the
"Other" in* Autobiography of Red

> *The reticent volcano keeps
> His never slumbering plan—
> Confided are his projects pink
> To no precarious man.*
> —EMILY DICKINSON, EPIGRAPH FOR
> "AUTOBIOGRAPHY OF RED: A ROMANCE"

1. Clearing Up the Question of the Relationship between Carson's *Geryoneis* and Stesichoros's

Either Carson derived the "Red Meat: Fragments of Stesichoros" from the extant fragments of Stesichoros's *Geryoneis* or she did not.

If she did not, Carson overwrites Stesichoros's fragments with her own, and in thinking we are studying Stesichoros we study Carson, and we as readers are either blinded or enlightened, or if not, not.

Almost nothing in Carson's "Red Meat: Fragments of Stesichoros" resembles English versions of the *Geryoneis* fragments by Diane Rayor (1991), David Campbell (1991), Paul Curtis (2011), and others, in any way. If these are translations, they are very strange translations indeed; if they aren't, what they are is even stranger. We're not winged eyewitnesses yet to the volcanic innerness of *Autobiography of Red*.

Reviewers and critics have had to take Carson's word for it that the "Red Meat" fragments provide some glimpse into Stesichoros's *Geryoneis* fragments. (To the extent that we *need* translations, we're least able to evaluate their reliability.) Sébastien Ducasse calls them "translated fragments of Stesichoros's *Geryoneis*"; Bruce Hainley writes that "Carson's translation of the penultimate fragment of Stesichoros reveals the 'Total Things Known About Geryon.'" Some critics recognized that the translations were "very free," "wildly free adaptations and in some cases outright inventions" (Bernard Knox), or that "taking liberties [with Stesichoros's texts] must be her idea of a hot time" (William Logan).

But it's not that these are "loose" or "wild" or "free" translations, or versions of Stesichoros incorporating deliberate anachronisms (hot plates, taxis, weekends); only two of Carson's sixteen "Red Meat: Fragments of Stesichoros" bear any recognizable relationship to the *Geryoneis* fragments. Carson creates fragments of a nonexistent poem under the camouflage of translation and then comments and riffs on it, taking liberties not with Stesichoros but with her own imaginative creation of how a Stein-infused "Stesichoros" ought to sound. Translations of the very idea of translation, Carson's sixteen fragments sing a palinode to Stesichoros's fragments: part parody, part pure invention.

Reading Carson's "Red Meat" alongside the red meat of Stesichoros's fragments in Campbell's forty or so fragments or Curtis's twenty-five, we find the only similarities in her sections XIV, "Herakles's Arrow," a loose/wild/free translation of Herakles's slaying of Geryon, and VII, "Geryon's Weekend." The latter appears as follows in other English translations:

And taking a small cup he drank, holding high the measured three flagons—the draught Pholos had mixed and handed to him. (Curtis)

And taking the bowl-cup with the capacity of three flagons he drank it, holding it to his lips—the bowl-cup which Pholus had mixed and handed to him. (Campbell)

For Carson, it goes like this:

VII. GERYON'S WEEKEND

Later well later they left the bar went back to the centaur's
Place the centaur had a cup made out of a skull Holding three
Measures of wine Holding it he drank Come over here you can
Bring your drink if you're afraid to come alone The centaur
Patted the sofa behind him Reddish small alive animal

Not a bee moved up Geryon's spine on the inside
(Carson, 11)

Carson takes from Stesichoros only the occasion—someone drinking from a cup handed to him by the centaur Pholos. Campbell and Curtis both interpret the fragment as a scene with Pholos and Herakles; Carson locates the scene as one of *Geryon's* erotic encounters. The bar scene, the seduction, the chilling image of sensation-through-negation ("Not a bee moved up Geryon's spine"): all are pure Carson, uncontaminated by Stesichoros. In an interview with John D'Agata Carson uses the phrase "costumed in normalcy" (D'Agata, 14); the "Red Meat" fragments are costumed in the normalcy of being the translations they aren't. Like Geryon pinning back his wings to conceal his anomalous body, Carson lulls us into a genre whose rules and promises we think we know. We think again.

Stesichoros, meanwhile, gets costumed in strangeness: his fragments made to seem the way Carson describes them: "as if Stesichoros had composed a substantial narrative poem then ripped it to pieces and buried the pieces in a box with some song lyrics and lecture notes and scraps of meat." The red meat here is all Carson, and the song lyrics, and the lecture notes. Only the ripped-to-pieces substantial narrative poem is Stesichoros's. Little of the radical fragmentation of the *Geryoneis* fragments remains, though, as in Campbell's translations: "head; . . . ; . . . a man . . . heart . . ."; "So s/ he spoke . . . answering."

Like Virgil and Dante descending on Geryon's back to the realm of the deceivers in Dante's *Inferno* XVII, Carson rides on the back of Geryon, deceiving us as she mounts the monstrous steed of Geryon's ruined mythic ancient text. Carson tells us in the first "Red Meat" section ("Red Meat: What Difference Did Stesichoros Make?") how Stesichoros's fragments sound and promises we can confirm that judgment ourselves "by considering his masterpiece. Some of its principal fragments are below. If you find the text difficult, you are not alone."

Yet the principal fragments are *not* "below," and what we "consider," when we consider the "Red Meat" fragments, isn't Stesichoros's masterpiece, but, almost wholly, Carson's. "To fill a Gap," Dickinson advises, "Insert the Thing that caused it— / Block it up / With Other—and 'twill yawn the more—." Carson not only fills the gaps in Stesichoros's narrative with a radical contemporary revision, but she elides even the few coherent fragments of the *Geryoneis* we have and overwrites them with startling but non-Stesichorean lines like "The sound / Of the horses like roses being burned alive" (12) and "Geryon walked the red length of his mind and answered No." We're asked to judge an ancient poet as if he were a postmodern follower of Gertrude Stein and to confirm that judgment by reading Carson's fragments as Stesichoros's. But any judgment we base on the illusion of scholarly evidence in the "translations" would be absurd. Carson's "projects pink" include concealing *her* red meat as Stesichoros's; that's just the beginning of the wild "concealment drama" (Carson, 147) at work in *Autobiography of Red*. This text is trickier, more subversive, more deeply parodic of scholarly authority and readerly and critical passivity than most reviewers and critics yet acknowledge.

2. The Reticent Volcano: Icchantikas and the *Yazcol Yazcamac* (Out of the Red Place and into the Red)

Autobiography of Red seizes Geryon from among the ruins of his textual entrapment and brings him crashing into twentieth-century North America. In the process, Carson also frees him from one mythology only to deposit him into another with the puzzling and thus little-discussed ending in which Geryon undergoes rhetorical transformation into a character in a different mythology: survivor rather than victim, hero-Herakles of his own myth, immortalized rather than slain. Carson strands her Geryon somewhere ambiguously between *being* the red-winged monster of ancient myth and the *Geryoneis* and merely *identifying*, in his sense of difference and vulnerability, with his mythic namesake, his monstrosity sometimes figurative, sometimes quite literal. Geryon mishears the statement "looks like time for you to get home to bed" as "Who can a monster blame for being red?" (Carson, 104). In Carson's mythic redefinition of Geryon's monstrosity from Sicily to Andean Peru, the answer to that fundamental question shifts radically.

Carson includes in her "fragments of Stesichoros" a list—presented as if Stesichoros had compiled it—of "Total Things Known About Geryon." The final "Stesichoros" fragment goes, "The red world And corresponding red breezes / Went on Geryon did not" (Carson, 14). Already as a child Geryon sees the meaning of his life prescripted in that mythic end. Geryon begins his autobiography with his own "Total Facts Known About Geryon" wherein he prefigures his own end, caged already in the myth that will doom him: "Herakles came one day killed Geryon got the cattle." When his mother asks, "Does he ever write anything with a happy ending," Geryon writes his own palinode to the ode of his mythic fate, writing his slaying out of the story: "New ending. All over the world the beautiful red breezes went on blowing hand / in hand" (Carson, 38).

Carson frees Geryon from the mythic (and Stesichorian textual) cage in which he's trapped, with her own palinodic act; like Geryon and Stesichoros, she reimagines the tragic ending and wrenches Geryon out of the Greek myth that dooms him and into a purportedly Peruvian Quechua myth that will reexplain his monstrous origins—and redefine him from mortal to immortal. Ancash tells Geryon of a legend of Eyewitnesses—"*Yazcol Yazcamac it means /* *The Ones Who Went and Saw and Came Back*"—people thrown into the volcano Icchantikas as a sacrifice to the gods who survive and return "as red people with wings, / all their weaknesses burned away— / and their mortality" (128–29).

"Purported," because exactly nothing in Carson can be taken at face value. The name of the volcano, Icchantikas, as Sophie Mayer points out (Mayer, 2008), is the name of no volcano, Peruvian or otherwise, but is a Buddhist term for those of incorrigible unbelief in the sutras. The term Carson assigns to the Eyewitnesses—Yazcol Yazcamac—appears, it seems, only in quotations from *Autobiography of Red*. Is the legend as invented and cryptically named as the volcano it supposedly concerns? In Carson's version, Geryon is winged and red not because of his heritage from his grandmother Medusa in the Greek version, but because he is a Peruvian sacrifice-survivor, a surviving descender into incorrigible unbelief in the Buddhist renunciation of desire. By the end of *Autobiography of Red* we have left one mythological cage and entered another, and the text has become Anne Carson's palinode to the Fire Sermon (both the Buddha's and Eliot's). *This* Geryon is immortal, transfigured by the fires of desire the Buddha warned against in his Fire Sermon. Ancash gives Geryon a new and liberating mythology. It's Carson, though, who writes Ancash's myth, and, like most of the "Red Meat" fragments, this legend may well be invented, imagined, belonging to Carson's innerness rather than Peru's outwardness. Carson becomes Geryon's new Stesichoros, springing Geryon free from Stesichoros's cage inside a textual and mythical cage of her own. *Cage*, after all, is

Geryon's favorite weapon and can be a potent one, if one means by it entrapping others rather than entrapping oneself.

3. White Gristle

"To fill a Gap / Insert the Thing that caused it—": It's Time that caused the gaps in Stesichoros's massive poem. We don't know what would fill those gaps, or how many gaps exist for which we have no trace. Carson fills the gaps in Geryon's story, the monstrous *deprivations* of Stesichoros's textual body replaced by the monstrous *excesses* of hers. Honoring the fragment, she nevertheless defragments the *Geryoneis*. She makes of it a Chimera of a text, seething with multiplicities; she parodies, interrogates, subverts, and inverts genre after genre—novel, epic, lyric, interview, postcard, syllogism, bildungsroman, autobiography, photograph, translation, scholarly essay. Carson's version de-monsterizes Geryon, eliminating his three conjoined bodies, his gigantism, with even his wings and redness—markers of his monstrosity—downplayed throughout much of the narrative. "You wish she'd made more of Geryon's being a monster," complains William Logan (Logan, 67); "I wanted the wings (and the whole 'monster' premise) to play a less passive role, and affect the book's narrative events. Geryon could have done everything he does here (except fly, once) without them," writes Sharon Wahl (Wahl, 83). But Carson's mind, and *Autobiography of Red* itself, are the real monstrous figures here: hybrid, multiple, contradictory, unassimilable, full of deliberate mistakes, deceptions, category errors.

Geryon's multiplicity and strangeness undergo translation into the monstrous excess of Carson's text itself: its proliferation of bewildering and contradictory documents and genres, its pretenses of authority that self-destruct as we read. A normalized Geryon finds his place in a highly abnormal text. Adam Kirsch, in a prominent review of *Autobiography*, argued that "Stesichoros is completely unnecessary for *Autobiography of Red*" and that the appendices, translations, syllogisms, interview, etc. are "showy, deliberately exterior to the main enterprise." Carson's erudition and intelligence, he argues, "wreak havoc on poetry." Critics like Kirsch want to normalize, demonsterize, the text, by removing its stranger and less assimilable excrescences. He wants, like Geryon, to clothe "himself in this strong word *each*" (Carson, 26), but the boundaries between what

Carson calls in an interview "the academic and the other" in her writing (D'Agata, 9) keep disintegrating, as does the word *each* for Geryon. Kirsch wants all the red meat of the extended narrative story of "wrong love" and not the gristle of the scholarship-translation-interview apparatus. But it's the havoc that Carson wreaks (and misdirects us by telling us Stesichoros wreaked) that is the rampage that makes *Autobiography of Red* such a classic monstrosity. As China Mievelle puts it in his recent "Theses on Monsters": "Monsters demand decoding, but to be worthy of their own monstrosity, they avoid final capitulation to that demand. Monsters mean something, and/but they mean everything, and/but they are themselves and irreducible. They are too concretely fanged, toothed, scaled, fire-breathing, on the one hand, and too doorlike, polysemic, fecund, rebuking of closure, on the other, merely to signify, let alone to signify one thing" (Mievelle, 143).

In Carson each eachness, each separable body, interpenetrates, won't stay apart. The academic and the unotherable "other" of essay/novel/poem/translation overlap, their categories in a permanent state of error. Dickinson's "The reticent volcano keeps" haunts *Autobiography of Red* the way Catullus 101 haunts *Nox*, naming its epigraph poem and its final photograph. In a book rounded by a meditation on reticence, secrets, underground projects and plans, untold tales, Carson herself, not Stesichoros, is the "reticent volcano" who confides her "projects pink" to no precarious man, who seethes, with buckled lips.

And the beautiful red breezes go on blowing, hand in hand.

Works Cited

Campbell, David. *Greek Lyric III: Stesichorus, Ibycus, Simonides, and Others*. Cambridge: Harvard University Press, 1991.

Carson, Anne. "A _____ with Anne Carson." Interview by John D'Agata. *Iowa Review* 27.2 (Summer–Fall 1997): 1–22.

Carson, Anne. *Autobiography of Red: A Novel in Verse*. New York: Knopf, 1998.

Curtis, Paul. *Stesichoros's "Geryoneis"*. Leiden: Brill, 2011.

Dickinson, Emily. *The Complete Poems of Emily Dickinson*. Ed. Thomas Johnson. Boston

Ducasse, Sebastien. "Metaphor as Self-Discovery in Anne Carson's *Autobiography of Red: A Novel in Verse*." *EREA: Revue Electronique d'Etudes sur le Monde Anglophone* 5.1 (Spring 2007): 78–84.

Hainley, Bruce. "Monster Heart." *The Nation* 266.20 (June 1, 1998): 32-34.

Kirsch, Adam. "All Mere Complexities." *New Republic* 218.20 (May 18, 1998): 37–41.

Knox, Bernard. "Under the Volcano." *New York Review of Books* 45.18 (November 9, 1998): 57–61.

Logan, William. "Vanity Fair." *New Criterion* 17.10 (June 1999): 60–67.

Mayer, Sophie. "Picture Theory: On Photographic Intimacy in Nicole Brossard and Anne Carson." *Studies in Canadian Literature* 33.1 (2008): 97–117.

Mievelle, China. "Theses on Monsters." *Conjunctions* 59 (2012): 142–44.

Rayor, Diane J. *Sappho's Lyre: Archaic Lyric and Women Poets of Ancient Greece.* Berkeley: University of California Press, 1991.

Wahl, Sharon. "Erotic Sufferings: *Autobiography of Red and Other Anthropologies.*" *Iowa Review* 29.1 (Spring 1999): 180–88.

GRAHAM FOUST

"Some Affluence"

Reading Wallace Stevens with
Anne Carson's Economy of the Unlost

The more I reread Anne Carson's *Economy of the Unlost*, the more I find it impossible to write *about*. Rather, I write around it, through it, under its spell. The problem—"a good problem to have," as they say—is that Carson's long essay has leant certain contours to my mind rather than having simply filled it with content. I'm also tempted to say that it leaves me wanting, but what I mean is that one of its pleasures is its lack of delusions of completeness. As Erazim Kohák writes, "A book succeeds when its margins are full."[1] To be sure, Carson's book is illuminative, and perhaps one reason for this is that it's got some holes in it. (Picture a lantern made by driving nails through a coffee can . . .)

For example, while Heraclitus of Ephesus makes several appearances in *Economy of the Unlost*, the one fragment of his that makes reference to money is never mentioned. Similarly, Wallace Stevens's famous notion that "money is a kind of poetry," while nowhere to be found in *Economy*, seems to haunt Carson's arguments from beginning to end.[2] While thinking through these present absences, I realized that while neither Heraclitus nor Stevens mentions money very often, both men happen to speak of it in the context of fire. Heraclitus's Fragment 90 reads as follows:

> All things are an equal exchange for fire and fire for all things, as
> goods are for gold and gold for goods.[3]

Here we see that Heraclitus gets right money's odd status as an object both homogenous and heterogeneous to itself. As Marc Shell writes:

> Insofar as gold is considered a metal, it is a good (or commodity)
> like all other goods. Insofar as it is considered as coined money,

it is a good unlike any other goods; perhaps, according to Heraclitus, it is not a good at all but rather a mere token or measure. Gold is thus both a good and a nongood, as fire is both a thing and an exchange for all things.[4]

If Stevens's quip about money and poetry is fairly well known, only four lines of his poetry make reference to currency.[5] The following poem is of most interest to us here:

At San Miguel de los Baños,
The waitress heaped up black Hermosas
In the magnificence of a volcano.
Round them she spilled the roses
Of the place, blue and green, both streaked,
And white roses shaded emerald on petals
Out of the deadliest heat.

There entered a cadaverous person,
Who bowed and, bowing, brought, in her mantilla,
A woman brilliant and pallid-skinned,
Of fiery eyes and long thin arms.
She stood with him at the table,
Smiling and wetting her lips
In the heavy air.

The green roses drifted up from the table
In smoke. The blue petals became
The yellowing fomentations of effulgence,
Among fomentations of black bloom and of white bloom.
The cadaverous persons were dispelled.
On the table near which they stood
Two coins were lying—dos centavos.[6]

Heat, fire, smoke; and in what feels like a flash, two upright people are replaced by two prone objects.

"Attempt to Discover Life" ends in a language other than the one in which Stevens usually writes, and its final line both is and is not a translation, for although a "centavo" *is* a coin, the word "centavo" doesn't *mean* "coin." (That would be "moneda.") In other words, Stevens's "other" word both restates what the objects are, while also specifying both their worth and that worth's geographical limits. The poem's narrative, then, leaves us to consider two distinct coins with identical value, and it does so by way of two very different words that point to the same things. From closure to origin—how else to think through a poem if not *back* through it?—the poem is shot through with doubleness, this *and* that: "dos centavos"; "two coins"; "black bloom" and "white bloom"; "smiling and wetting"; "fiery eyes and long thin arms"; "brilliant and pallid-skinned"; "bowed, and bowing, brought"; "blue and green, both streaked." More doubling: Stevens uses the name of a real place to refer to an unreal place—in a reply to José Rodríguez Feo, whose letter inspired the poem, he claims that "the San Miguel of the poem is a spiritual not a physical place"—and the poem's title can of course be read as both a noun and a command.[7]

In his letter to Stevens, Rodríguez Feo describes a health resort at which he is convalescing. Here is what he writes:

> The vegetation is very puritanical in appearance; mostly palm trees—no flowers . . . most of the time I just sit and watch the modest citizens (really very poor) walk about, selling lottery tickets or marching about the streets with their sad-looking horses to incite some rich sick-visitor to take a hike on horses and win therefore a few pesos.[8] (82)

Having read this description, we see that Stevens's poem has both expanded the color palette of his correspondent's narrative and slashed the income of San Miguel's service industry, as an abundance of flowers is now present in a place where Rodríguez Feo says there are none and "a few pesos" has become "dos centavos." Moreover, the "rich sick-visitor" has become two "cadaverous persons" who leave coins behind in one of two—or two of two—ways. On the one hand, "dos centavos" could simply be their rather meager payment for the waitress's services; on the other hand, the coins could be all that's left of them after they've been "dispelled" by the eruption of the flower volcano.[9] That said, the former reading can easily be sublated into the latter, as it's not difficult to imagine these coins ending up in the waitress's pocket either way. The second of these readings, then, is in some way both readings, thus rendering the centavos both remainder and payment, allowing them to echo their own structure as money, which is to say their being "as much proposition as thing."[10]

Walt Whitman contradicts himself, boasts that he "contain[s] multitudes"; Karl Marx, as Carson mentions, claims "money can exchange any quality or object for any other, even contradictory qualities and objects."[11] Perhaps Stevens found these two ideas compatible when he called money "a kind of poetry." If the "dos centavos" of "Attempt to Discover Life" is one of Stevens's mere two poetic references to money, one of his well-known late poems, "The Planet on the Table," might be said to gesture toward money by way of its seemingly contradictory comments on poetry:

> It was not important that [Ariel's poems] survive.
> What mattered was that they should bear
> Some lineament or character,
>
> Some affluence, if only half-perceived,
> In the poverty of their words,
> Of the planet of which they were part.[12]   (450)

At poem's end, we find ourselves in rather ambiguous syntactical territory: Is "some affluence" an appositive that describes "some lineament or character," or is it a second item in a list, "lineament or character" being a kind of inscription and "affluence" being some sort of wealth? The answer is, of course, two answers in one: it's both.

We can see why this is so by thinking about Stevens's aphorism about money and poetry, money and poetry both being *written* things. Ariel's poems' bearing of "affluence" may well be the result of their also bearing "some lineament or character, " much in the same way that the monetary "proposition" printed on a dime or a $100 bill gives a piece of metal or paper a value far beyond its material worth. If the idea of "impoverished" words bearing the world's affluence seems strange, we need look no further than Carson's *Economy* to remember that "the profoundest of poetic experiences [is] that of *not* seeing what *is* there."[13] The hope for this possibility is perhaps best expressed by the poet Jack Spicer in his book *After Lorca*, in which he writes:

> I would like the moon in my poems to be a real moon, one which could be suddenly covered with a cloud that has nothing to do with the poem—a moon utterly independent of images. The imagination pictures the real. I would like to point to the real, disclose it, to make a poem that has no sound in it but the pointing of a finger.[14]

In other words, when we encounter words, we see *beyond* what's on the page *by way of* what's on the page; that is, the word "moon" points us toward the actual moon in the way that the writing on a $100 bill allows us to see beyond the bill's status as words and pictures on a piece of paper and into the realm of *value*, which, while even more difficult to touch than the moon, is nevertheless a very real force in the world. In poetry, as in money, language's poverty is not complete, for language's poverty lacks language itself, and so gives rise to the affluence we call reference.[15] Or, as the poet Allen Grossman says, "Poetry can never take its medium as its whole subject. Language always means something else."[16]

Works Cited

Carson, Anne. *Economy of the Unlost: (Reading Simonides of Keos with Paul Celan)*. Princeton: Princeton University Press, 1999.

Coyle, Beverly, and Alan Filreis, eds. *Secretaries of the Moon: The Letters of Wallace Stevens and José Rodríguez Feo*. Durham: Duke University Press, 1986.

Grossman, Allen. *The Sighted Singer: Two Works on Poetry for Readers and Writers*. Baltimore: Johns Hopkins University Press, 1991.

Kirk, G. S., ed. *Heraclitus: The Cosmic Fragments*. New York: Cambridge University Press, 1978.

Kohák, Erazim. *The Embers and the Stars*. Chicago: University of Chicago Press, 1984.

Marx, Karl. *Selected Writings*. Edited by David McLellan. London: Oxford University Press 1977.

Shell, Marc. *The Economy of Literature*. Baltimore: Johns Hopkins University Press, 1978.

Shell, Marc. *Money, Language, and Thought: Literary and Philosophic Economies from the Medieval to the Modern Era*. Baltimore: Johns Hopkins University Press, 1982.

Spicer, Jack. *My Vocabulary Did This to Me: The Collected Poetry of Jack Spicer*. Edited by Peter Gizzi and Kevin Killian. Middletown, CT: Wesleyan University Press, 2008.

Stevens, Wallace. *Collected Poetry and Prose*. New York: Library of America, 1997.

Notes

1. Erazim Kohák, *The Embers and the Stars* (Chicago: University of Chicago Press, 1984), 223.
2. Wallace Stevens, *Collected Poetry and Prose* (New York: Library of

America, 1997), 905. For more on this aphorism, see my "Wallace Stevens's Manuscript As If in the Dump," *Jacket* 14 (July 2001), http://jacketmagazine.com/14/foust-on-stevens.html (visited May 31, 2013).

3. G. S. Kirk, ed., *Heraclitus: The Cosmic Fragments* (New York: Cambridge University Press, 1978), 345.

4. Marc Shell, *The Economy of Literature* (Baltimore: Johns Hopkins University Press, 1978), 54.

5. "Examination of the Hero in a Time of War" contains the phrase "twelve dollars for the devil"; "New England Verses" contains a reference to "a weltanschauung of the penny pad"; and "Owl's Clover, A Duck for Dinner" mentions "[a] penny sun in a tinsel sky." I do not count the bucks "clattering / Over Oklahoma" in "Earthy Anecdote" as a reference to currency.

6. Stevens, *Collected Poetry and Prose*, 320–21.

7. Beverly Coyle and Alan Filreis, eds., *Secretaries of the Moon: The Letters of Wallace Stevens and José Rodríguez Feo* (Durham: Duke University Press, 1986), 91.

8. Coyle and Filreis, *Secretaries of the Moon*, 82.

9. In its definition for "centavo," the *OED* cites an issue of *Chambers's Journal* from 1920 that mentions the following: "two centavos to the escudo is the 'assistance' tax in hotels and restaurants."

10. Marc Shell, *Money, Language, and Thought: Literary and Philosophic Economies from the Medieval to the Modern Era* (Baltimore: Johns Hopkins University Press, 1982), 171.

11. Karl Marx, *Selected Writings*, ed. David McLellan (London: Oxford University Press 1977), 111.

12. Stevens, *Collected Poetry and Prose*, 450.

13. Carson, *Economy of the Unlost*, 62.

14. Jack Spicer. *My Vocabulary Did This to Me: The Collected Poems of Jack Spicer,* ed. Peter Gizzi and Kevin Killian (Middletown, CT: Wesleyan University Press, 2008), 133.

15. I borrow here from an aphorism by Antonio Porchia: "My poverty is not complete: it lacks me."

16. Allen Grossman, *The Sighted Singer: Two Works on Poetry for Readers and Writers* (Baltimore: Johns Hopkins University Press, 1991), 229.

KARLA KELSEY

To Gesture at Absence
A Reading-With

To think the definitionally unthinkable, to delineate and access that which is beyond-thought. Nothingness. The void. The signaled-by-negation. The no-longer-present because absent, lost. The empty space in a universe, atom, room. These phrases gesture, attempt to catch nothingness with a form we can access.

As exploration of nothingness *Economy of the Unlost (Reading Simonides of Keos with Paul Celan)* reminds us that this attempt courses through philosophical and poetic history. Parmenides: "You must gaze steadily at what is absent as if it were present by means of your mind" (103). Henri Bergson: "philosophical speculation makes use of the void to think the full" (104). Simonides: "Being man, you can't ever say what will happen tomorrow / nor, seeing a man prosper, how long it will last" (104). Paul Celan: "A / star / has probably still light. / Nothing, / nothing is lost" (118).

Two questions frame the tradition of thinking about nothing: can something come out of nothing? And, does thinking about nothing make it something? These questions date back to Thales, regarded by Aristotle to be the first Western philosopher, and turn the topic both material (can matter come from nonmatter?) and personal (how does my thinking not only access, but create, objects of thought?). As such, the questioner occupies a precarious position. To access the emptiness *out there* the questioner must be aware that she stands at its edge and implies her self with its naming: "a negative is a verbal event . . . that depends on the act of an imagining mind" (102).

The fragmentary nature of Simonides's and Celan's texts necessarily places Carson's project on this edge between presence and absence. To the fragments themselves Carson applies the tools of the scholar, working *into* the textual-material landscape in order to work *outward* toward absence. The extent to which Carson grafts fragments into a larger textual context is evidenced in the volume's eight-and-a-half-page bibliography citing primary and secondary texts written by poets, philosophers, literary critics, art critics, historians, and economists in French, German, Italian, Spanish, ancient Greek, and English. Along the bottom of its 134 pages rustle an accumulation of 256 footnotes.

Simonides's text comes to us literally fragmented: while known to be a prolific writer, his extant corpus consists of just 1,300 legible words. Carson-the-scholar presents his work in ancient Greek alongside translations primarily her own. She then builds outward from this materiality, explicating while filling in gaps and voids with discussion of translation, syntax, philology, and context. The context she provides is sometimes material, as when she writes about his epitaphs—one of the many genres in which he excelled—describing the economies of stone carving and stone reading. At other times, Carson works backward from context, such as Plutarch's brief mention of Simonides's lost poem about Theseus, to well-reasoned speculation about a no-longer extant text.

Because nearly contemporary and intentionally fragmented, Celan's work requires less contextual scholarship. Yet Carson's approach to Celan is no less scholarly, presenting original German alongside English translations, delineating issues of translation, syntax, philology, and context. Her scrupulous close-readings serve to unpack Celan's difficult poems, which, coded and dense, resist settling and defy singular definitive meaning. In addition to analyzing some of his more familiar poems, she also fills in our sense of Celan's oeuvre by including less frequently analyzed work as well as speeches and prose texts.

As such, with great generosity of intellect particularly of service to readers without training in the classics, Carson-as-scholar brings what is absent (because lost, unsettled, multiple) into presence. But this scholarly action comprises only one mode of Carson's engagement with the multiple voids surrounding these texts. For even as she cites, footnotes, and explicates she simultaneously unfurls *Economy of the Unlost* with lyric invention. These innovations include the very project of juxtaposing two such radically different writers. Additionally, Carson structures her chapters as constellations of titled sections that, while thematically linked, do not necessarily build linear arguments. Instead, the chapters work like a poem's architecture of stanzas—a series of rooms.

Tone, generating relationship between writer and source-text, writer and reader, becomes lyric tool. While always recognizably

"Anne Carson," Carson smoothes her voice over a broad register. At times she creates the cool distance between author/source text/ reader appropriate to the classics scholar: "The metrical units are reduced, from choriambic metra with dactylic expansion in verse 1, to choriambic metra alone in verse 2" (104). At other times she confides and whispers intimately. About herself she confesses: "I do not want to be a windowless monad—my training and trainers opposed subjectivity strongly, I have struggled since the beginning to drive my thought out into the landscape of science and fact where other people converse logically and exchange judgments—but I go blind out there" (vii). About a Celan poem she utters: "The poem as a whole, recapitulating the first stanza, has the rhythm of a blood-sail, sailing forward in waves from gorselight to gorselight to you" (6). In one of her most engaging turns she dares to fold us, her readers, into Celan's pronoun, this you: "That is why the whole of Celan's poem gathers us into a movement—toward you—that sails to the end. But you, by the time we reach you, are just folding yourself away into a place we cannot go: sleep. Blank spaces instead of words fill out the verses around you as if to suggest your gradual recession down and away from our grasp" (9).

One of the difficulties of thinking about nothing extends from its inaccessibility to the senses. And so how to enter its contours its movement its essence? Further, how to aptly figure emptiness in language, an act that hinges on making present? In the midst of such difficulty Ancient philosophers debated the concept of an ubiquitous primeval material, an ur-matter composing the basis of the universe. Because the universe exists it was thought that ur-material must also exist because something, thinkers such as Thales logicked, cannot come from nothing.

Air was a popular contender, but because it is invisible questions arose as to whether or not air was really a substance or simply empty space: nothingness. Story has it that Empedocles, in the middle of the fifth century BC, thought to measure air, for if it could be measured then it was not nothing, but was substance, albeit invisible. With the aid of a tank of water and a "water thief," or clepshydra—a glass tube open at one end and enclosed with a sphere on the other—Empedocles began to experiment. He found that no water could enter the hydra until air had left, which proved that air was something occupying space, rather than emptiness itself.

As Empedocles's experiments with glass and water allowed him to more accurately know the unsensible, Carson's juxtaposition of Simonides and Celan affords access to what cannot be sensed directly: "With and against, aligned and adverse, each is placed like a surface on which the other may come into focus. Sometimes you can see a celestial object better by looking at something else, with it, in the sky" (viii). *Economy's* comparison of these two very different figures' often arrestingly similar relationships to death, alienation, negation, invisibility, and other void-centric topics overtly probes the topic of nothingness. However, the most compelling comparison lays bare through difference, exposing the great void between them. This ultimate revelation comes with the last question of the book: Do words hold good? "Every time a poet writes a poem he is asking the question, Do words hold good? And the answer *has to be yes*: it is the counterfactual condition upon which a poet's life depends" (121).

Do words hold good: anxieties energizing this problem strikes a contemporary frequency, and Carson's juxtaposition presents a case study in a fundamental way that poetry's relation to "holding good" has shifted since antiquity. Simonides's answer to this question is a resounding yes: "Simonides's lack of despair is noteworthy. Do words hold good for him? Yes they do and, on the basis of this goodness, he invented a genre of poetry" (122) the epinikion—the formal praise poem or epinician ode, delivered at the closing of Olympic and other athletic games to honor the victors.

Carson's description of epinician odes conveys the extent to which this genre was less a form of writing than it was a communal event:

> The odes were given in choral performance—combining music, song and dance—to an audience that might include the victor, his kinsmen, fellow competitors, fellow citizens and other spectators. It is hard to overestimate the social, ethical, and epistemological importance of these performances to the community in which they took place. Indeed community is constituted by such acts. (122)

In virtue of the communal importance of this role, epinician poets were compelled to "take seriously their own function of counterbalancing private emotion with communal reasoning"

(122). It is this public role of balancing that affords the poet—and the words upon which he stakes the validity of his own being—goodness. Do words hold good, is the life of the poet a good—a good enough—life to guarantee a life of something rather than nothing? Yes, yes, and more yes, says Carson for Simonides: the language-workers of his time are not only taken seriously but are needed, for "in words he knows how to clear away everything ugly, blameworthy, incommensurable or mad and manifest what is worth praise" for an entire community (126).

To Simonides's public, communal ode-making Carson contrasts Celan's private, interior lyric utterance. "Who needs a Celan?" Carson writes, posing a rhetorical question. "It would be an understatement to say the function of praise is denied to the modern poet. Not only because all epistemological authority to define a boundary between blameworthy and praiseworthy has been withdrawn from him, but because the justice and health of his community are regarded as beyond redemption" (126).

"Negation," Carson writes, "requires this collusion of the present and the absent on the screen of the imagination. The one is measured against the other and found to be discrepant; the discrepant datum is annihilated by a word meaning 'No'" (102). By juxtaposing the vivid communal performance of poetry in antiquity with the utter lack of such arena in contemporary times, Carson allows us to experience the weight and pull of negation. We do not just intellectually understand—but internally feel—the lack of such communal activity and space when our imagination compares the ode-filled festivities of an Olympian closing ceremony to April 20, 1970, a lone desk in an empty room, a biography of Hölderlin open to a page where Celan has underlined the phrase "Sometimes this genius goes dark and sinks down into the well of the heart" as one of his last gestures before taking his own life by drowning (120).

As with the inherent impossibility of describing emptiness, nothing that can be said is adequate to the raw edge of such lack. Words fail despite gestures of holding, such as Celan's poems held to and for others: Hölderlin, Martin Buber, Rosa Luxemburg, Heidegger. Words fail despite the fact that Carson herself holds Celan's poems to the light.

When Carson asks, "Do words hold good?" she ultimately asks us whether or not words hold good now: is it possible, absent communal poetic function, for language to bear this weight. While she does not answer this question overtly, I read her overall project (here and across the body of her work) as passionate attempt to say yes and to make it so, while at the same time bearing witness to the devastation of failure. By including, and writing into, a community of voices—poets, scholars, and other varieties of language-makers— Carson holds open textual space to the praise of thought and song that otherwise might be lost.

Work Cited

Carson, Anne. *Economy of the Unlost*. Princeton: Princeton University Press, 1999.

"Parts of Time Fall on Her"
Anne Carson's Men in the Off Hours

Perhaps no other book in Anne Carson's body of work is more obsessed with death and gender than *Men in the Off Hours*. Ending poignantly on a lyric essay titled "Appendix to Ordinary Time," the poet meditates on the death of her mother, Margaret Carson, at the same time evoking Virginia Woolf's response to the death of a parent in *Moments of Being*, equivocating the grief crafted into words with "the strongest pleasure." Indeed, Carson seems to only mordantly underscore Woolf's pleasure: "And whom do we have to thank for this pleasure but Time" (165).[1] Rather, Carson's appendix affirms the temporal spaces of the mother and the daughter in the last moments of the mother's life, before turning that experience into death in textual crossouts: "death lines every moment of ordinary time" (166). Indeed, in *Men in the Off Hours*, Time as a feminine, internal, emotional, polluting, and boundary-shattering potency is obsessively juxtaposed against Time as a patriarchal, external, empirical, sanitized, and contained impotency. From the beginning of the book, Time is observed and narrated in the patriarchal, with historiographical purposes attuned to framing *chaos* by local lenses, where in the feminine, Time serves to collapse all past, present, and future in attuning to *kosmos*.

In "Ordinary Time: Virginia Woolf and Thucydides on War," Carson explicates how Thucydides's historiographical project was to mark a "beginning" of patriarchal time with the Peloponnesian War while synchronizing competing chronologies of the city-states of Argos, Sparta, and Athens. The war results, in one year's time, in untold numbers of deaths of Athenians, which Pericles in a funeral oration describes as "the vanishing of young men from the country was as if the spring were taken out of the country" (8). This, and her discussion of the "erasure" of the Thebans at Plataea, finds its correspondence in her discussion of typographical crossouts at the end of the book (in "Appendix to Ordinary Time"), where death is formally constituted in Carson's reproduction of marginalia and edits "read" from *Women and Fiction* (in the Fitzwilliam Museum's autograph manuscript of *A Room of One's Own.*

such
abandon ~~Obviously it is impossible, I thought, looking into those~~
ment ~~foaming waters, to~~
such ~~compare the living with the dead make any comparison~~
rapture ~~compare them.~~

The full text from *A Room of One's Own* reads:

> In a sort of jealousy, I suppose, for our own age, silly and absurd though these comparisons are, I went on to wonder if honestly one could name two living poets now as great as Tennyson and Christina Rossetti were then. Obviously it is impossible, I thought, looking into those foaming waters, to compare them. The very reason why that poetry excites one to such abandonment, such rapture, is that it celebrates some feeling that one used to have (at luncheon parties before the war perhaps), so that one responds easily, familiarly, without troubling to check the feeling, or to compare it with any that one has now. But the living poets express a feeling that is actually being made and torn out of us at the moment.[2]

Carson notes that Woolf's defense of her valorization of Victorian poetry as contacting with a reality before the horrors of World War I is a deferral from patriarchal time. Woolf cannot find affinity with poets whose very utterance shall be historicized by war. Anne Carson reads Woolf's perception of the war (in "The Mark on the Wall") as a feminine critique of patriarchal madness, where "Once a thing's done, no one knows how it happened." Though Carson suggests it may be "incidental," Carson sees significance in the fact that the figure who stands over Woolf and states, "I'm going out to buy a newspaper" is a *man*—none other than Leonard Woolf. Virginia Woolf reads Victorian poetry to remember the world before the war; Leonard reads the newspaper, it is implied, to "follow" the war.

Nevertheless, if Woolf's affinity to an older poetry is an act of refusal, Carson prefers the palimpsest of time represented in the crossout, accepting that "death lines every moment of ordinary time." The intersection of feminine and patriarchal conceptions of time lies in this ordinary time, where all is defined by temporal limit—where death is an end of subjectivity. In a poem such as "Epitaph: Annunciation," the act of "annunciation" collapses time, and Mary muses on immaculate conception ("a blush feels / Slow, from inside") (14). The annunciation marks the beginning of the "motion" that "swept the world aside" (14), yet contact between patriarchal and feminine time is procreative in moving "ordinary" time to its terminal, from *oikoumene* to *kosmos*. If Carson's project is to place women into contact with patriarchal historical forces, in "Dirt and Desire: A Phenomenology of Female Pollution in Antiquity" the poet suggests that such contact "is crisis" (130). Carson frequently merges her critical philhellene lens with lyric, resulting in dense lyric essays such as those that bookend *Men in the Off Hours*. Carson's placement of this "critical essay" in the binding (or bounds) of a book of poetry signals her unusual status as a practicing classicist scholar of renown. The stakes of her original scholarly and poetic inquiry into Time itself seem to have been shaken by the startling fact of her mother's death. "Dirt and Desire" provocatively situates women as "matter out of place," and by extension, out(side) of time. Women are, within the male gaze, "pollutable, polluted, and polluting in several ways at once," resulting in patriarchal fear of their "formless selves" that lack "personal boundary." As "units of danger," women are "penetrable, porous, mutable, and subject to defilement." All of these terms work to further define feminine thinking and feminine constructs of time in apposition to male attempts to historicize a *kosmos* of "good order" through the binding of perceived threats to that order. Here she explores the importance of the metaphor of women's headgear to the ancient Greek patriarchal order and in particular the symbolism of the headbinder for Sappho as a hermetic lid on female purity to prevent "leakage." Carson admits she is unsure whether or not Sappho's use of the image is meant to condone or to critique—rather, it "confirms" the Greeks' beliefs that the female "plays havoc with boundaries and defies the rules that keep matter in place" (152).

Thus, Anne Carson's *Men in the Off Hours* always suggests the limits and destructive agenda of patriarchal time. The poem "First Chaldaic Oracle" enacts a Gnostic meditation on our subjective relationship with the cosmos, suggestive of the idea that oracular vision, or *vates*, is dependent upon a feminine mindset. As the Chaldean Oracles were a syncretic merging of Eastern (Persian or Babylonian) philosophy associated with the feminine and Western (Neoplatonic) philosophy associated with the patriarchal, the poem enacts a feminine critique or correction of patriarchal "thinking": "There is something you should know. / And the right way to know it / is by a cherrying of your mind" (10). "Cherrying" engenders the mind with feminine discourse. The vatic mode is dependent upon a feminine emptying of the mind to "use the hum / of your wound / and flamepit out everything / right to the edge." This is an equivalent to attuning into (and attending to) the Gnostic "world-soul." On the other hand, turning phenomena into objects is enacted in the poem with patriarchal language ("kings your mind"). "Staring hard" is an empirical gesture—a violent "pressing" of the mind on a "thing"—which only results in a tautological trap: "try to know / that thing / as you know a thing, / you will not know it" (10). The vicious outcome is characterized as "kills on both sides" and destruction of that phenomena in "Scorch is not the way / to know / that thing you must know." Indeed, irony seems to inform the speaker's insistence that the only way the *totalitarian* patriarchal mind ever sees phenomena is as "thing," and this is underscored in her keening of the Velvet Revolution–era Prague into "Praguing the eye / of your soul and reach" (10). Indeed, Carson seems intrigued with patriarchal "thinking"; it is naive or refuses to acknowledge how its conceptualization of phenomena into "things" is destructive.

In "Irony Is Not Enough: Essay on My Life as Catherine Deneuve," Carson immerses persona into director André Téchiné's 1996 film *Les Voleurs,* where Catherine Deneuve, in the role of a philosophy professor (in the film named Marie), finds her seminars dismantled by her desire for a student referred to as "the girl" (who in the film is named Juliette). Carson is more interested in the *real* of Deneuve than the role of Marie, where in the spectacle of viewing the film one imagines the speaker never saw *other* than Deneuve, so the name "Marie" is never mentioned, nor are any other characters named. The time associated with Juliette, "the girl," is feminine; "the girl" is always late to the seminar, whose schedule is collapsed into feminine boundless "void at the middle of MonWedFri" as "parts of time fall on her" (120). Deneuve loses track of time, the clocklike turnstiles resisting her entry to the subway; she rides the train past her stop. The time associated with Juliette's male lover Alex (and Catherine Deneuve's future lover) is patriarchal and appointed: "A note is stuck under her door. From a boy who can't come to seminar today *But can I see you at 5 p.m.* scrawled on a page torn out of *Der Spiegel*" (125). Later, Carson dramatizes the violent vacillation between feminine and patriarchal time that will lead (in the film) to Marie's suicide in fatidic tolling: "She turns at the sound of the five o'clock bell. Comes a knock at the door." Marie's suicide is more hauntingly evinced when "love," which is exerted from the lungs (which Carson notes is mistranslated as "heart" by most contemporary translations), is linked to life by Sappho: "To stop breathing is bad. / So the gods judge. / For they do not stop breathing" (125). As Deneuve ruefully observes in a section of the poem subtitled "*hommes*," "Sokrates died in jail. Sappho died in a leap off the white rock of Leukas (for love) so they say" (122). Later in *Men in the Off Hours*, Woolf's suicidal depression, described in a diary entry from March 1, 1937 as comparable to being "exposed on a high ledge in full light" (165), "comforts" Carson, even if Woolf's diaries eventually "led her, after all, to the River Ouse" (165).

Yet Carson also tonally sympathizes with the patriarchal construct of time—its yearning to bring nonlinearity, experience, and phenomena into a contained and ordered whole. Indeed, Carson's project is not so much a feminist critique of a patriarchal construct of time as it is a mimesis of this dualism. In an interview in the *Paris Review*, she states, "I think that at different times in my life I located myself in different places on the gender spectrum, and for many years, . . . I didn't have any connection to the female gender. I wouldn't say I exactly felt like a man, but when you're talking about yourself you only have these two options."[3] In a series of ekphrastic responses (titled "Hopper: *Confessions*") to Edward Hopper's "urban pastoral" paintings, the subject's framed experience is synthesized with excerpts from a nineteenth-century translation of Augustine's *Confessions* at the ends of the poems. Augustine's meditations on divine time, where past, present, and future are fluidly perceived at once, are dependent on the notion that the soul has the vatic capacity to connect to divine time; yet Augustine's meditations are filled with consternation that our mortality and subjectivity cannot behold divine time—that we perceive time in very limited terms: "Whatsoever of it has flown away is past. / Whatsoever remains is future" ("The Barber Shop," 53). Augustine describes an hour passed by as "flying particles." Time is smeared into a blur. The goal to violently capture the *eikos*—the veridical surface of our experience—is threatened by the mutability of the cosmos. Hopper's subject "sit[s] very straight / till the pictures are through" ("Western Motel," 54).

Patriarchal time is in opposition to this mutability; feminine time embraces it. The feminine subject expresses little anxiety in the divide between past and present. By comparison, Carson's ekphrastic treatments of Hopper's brushstrokes result in violent imagery such as a "summer smeared" or "autumn that pierces bones." In "The Barber Shop," the prosodic enactment of patriarchal (fatherly) scissors fiercely cutting is juxtaposed against the presence of a feminine (daughterly) "quiet" repose:

> His scissors blaze on open black water.
> She
>   likes
>   the
>   quiet she
>   may
>   be
>   his
> daughter.

The scissors find a later iteration as pruning shears in "Appendix to Ordinary Time," where in her last diary entry Virginia Woolf notes, "L. is doing the rhododendrons" (166).

Though Carson empathizes with the desire to freeze time into the artistic frieze in the Hopper poems, in "Appendix to Ordinary Time," she also decries the truth that it is "too late now" to call her mother; Time—this time expressed in the metaphor of a body of water—has become a "lake" that "trickles on" (165). The image of the lake resonates later in the book's final placement of a photograph of Carson as a child with her mother, dipping toes in a lake, and captioned with the phrase "*Eclipsis est pro dolore,*" meaning

It (she) is crossed out	*in the face of*	sorrow
	because of	pain[4]
	from	
	on behalf of	

The openness of this epitaphic phrase, in all of its permutations for reading Carson's grief, defines "ordinary time," which is experienced on such personal terms that it is offset against any attempts to inquire into the tensions inherent in the relationship of feminine and patriarchal time; for it was during this lyric investigation into time that Carson's mother died: "My mother died the autumn I was writing this. And *Now I have no one*, I thought" (165). Such is the sense of abandonment and rapture felt—in ordinary time.

Works Cited

Carson, Anne. "The Art of Poetry, No. 88." Interview by Will Aitken." *Paris Review* 177 (Fall 2004). http://www.theparisreview.org/interviews/5420/the-art-of-poetry-no-88-anne-carson. Accessed August 15, 2013.

Carson, Anne. *Men in the Off Hours.* New York: Knopf, 2000.

Mayer, Sophie. "Picture Theory: On Photographic Intimacy in Nicole Brossard and Anne Carson." *Studies in Canadian Literature / Études en littérature canadienne* 33.1 (2008): 97–116.

Woolf, Virginia. *A Room of One's Own.* New York: Harcourt, Brace, 1929.

Notes

1. Page numbers, unless otherwise noted, refer to Anne Carson's *Men in the Off Hours* (New York: Knopf, 2000).

2. Virginia Woolf, *A Room of One's Own,* 22–23.

3. Anne Carson, "The Art of Poetry, No. 88," interview by Will Aitken, *Paris Review* 177 (Fall 2004).

4. Translation by Sophie Mayer, "Picture Theory: On Photographic Intimacy in Nicole Brossard and Anne Carson," *Studies in Canadian Literature / Études en littérature canadienne* 33.1 (2008).

DOUGLAS A. MARTIN

Lacuna Is for Reign

I have a couple of connections to the book upon which I will be centering—or de—a discussion of the depths of Anne Carson's authorship. (Thucydides to Virginia Woolf: "That's a terrible singsong now. Tone has to be colder. But tense.")[1] The collection ends with a prose poem, "Appendix to Ordinary Time," a piece the first edition dust jacket situates in author autobiography. Essay, it also appears to me despite lacking such a designation Carson is known to give, in this volume's pages to four other works, two lineated, two subtitled, one around a speaker as Catherine Deneuve as teacher. This latter is a source of our ever having been danced together.[2]

Another source of connection: when I still had that someone he was. He was her student before. There a note on the wall was her handwriting tacked by his desk—desire, a spindle, if I remember correctly. This was back when a lot of us still wanted to be her version of Geryon presented in *Autobiography of Red*. At the bottom of the Strand, I found a review copy advance of her next collection published and as a present gave to the someone I'll call The Poet in reference forward, hoping so (as Sappho has it in an episode of that "TV Men" series Carson scripts inside): "He She Me You Thou disappears."[3]

The Dock

With a photograph of child beside mother, an author in formation I project, by some appearance a happier moment the book concludes, though mother is laid back, in sunglasses looking darkened, almost prone reclining at a somewhat odd angle arm akimbo crooked, a skirt element to the bathing suit. The child's feet dangle in the lake. Left arm reaches out somewhere around the thigh, and it's back behind in gray area, if they touch at all. I find her shaded somewhere between laughing or crying squinting forward meeting the camera's eye. Whoever is behind this (*The mind has no eye*, Hektor declares in a Carson treatment)[4] catches the two towards relaxed together.

She has an inner tube around her waist still, or resting shell floats. She has climbed up out of the water recently perhaps, hat on head—does it match mother's, onto the wooden peer, for sunnapping.

This is where the book has been brought toward in ending. Not Mrs. Ramsey in *To the Lighthouse*, holding onto James and reading to him, nothing like those photographic representation of Woolf's sister and sister's son Julian (Madonna and Child) I've seen: cherubic, frame of an open window, posed on a mother's knee, folds of fabric dress drape. Woolf's sister, Bell, looks not up out of the frame but into her child's face, oblivious seemingly lowered to any other gaze outside together a hold they make.

Author remembers "she would have been at this hour alone in her house, gazing out on the cold lawns and turned earth of evening, high bleak grass going down to the lake."[5] Related is debating whether or not to try to call the mother on the phone. Memories animated, the author in a paragraph shifts to take the text back to Woolf, and begins more afloat there moving forward, text on all levels, a line in letters repeated, more letter lines, remaining fragments (Leonard the husband does not do what he is instructed to and destroy all her papers), weeding, getting her to the meditation on textuality Carson will begin to sustain, this subject now ostensibly essayed, way roundabout to arrive back at the mother: an experience in time gathered around Woolf's crossouts (the trace of them both in her mind joined).

"There Is Too Much Self in My Writing"

The *Off Hours* book contains many epitaphs, but the one embedded in the conclusion of the closing text is a repurposed, reapplying of one such Woolf crossout.[6] Carson's work itself produces a kind of *cross under* in tone, towing around the way words knot. I think of shoe lacing, Artaud arrested at the point of entry, "holding his shoe,"[7] her early pilgrimages, the essay on the road to Compostela in *Plainwater* in particular, and a wonderful dusty author photo in the early Brick Books edition of *Short Talks* (1992), where she is also identified as a painter of volcanoes and posed in front of one.[8]

There is cosmology here, one mirrored when the eyes ripple up along a line, see things align or out in relief skate.[9]

With her mother's epitaph at hand, the words reflect in ways the bodies positioned on the facing page: stacked in the left margin at the bottom of the left page is Carson in words upon words, one day to leave home, stage left Woolf's longer lines on the subject of equivalencies stricken in long-limbed strokes.

The caption to the picture on the last page ("Margaret Carson / 1913–1997") finds support, glossed in a way with the italicized sentence beneath, "*Eclipsis est pro dolore*,"[10] beats beading out . . . One body translates, moves in front of another, before another because of and for sadness. Pane put upon pain, I want to play. I wonder about the origin of many of these texts, the orders under which Carson writes, revises, publishes, and settles . . . cites surface again, to find their excavation in other times and places, my already curtained "TV Men" series one example. (I don't get what she's doing there, as The Poet once said to me.) Underlying authority is necessarily disguised in all kinds of ways. A draft is something that happened in time, a medium cloaking other things. Root change artful, TV is a transvestite.

Hector

It was SS who told me in one gossipy moment her theory of why my paper for a conference was not accepted. One of the organizers hated one of the women I wanted to look at in connection. I was going to write a big book, a line I wanted to see myself in that would end in Carson. Part of the thesis would be how an image one cultivates determines in large part how writing gets received: I mean absent author photos, words on the page stand more in for any face. Strategies, though, change. *Decreation* has three pictures, a three-headed sensibility: of a piece of art, a still from a film (four figures of Beckett dancing one point), three figures from director Antonioni (one face seen: Monica Vitti in character), the stills glossed with poetic relevance to/from accompanying essay. *Nox* is arguably a box of pictures.

Or the thing I was going to do with Carson was something about intellectual intimidation, feeling when reading her I must not be smart enough. I need to learn more things, or I just trust she knows best, most. I might modify this to intellectual selection: now what is abjured—what abjected (Kristeva)—incorporated. The diary quote used by Carson in "Appendix to Ordinary Time" I listen to a scholar at a lunchtime lecture relate to a first scene of childhood molestation of Woolf.[11] From her diaries: "Began reading Freud last night; to enlarge the circumference, to give my brain a wider scope: to make it objective; to get outside" (December 2, 1939). "I tried to center by reading Freud" (June 27, 1940). The crossouts are a qualified exposure. Woolf, in "The Decay of Essaywriting": "Confronted with the terrible spectre of themselves, the bravest are inclined to run away or shade their eyes. And thus, instead of the honest truth which we should all respect, we are given timid side-glances in the shape of essays, which, for the most part, fail in the cardinal virtue of sincerity."

When the choreographer Bill Forsythe was looking for something to adapt, he was struck by the cover of my first book in the window of Shakespeare and Co. Hoping for a Damien Hirst spot painting, I had got instead the better use of blood, gold leaf, and resin by Jess von der Ahe (her menstrual blood). A quote from Carson's *Autobiography of Red* concerning Geryon and photography led off inside and her work was sought by him in pairing.

When the piece created comes to a New York premier, we are up in the balcony seats.[12] Collaborators have gathered round. My mother has come to the city from her rounds at the hospital. At intermission, a man walks by, saying something about how little this is doing for him. He says it much more strongly. It is one of three or four nights, and the space upstairs is selling Carson's books not mine. My mother also bravely sits through the special postshow performance of "Cassandra Float Can" Carson gives one night. (Collaborators walk through the crowd, holding up photographs.)

"That's some text," walking by my mother and me, Carson says. (TV Men: "discover all that is 'feminine,' all that reaches forward / in supplication within us" [Artaud];[13] "in a voice wavering, collapsing, sucked under here and there / by secret" [Sokrates].)[14] I remember the poet saying it in her characteristic deadpan, so it was hard for me to know the degree of sincerity. I always remember something I read in a book at school about Virginia Woolf, I paraphrase: *autobiographical traces resist modernist purity.*[15]

One night after a performance we are all in a restaurant. I am afraid she does not want my mother and me there, but when the choreographer who has given me so much invites, I say yes. I might do a series of images now that would set a tone all in irony (fish out of water, blued under it—I notice in her work how many times these affects fall, where, to what saturation imbued). Mother drowning, not drowning, mine sits there with me, mostly silent. Particular lines in the ballet must have been especially hard for her. Many of the dancers have been earlier that day in the city for a showing of Matthew Barney's *Drawing Restraint 9*. I will try to sound adept, thinking I might then have something to contribute. You heard those stories about how Lars Von Trier so traumatized Björk supposedly she'd never act again? Well here is this thing this person who loves her was doing for her, giving it back to her. (I surely don't use the words from psychoanalysis.) You could see her blush, and he gave that to her, when they began to trust each other with the flensing knives, next to each other, at each other's legs. ("We have time to open the whole of our mind wide to beauty," Woolf praised early cinema.) They both do it to each other, I gush! Two plains nourished each other, in a place of similar reflection.

And that's art? Carson questions.

Notes

1. Anne Carson, *Men in the Off Hours* (New York: Knopf, 2000), 116.

2. "Kammer/Kammer" had its world premier at the Bockenheimer Depot in Frankfurt, 2000. It is comprised of the text of Carson's "Irony Is Not Enough" and a chapter ("The World") of my first novel, *Outline of My Lover*.

3. Carson, *Men*, 118.

4. Anne Carson, *Glass, Irony and God* (New York: New Directions, 1995), 56.

5. Carson, *Men*, 165.

6. The quotation that makes the subhead for this section is from Anne Carson, *Economy of the Unlost* (Princeton: Princeton University Press, 1999), vii.

7. Carson, *Men*, 74.

8. For more on the shoe, see Fredric Jameson on representations by van Gogh and Warhol ("The Deconstruction of Expression" section in "Postmodernism; or The Cultural Logic of Late Capitalism," New Left Review 146 [July–August 1984]: 53–92).

9. I see the "eclipse" there too, in her other languages, an event as metaphor of subjectivity taken up and set down in another book to come: Carson's *Decreation* ("Totality: The Colour of Eclipse") where Woolf also plays a named part, but we can find Woolf's presence all the way as far back as in *Eros the Bittersweet* (1986).

10. Carson, *Men*, 167.
11. Louise DeSalvo at Hunter College, New York. September 17, 2003.
12. Brooklyn Academy of Music, 2006.
13. Carson, *Men*, 66.
14. Carson, *Glass, Irony and God*, 68.
15. Maggie Humm, *Modernist Women and Visual Cultures* (New Brunswick: Rutgers University Press, 2003), 10.

ANDREA REXILIUS

The Light of This Wound
Marriage, Longing, Desire in Anne Carson's The Beauty of the Husband

Dancers of the tango profess that to dance is to have a conversation, a dialogue that occurs silently on the level of mood, feelings, interpretations, and adjustments. The dance is improvisational; the communication is an agreement of sorts, a union that fluctuates and builds. What is agreed upon erupts from the dancers, revealing the tensions, passions, longing, and lingering of the couple. When watching performances of the tango, you will see the pursuit, the sexuality, the entanglement of this dance.

Anne Carson's *The Beauty of the Husband: A Fictional Essay in 29 Tangos*, is a complex translation of "the tango" into a text. Her text moves quickly through a series of vignettes about a heterosexual relationship, pierced by Greek mythology, contemporary cultural references, and Keats's idea that "beauty is truth, truth beauty." The lovers we witness dance a tango fraught with karmic irresolution, but it is a karma, Carson seems to suggest, that we all (we being lovers) are bound to. In this particular rendition of the karma, the tropes focus on "failed," or perhaps successful within their failure, love affairs, the tragedy, the brutality beneath the extreme power of the dance. To some extent these tropes are limiting because they focus primarily on the stories/myths/classifications of heterosexual love relationships. The dance goes like this: courting, engagement, marriage, affair by the husband, separation, reunion, more affairs, an affair by the wife with the husband's best friend, separation, divorce, possible reunion. While reading, I couldn't help but wonder if other types of pairings would have the same "karmic" patterns. Perhaps. Perhaps not.

What exactly is Carson doing with this karmic pattern? She must be piercing it in some way, right? She isn't just reiterating the same stereotypical cultural mythologies about men and women and what is destined to happen between the sexes, I'd hope. This question was the most difficult for me to parse. Carson's text does not seem to provide a solution, a way out of the tango toward a healthy version of desire. Desire here is robust, brutal, and addictive. References to the Greek gods make desire cruel, vindictive, impossible to satiate. What helps is that eroticism as lack is compelling. And as she writes in *Eros the Bittersweet*, eros requires a triangulation. *The Beauty of the Husband* is just one example of the possibilities of that triangulation. And it is perhaps the most common triangulation that persists in our mythological and pop-culture renditions of male/female relationships.

Roland Barthes takes up a similar investigation in his book *A Lover's Discourse*, in which he distinguishes the various "figures" (tropes, states of mind) that lovers move through in their relationships with one another.

Barthes writes:

The amorous subject draws on the reservoir (the thesaurus?) of figures, depending on the needs, the injunctions, or the pleasures of his image-repertoire. Each figure explodes, vibrates in and of itself like a sound severed from any tune—or is repeated to satiety, like the motif of a hovering music. No logic links the figures, determines their contiguity: the figures are non-syntagmatic, non-narrative; they are Erinyes; they stir, collide, subside, return, vanish with no more order than the flight of mosquitoes.[1]

I like thinking about this "flight of mosquitoes" as a more erratic description of the tango. And so, Carson and Barthes similarly define the "dance of desire" as they investigate these tropes.

Carson:

The ruse of inserting a rival between lover and beloved is immediately effective. . . . to represent eros as deferred, defied, obstructed, hungry, organized around a radiant absence—to represent eros as lack.[2]

Barthes:

Annulment: Explosion of language during which the subject manages to annul the loved object under the volume of love itself: by a specifically amorous perversion, it is love the subject loves, not the object.[3]

Carson:

But the ruse of the triangle is not a trivial mental maneuver. We see in it the radical constitution of desire. For, where eros is lack, its activation calls for three structural components—lover, beloved and that which comes between them. They are three points of transformation on a circuit of possible relationship, electrified by desire so that they touch not touching. Conjoined they are held apart.[4]

Barthes:

Embrace: The gesture of the amorous embrace seems to fulfill, for a time, the subject's dream of total union with the loved being.[5]

Carson:

The third component plays a paradoxical role for it both connects and separates, marking that two are not one, irradiating the absence whose presence is demanded by eros.[6]

Barthes:

Errantry (the Ghost Ship): Though each love is experienced as unique and though the subject rejects the notion of repeating it elsewhere later one, he sometimes discovers in himself a kind of diffusion of amorous desire; he then realizes he is doomed to wander until he dies, from love to love.[7]

According to Carson and Barthes then, the tango that desire marks is the presence of absence, the inability of effective culmination. Desire dies when it is no longer wandering, when the tension eros requires falls away into the mundane, into that which is lacking the triangulation of lack. As Carson defines it in *The Beauty of the Husband*, the dance of marriage, triangulates around the following movements: courting, an affair by the husband, separation, reunion, an affair by the wife, separation, divorce, longing. All of these situations call attention to the space between the two lovers, to the impossibility of them becoming one. These movements heighten their state of longing.

Longing, as Carson defines it in this book, is predicated upon karmic, mathematical, uncontrollable urges that move within us. We are bound to this wound via impulse. Impulse being the gravity of desire. Carson writes on page 49:

> Why did nature give me over to this creature—-don't call it my
>   choice,
> I was *ventured*:
> by some pure gravity of existence itself,
> conspiracy of being![8]

On page 79:

> Note these two people
> who are not yet married
>
> stand embedded in the destiny of husband and wife as firmly
> as any two contiguous molecules in a chain reaction[9]

On page 49 again:

> Yes a cliché
>
> and I do not apologize because as I say I was not to blame, I was
>   unshielded
> in the face of existence
> and existence depends *on beauty*.
> In the end.
> Existence *will not stop*
> until it gets to beauty and then there follow all the consequences
>   that lead to
> the end.[10]

And on page 89:

> so ingenious are the arrangements of the state of flux we call
> our moral history are they not almost as neat as mathematical
> propositions except written on water—-[11]

"A wound gives off its own light," is the first line of *The Beauty of the Husband*. What we see throughout is the light of this wound:

marriage, longing, desire. It is a beckon that calls to us throughout the darkness of existence. Wound is lack. Wound is life force.

Fiction forms what streams in us.
Naturally it is suspect.
What does *not wanting to desire* mean?[12]

I want to leave this question lingering in this essay, just as it lingers in Carson's text, for each of us to answer silently, within the body, on our own.

The Beauty of the Husband also speaks of language as a wound. Our relationship to language mirrors the relationship between the dancing couple. Language is also erotic lack. On page 93, Carson describes the movement of language as "little holes that show where the rain hits." / "Little holes that widen and break." The relationship between the husband and wife in this story are predicated upon language: love letters, lies, apologies, invocations, pleas, etc. The tango is an unspoken movement, but also a dialogue, and Carson plays up this parallel throughout her text:

> In a letter both reader and writer discover an ideal image of themselves, short blinding passages are all it takes.[13]

> Husband and wife may erase a boundary.
> Creating a white page.[14]

> Philosophers say man forms himself in dialogue.[15]

And in a line that speaks most directly to this dual idea of the tango:

> [The tango or dialogue,] Which, like the chain of Parmenides' well-rounded Truth you can follow around in a circle and always end up where you began, for "it is all one to me where I start—I arrive there again soon enough."[16]

The story ends with the husband calling the wife. They are now divorced and he has a new family. "So many versions of the same story, trading sections back and forth."[17] And now the wife is becoming the mistress in their triangulation of desire. The dance begins again.

The Beauty of the Husband also ends with analogies of war. A third trope running throughout this theme of desire. And one that most adequately provides an answer about why this disillusion between the two sexes persists, why the tropes, the clichés, the stereotypes continue between them. First we have the clichéd analogy of the predator (male) /prey (woman) relationship;

> what broke wasn't glass, what fell to earth wasn't body.
> But still when I recall the conversation it's what I see——me a
>   fighter pilot
> bailing out over the channel. Me as kill.[18]

> He sought her. He sought her everywhere. Through the
>   nakednesses
> of his imagination. In sorrow. In foxholes. As deer flicker way off
>   in a wood in
> late
> Winter.

> He knew he would destroy the deer.[19]

In the context of insatiable desire, this hunting/war cliché carries more weight, is slightly moving. The two end lines "me as kill" and "he knew he would destroy the deer" speak to the power of longing, the shattering collision of touching not touching. The death of desire when the lack/longing toward is gone. The game between the sexes.

Finally, Carson writes:

> But you overlook
> an important cultural function of games.
> To test the will of the gods.
> Hulzinga reminds us that war itself is a form of divination.[20]

The purpose then of the tango / the flight of the mosquito, the longing of the erotic, the bittersweet beauty of the husband is to test the limits of that karmic lack, to "erase a boundary / Creating a white page."[21] Desire is that divining rod which allows us to see a wound's light. Desire is that light.

Notes

1. Roland Barthes. *A Lover's Discourse: Fragments*, trans. Richard Howard. (New York: Farrar, Straus and Giroux, 1978), 7.
2. Anne Carson, *Eros the Bittersweet* (Normal, IL: Dalkey Archive Press, 1986), 18.
3. Barthes, *Lover's Discourse*, 31.
4. Carson, *Eros the Bittersweet*, 16.
5. Barthes, *Lover's Discourse*, 104.
6. Carson, *Eros the Bittersweet*, 16.
7. Barthes, *Lover's Discourse*, 101.
8. Anne Carson, *The Beauty of the Husband: A Fictional Essay in 29 Tangos* (New York: Vintage Books, 2001), 49.
9. Carson, *Beauty of the Husband*, 79.
10. Carson, *Beauty of the Husband*, 49.
11. Carson, *Beauty of the Husband*, 89.
12. Carson, *Beauty of the Husband*, 7.
13. Carson, *Beauty of the Husband*, 94.
14. Carson, *Beauty of the Husband*, 101.
15. Carson, *Beauty of the Husband*, 117.
16. Carson, *Beauty of the Husband*, 99–100.
17. Carson, *Beauty of the Husband*, 130.
18. Carson, *Beauty of the Husband*, 16.
19. Carson, *Beauty of the Husband*, 57.
20. Carson, *Beauty of the Husband*, 102.
21. Carson, *Beauty of the Husband*, 101.

J. MICHAEL MARTINEZ

Who with Her Tears
Soaks Mortal Streaming
Anne Carson and Wonderwater

Anne Carson writes, *"Cling to the roses*. I dreamed Hölderlin said this. He did not, but it contains a likeness of him and sometimes that is more sustaining[1]." Carson, stirred by Hölderlin, dreams his words. And they are not his words. From her admiration, the love of his work, this dream speech and its infidelity become closer to Hölderlin than Hölderlin's genuine language. The question: how does a simile, containing only a likeness and not the *thing* itself, develop beyond the *thing*? That is, how does a phrase resonating with Hölderlin, but not written by him, become more than Hölderlin himself could articulate?

The *likeness* to a Hölderlinian line, "Cling to the roses," reproduces Hölderlin; though he didn't write this line, it becomes all the more Hölderlinian, for he has withdrawn into the likeness itself inherent in Carson's line. How? Through Love and Strife: the love behind Carson's admiration and the implicit strife of the dream's infidel claim (to be something that it is not). Carson's fantasy, the inauthentic foreign claiming authenticity, turns out to be the impure home Hölderlin is sustained within. Isn't this what is implied by Carson's dream?

Could it be that Carson's text embodies Hölderlin's entreaty for the artist, in work and life, to reconcile Love and Strife, the particular and the universal to the degree that those opposites, refusing synthesis or negation, become foreign unto themselves? Anne Carson, throughout *Wonderwater*, clues the reader to the German poet's aesthetic entreaty: when she pairs the eternal attentiveness of flowers against the daily whisper of Hölderlin's slippers on his way to a tryst, or when she states, "Love and hate are side-by-side surprises, are they not."[2] These incidental moments in *Wonderwater* are embodiments of Hölderlin's teachings. Hölderlin writes in "The Basis of Empedocles," "When life is pure, nature and art oppose one another merely harmoniously."[3]

Art perfects nature. Nature is raised to the divine in this aesthetic act through art's particularity, its supplementing of what nature lacks. Art, in pursuing to represent and perfect nature, becomes the idealized natural and, thus, no longer the aesthetic. The natural, achieving the pinnacle of ideality through art, is no longer itself. A pure life, according to Hölderlin, is when the oppositional natural and the aesthetic reconcile and divest themselves of themselves in each other.[4] In that middle ground between the opposites emerges the divine.

In between the turned backs of the gods and men emerges a null space, a sacred emptiness where a divinity outside the divine emerges. It is the sacrilegious sacred, for it is impossibly outside the omnipresent divine: this rupture posits an ontological vacuum within the divine's totalizing presence.

The null space, the sacred outside existing between the turned backs of humanity and the gods, is also the very space where they, in their twin refusals, are the most similar. This is the "pure life" of harmonized contradictions Hölderlin enunciates and models in *Empedocles*. This tragedy enacts the clashing and reconciliation of two powerful conflicting forces, Love and Strife.

In this sense, Anne Carson's *Wonderwater* embodies Hölderlin's conceptions, for the work itself is interpenetrated with those active forces: Hölderlin's relationship with Gontard, as told in fragments by Carson, represents the enactment of those forces. Her work is interpenetrated by three elements: Hölderlin and Gontard's tragic romance, Hölderlin's work on *Empedocles*, and Carson's own considerations; much like rock may be veined with mineral gold, so too is *Wonderwater* veined with the life of these commanding histories.

Hölderlin writes, "Everything that *is* interpenetrates as soon as it becomes active."[5]

In the accounts of the historical Empedocles's teachings, it is stated he wrote, "all things unite in one through love."[6] It is important to note for Empedocles, *Love* is not simply a sentimental feeling or an ethical imperative. It is the cosmic force, along with the destructive *Strife*, materially (re)organizing the universe. Moreover, these cosmic forces, creating and ordering "trees and men and women, beasts and birds and water-bred fishes, and the long-lived gods too," also inhabit and order the individual lives of humanity.[7]

As Anne Carson dreamed of Hölderlin, Friedrich Hölderlin dreamed of Empedocles. Hölderlin wrote, "Empedocles is a son of the heavens. . . . a human being in whom those opposites are united so intensely that they become one in him, divesting themselves of their original distinguishing form and thus reversing themselves."[8] Here, Hölderlin speaks not only of Love and Strife uniting, but also of the universal and particular. In Hölderlin's "The Basis of Empedocles," nature is the tendency toward the universal, whereas "man" resides in the particular.

For Hölderlin, Empedocles is the form that takes shape as an excess of intensity in the opposition of nature and art, in which each pole takes a temporary, changed, or not fully original form. Empedocles is the historical manifestation of the aforementioned "null space" or sacred between. However, he is still only a man, transient and mortal. Thus, the suicide of Hölderlin's Empedocles is an exhibition of this "*momentary unification*" of the cosmic forces Love and Strife, the universal and the particular.[9] Empedocles is only a momentary embodiment of this unification, for this union, which appears to dissolve distinctions, in order to fully exemplify itself, demands its own disintegration.

As Empedocles dies, the excess of intensity that made the union of extremes possible cancels itself, leaving "a more mature, true, purely universal intensity."[10] This is to say, a more pure Strife beckons and alienates him from the humanity he cherishes; a broader Love pulls Empedocles to unify with the volcanic earth to which he casts himself. Empedocles disavows the negation Love and Strife achieved *as his person* and, in so doing, distills a Love more profound, a kind of purified immanence.

In the final pages of *Wonderwater*, Carson presents an expression from geometry, the term "anexact." Anexact, defined by Carson, is "an impure version itself purely represented."[11] That is to say, the "anexact" is the *thing* whose idealization has been completely absorbed into its image/representation. It defies conceptual negation, for it has negated the concept into itself; it is of the world and irreducible from it. The "anexact" has absorbed and been removed from the eidetic into that pure impurity of representation. The *thing* withdraws into its likeness. It is the geometrical rendering of the integrated antinomy of Love and Strife.

"Her, The Water, And Me" begins with Anne Carson ruminating on Empedocles's cosmogony. "Earth Air Fire Water" are, in Empedocles's cosmogony, the primary elements of the manifest universe. Love and Strife are the two forces integrating and rescinding the various unities of these elements. In this annotation, Carson focuses solely on Water. Carson writes, "No one knows what to make of Nestis."[12] "Nestis" may be the name of a goddess worshipped in Sicily; however, Carson states the Greek term is ordinarily used to mean "famine" or "fasting."[13] "Nestis" is thus an expression for one of the primordial elements used in creation itself, and it is a term generally articulating a kind of lack through the absence of water or through intentional refusal of substance. "Nestis," the term, is another axis of contradictions: it is both the primary element of water and its absence.

> Nestis who with her tears soaks mortal streaming (Empedocles, Fragment 63)[14]

In "Her, The Water, And Me" Anne Carson notes the odd phrasing of "mortal streaming" and relates this to rivers and streams, as well as to the human body's sweat and semen. The "annotation" begins its revelatory turn when Carson, after unfolding "Nestis" within its ancient Greek context, engages the term to describe the ambiance within her kitchen:

> The sorrow of Nestis's tears . . . moves around me as I sit at my kitchen table reading bits of Empedokles on a cloudy afternoon, perhaps it is a sad time in my life—not that isn't why Nestis gets to me. Something to do with contradiction itself and how we use it, need it, pierce ourselves on it. Our mortal streaming, split, pierced, and caught.[15]

Nestis, one of the elements composing reality itself, inhabits the air of the domestic; the universal dwells in the spaces of the particular. Carson's sorrow excavates the tears of Nestis from the particular. Nestis, the universal, "gets" to her. The phrase "gets to" may seem innocuous; however, it pinpoints the very moment the universal begins its coupling with the particular, when Love and Strife begin a "momentary unification" in Carson's own text.

Anne Carson writes that "we" need contradiction and "we" pierce ourselves on it. She, as with Hölderlin's Empedocles, speaks for humanity: the "we" is the contradiction of the "I." Carson pierces her singular subjectivity with the necessity to articulate the "we." The pronoun itself is addressed; as such, it becomes the event and space where the foreign weds the native: it is "anexact."

The "we" must be read within the aforementioned poeticological theories of Hölderlin and Empedocles: Love and Strife organize all of reality; Love/Strife are the same forces operating within the individual subject as they are to the organizing and dissembling of stars and planets; thus, the "we" Carson speaks *is* the "we" of creation itself—it is the minuscule human and the explosion of nebulae both bound to the primordial coupling/divorcing of Love and Strife, birth and death.

Embodying mortal streaming by speaking of her own love affair gone awry, Anne Carson writes, "It began at a party when a man at a party said *I have to see you again.*"[16] In her relationship, she finds those forces of Love and Strife negotiating, unifying, and dissembling. Although these forces are timeless, they are still surprising in their power to bring together the contrary and unknown and, with just as much as mystery, tear them apart. Why? Carson writes, "Yes they tear us apart but otherwise nothing would ever happen. Yes we are to blame for it but way back at the start of us, not now."[17]

We are to blame for this suffering; however, it began at the beginning of us: at the beginning of creation itself—we are not subject to love and strife, we are Love and Strife. We are not to blame now, in our current manifestation; however, we are accountable, for we are ever the startled heralds of primordial forces operating since the first solar nebulae unleashed into solar flare.

Time itself could not begin without the very tearing Love must induce through the inevitable manifestation of Strife. Strife is, thus, not a form of adversity; rather, it is a kind of constructive suffering providing the necessary momentum for the event of Love.

Anne Carson writes, "But soon the relics began to stir—and certainly this cheats and baffles reason, how there can be relics at the dawn of time—yet we all know, as one moves into love, it gradually becomes impossible to identify with the other's innocence" (58). Reason is inadequate to gauge the primordial forces of Love and Strife. The relics stirred and awakened are the very impossibilities of identifying with the other's innocence. The love felt for the other awakens a kind of knowledge. This knowledge is that the beloved is never innocent, for the love itself is the derivation of ruin.

"From somewhere, outside it, stains soak through" Carson writes (58). The outside emerges from without innocence but from within love; innocence is stained with Love and, thus, with Strife. In perceiving the other's complicity and lack of innocence, I must also see, in *not* identifying with their innocence that I identify with their guilt and all of creation is stained through. As with Hölderlin's Empedocles, I identify with All. "Who am I?" Carson asks.[18]

Notes

1. Anne Carson, *Answer Scars, in Wonderwater: (Alice Offshore)*, by Roni Horn, Louise Bourgeois, Anne Carson, Hélène Cixous, and John Waters (Göttingen, Germany: Steidl Verlag, 2004), 143.

2. Carson, *Answer Scars*, 58.

3. Friedrich Hölderlin, *The Death of Empedocles: A Mourning-Play*, trans. David Farrell Krell (Albany: SUNY Press), 144.

4. A more literal analogy could be Roger Caillois's classic essay "Mimicry and Legendary Psychasthenia," where an insect, in mimicking plant life, is so diminished into its environment, the mimicry so complete, others of its ilk feed upon it as if it were the plant. Thus, dispossessed of those aesthetic distinctions defining it, the insect's aesthetic mimicry becomes the natural and, in being cannibalized, its very undoing.

5. Hölderlin, *The Death of Empedocles*, 6.

6. G. S. Kirk and J. E. Raven, *The Presocratic Philosophers* (New York: Cambridge University Press 1957), 327.

7. Kirk and Raven, *The Presocratic Philosophers*, 327.

8. Hölderlin, *The Death of Empedocles*, 146.

9. Hölderlin, *The Death of Empedocles*, 147.
10. Hölderlin, *The Death of Empedocles*, 148.
11. Carson, *Answer Scars*, 158.
12. Carson, *Answer Scars*, 158.
13. Carson, *Answer Scars*, 158.
14. Carson, *Answer Scars*, 158.
15. Carson, *Answer Scars*, 158.
16. Carson, *Answer Scars*, 58.
17. Carson, *Answer Scars*, 58.
18. Carson, *Answer Scars*, 58.

HANNAH ENSOR

Antagonistic Collaborations, Tender Questions

On Anne Carson's Answer Scars /
Roni Horn's Wonderwater

Wonderwater is a project by Roni Horn. It is a set of titles annotated separately by four artists in four editions, put together into a box of books. One of the annotations is by Anne Carson. Anne gives her book the title *Answer Scars*.

Or: Anne Carson wrote the book *Answer Scars* to titles provided by Roni Horn.

Wonderwater / *Answer Scars* moves; it's an odd beast to sit with, confusing and affable: I enjoy spending time with it (Gertrude Stein: "and do you happen to like to look at it").

Anne here is a collaborator; she works to a constraint. As a review of 2010's *Nox* says, "Many of Carson's past experiments with form were funky and intuitive: they found their own shape." Here, the shape is given and participated-with, though not un-pushed-against.

And the shape given by Roni Horn's titles creates an odd collection of things. *Answer Scars* is not coherent yet it coheres. Some of the titles seem to fit her wacky project (one of "facts" she might say: facts about Friedrich Hölderlin the German poet and translator, facts of his love affair and mental health, autobiographical facts, personal and interpersonal facts, facts of Hölderlin's work in translating the yet earlier Empedokles) so well that I can hardly believe they were there before Anne's writing to them. Some of the titles don't fit her needs at all and she skips them.[1] Some don't fit and she *does* write to them, so Aretha Franklin and Charles Mingus have dreamed of, spent time with, Hölderlin. A playful thing, this repartee and refusal. This fitting within and pushing against. Here is Anne in an interview: "The things you think of to link are not in your own control. It's just who you are, bumping into the world. But *how* you link them is what shows the nature of your mind." In *Wonderwater* /

Answer Scars, Roni's titles play too. Roni says *What will you do with this,* and Anne responds, *Here is what I will do.* Bump, bump. It is a little game.

Two of the titles have the name Roni Horn in them. Roni Horn writes the titles, writes herself into them. The first time Roni Horn shows up in a title it is this one:

IF ON A WINTER'S NIGHT . . .
RONI HORN . . .

And the response, alone at the bottom of the page:

No I don't want to deal with Roni Horn yet.

We all know "Bartleby." "Bartleby" is a weird story by Herman Melville. *Answer Scars* is a weird book by Anne Carson in the series *Wonderwater,* which is a collaborative project by Roni Horn among others. Anne would prefer not to talk about Roni Horn, not yet. We are allowed to ask, "Why not?" as we are allowed to ask this of the other blanknesses, the other titles left more or less alone, though we will not get a response. I find it all very charming. And also jarring: It's Roni Horn's project. Talk about Roni Horn. I mean, when she asks you to.[2]

Later she does, she decides she's ready. The title given is UNTITLED (RONI HORN). Anne writes many things in this section: first on *geist,* then chains, then Zeus; a Motown song shows up (*"chain of fools* they say in Detroit"), and Foucault, whom she describes as a "funny thorn,"

which rhymes with Roni Horn. Why is she thrusting herself into the midst of this? Same reason Foucault does. Pissed off at— *now that is a good question,* what Foucault and Roni Horn are pissed off at.

The section ends, too, with Roni Horn: "*Do you believe in reembodiment? I asked her and she said No.*"

I find this all terribly funny. Maybe because it's an antagonistic collaboration for at least a second, which is rare in artistic collaborations: some struggle on the page, a little bit of shiftiness. Who has the power? There is pulling, pushing, picking: Roni insists that Anne write about her. Anne says no, not yet, I don't want to (which is itself a start), and then does write about her, but not without a jab and a tug and a joke or two. Roni prints the book and her name is on it as on the rest. Here it all is! What do they think of each other? It's like reality television. How exciting!

Answer Scars is not about Roni Horn though it might be about Anne Carson. It is certainly about Hölderlin and also about Suzette Gontard.

The pages written to the title SAYING WATER begin with Suzette taking "a plain view of house facts and heart facts" once her lover Hölderlin was gone. Anne says that Suzette had grown to be less and less delighted by her children, particularly by Henry, after they were no longer under Hölderlin's tutelage. A scene:

> One afternoon [Henry] met his mother coming out of the room that had been Hölderlin's. She'd gone in to search for some scrap of her lover and found a few bits of paper, a little sealing wax, a white button and a piece of petrified rye bread—"true relics" she calls them and all of a sudden there was Henry.

Henry was, in that moment, "[a] sudden boy, a melancholy boy." Anne goes on to mention the ways in which Henry was ultimately lost to history (died young, accomplished little of note), and continues,

> Odd process, history. This net we throw on Henry. What do you think, maybe Henry flew into a rage as his mother vanished down the hall, maybe he waved his impertinent young fist at her and shouted "Monkey hustle!" Maybe not. It's a net of water thrown on water.

So far so odd, so beautiful, right? The last line, though, is what stuns me:

> I wonder what did he do for the rest of the afternoon.

Henry Gontard is lost to us, in almost all of the ways he could be—indeed, he is all the more lost for our having bits of him at all. When Anne translated Sappho she left blank what others before her had filled, noted the edges of what had been fragmented. In her words,

[Sappho's] addresses to gods are orderly, perfect poetic products, but the way—and this is the magic of fragments—the way that poem breaks off leads into a thought that can't ever be apprehended. There is the space where a thought would be, but which you can't get hold of. I love that space. It's the reason I like to deal with fragments. Because no matter what the thought would be if it were fully worked out, it wouldn't be as good as the suggestion of a thought that the space gives you. Nothing fully worked out could be so arresting, spooky.

To Anne, Henry is real and absent (not a dichotomy), and there and lost (ditto), and history has stripped him away into the space where a person would be but which we can't get hold of. The bits of paper, sealing wax, button, and rye crumbs, stand in for what remains not only as physical remnants of Hölderlin's presence in the Gontard household, but as what remains of Hölderlin, of Suzette, and of Henry, for us to contend with. What Frau Gontard has of Hölderlin is surrounded by what she doesn't.[3] What we have of Henry is surrounded by what we don't; what we have of history, of text, is surrounded likewise. Anne sees this and it is big around her. A louder voice to her than to others, perhaps; a louder voice to her because of what little is there.

"I wonder what did he do for the rest of the afternoon" is a beautiful question: it is tender and matter-of-fact; attentive and aware of its limits; ordinary—mundane, even—and startlingly unexpected: what other historians, critics, even poets, would ask this question, as if asking it of, say, a still-living person (i.e., Well, Henry, what did you do for the rest of the afternoon)? Just because this was "Not quite the 19th century yet"—as Anne puts it on the first page—and just because history gives us little reason to care about Henry Gontard (he died at the age of nineteen and, as his mother feared, amounted to very little) doesn't mean we can't wonder. But would we? On our own? History—the study of it and the fact of it—is comprised of skating past dead humans. Anne might skate but she skates sideways from the rest of us. As if her blades aren't even on straight. And a little less blindly in circles. I for one would have never thought of Henry Gontard again; we had our version of rye crumbs and a button and some papers, a relational existence (son of, tutee of), a few mentions in some letters, and in clear and simple order Anne has given us the negative space of a person. What *did* he do the rest of the afternoon? It is a simple enough question.

In *Answer Scars,* Anne watches her own methods. Asks "why do it this way," even while noting that this is a process of observation and "not a complaint." At one point, after cinching a question about Empedokles up to a personal narrative, she adds,

> I realize I'm being philosophically unfair. Empedokles is a cosmologist, not aiming to console me for the vagaries of love or its mortal pain. Still I take comfort from his images. A lover may become a monster. I need a way to think about that. Here are some lines from fragment 57 and fragment 61.

Elsewhere, "Love validates life, these people believe. Did I ever believe this? Do you? Why keep poking about in an eighteenth century relationship as if it can teach us the rules? Not a complaint. I just wonder."

She is as clear as can be: "I need a way to think about that." We all do. This is a bewildered text doing work; poking about; seeking to explain what appears and seems central (but why central: this is allowed to be a mystery). A compelling reason to write, it seems: "I need a way to think about that." Not a complaint. Huh. Yes.

Works Cited

Carson, Anne. "The Art of Poetry, No. 88." Interview by Will Aitken. *Paris Review* 171 (2004): 190–226.

Carson, Anne. *Answer Scars.* In *Wonderwater (Alice Offshore),* by Roni Horn, Louise Bourgeois, Anne Carson, Hélène Cixous, and John Waters. Göttingen: Steidl Verlag, 2004.

Horn, Roni. *Wonderwater (Alice Offshore).* Göttingen: Steidl Verlag, 2004.

Ratliff, Ben. "Lamentation." *New York Times,* June 11, 2010.

Rimanelli, David. "Wonderwater." *Artforum International.,* suppl. *Bookforum* 11.3 (2004): 53.

Stein, Gertrude. "Pictures." In *Poets on Painters: Essays on the Art of Painting by Twentieth-Century Poets,* ed. by J. D. McClatchy. Berkeley: University of California Press, 1998: 81–106.

Notes

1. In what may be the only review of *Wonderwater,* the reviewer declares John Waters's annotations superior to the other artists' because he is the only one who "bothered to write something for every entry." I will leave that claim entirely alone, except to say it has been made and not by me.

2. Of the four contributors, Louise Bourgeois writes about Roni Horn when she is asked zero out of two times, Anne writes on both out of the two (though one is this "I don't want to" refusal), Hélène Cixous has one out of the two pages filled (though there is handwriting on the latter page between Roni and Hélène regarding where in the book to put this page, and "HC" writes to Roni, "you can include it somewhere in the untitleds"), and if you're prone to reading footnotes you already know that John Waters annotated every page, including the Roni Horn ones.

3. Henry says, "You have already lost a great deal that used to be in this room."

COLE SWENSEN

Opera Povera
Decreation, an Opera in Three Parts

OK, so where is the music? And where are the sets? And the cos-
tumes? And all the rest of the over-the-top ornamentation that lets
us know that we're in the presence of an opera? What marks some-
thing as an opera is, above all, extremity; even minimalist produc-
tions, such as Robert Wilson's, depend on it by taking minimalism
itself to extremes. Opera must exceed.

And Carson's opera does, though in unexpected, even unprece-
dented ways. A minor one is formal: "Decreation: An Opera in
Three Parts" has, as advertised, three parts, which echoes the three
acts of a traditional opera, but it also has a double, a doppelgänger
in the form of the preceding essay, also titled "Decreation," but this
time, "Decreation: How Women Like Sappho, Marguerite Porete,
and Simone Weil Tell God." It opens with a clear statement: "This is
an essay about three women and will have three parts," and yet it
actually has four, so there's not only an excess, but it's also central-
ized, as the extra part falls exactly in the middle of the seven parts
that compose the whole of "Decreation." Excess, overflow, almost
by definition, must fall to the outside, and, though it may extend the
margins, it is nonetheless marginalized; here, on the contrary, we're
told and shown that it is central, which prepares us to look for the
key to this work in excess that operates in unusual ways.

But is that instance of excess sufficient to justify calling this an
opera? Or, put another way, how is the operatic essential to this
work? Perhaps the rationale lies in that very word: work—for in
Italian, the word *opera* simply means "work," with all its ambiguity
and multidirectional applicability. Does the work work? Are all its
working parts in sync? "Poetry is a machine made of words" (Wil-
liam Carlos Williams). Throughout the history of opera, machines
have played a crucial role, winging people aerially and whisking
them terrestrially across the stage, changing the scenery, and gener-
ally defying and transcending natural law.

The centrality of the machine to opera dates—as does much else in opera—back to Greek drama, specifically to the *deus ex machina*, a phrase that Horace used to refer to the apparatus (a *mekhane*), a little like a crane, that was used in Greek tragedies to deliver the gods onto the stage. Horace strongly advised against such devices; his complaint was of the artificiality of such gestures, but from our current perspective, such artificiality is appealing, and appears as the frank display of the work's construction and a blatant celebration of the parts of which it's composed. We see, as it were, the inner workings. And what kind of work are they doing?

Almost all work is based (like the *machina*, whisking someone across the stage) on some kind of crossing, either literal or figurative; in physical work, you move something from one place to another, or turn one thing into another, crossing a boundary of definition or category (a recipe turns into a cake, a blueprint into a building, steel into a girder), while in mental work, you try to get an idea across, or put a deal across, or again, turn one thing into another—statistics into information, evidence into a case, an inkling into an essay. And much that we call work crosses this divide, turning the mental into the physical, turning ideas into actions or objects. All these instances of work are not only crossings, but, as mentioned above, they're also often crossing boundaries—transcending a limitation of class, category, or definition.

In "Decreation" Carson both points to and does a lot of crossing of various sorts. Again, one of these is formal; she crosses from the genre of the essay to the genre of the opera, smudging the boundaries of each and interlacing them. Though crossing generic boundaries is something Carson has done throughout her work, here it is not only a formal move and not mainly an argument about genre limitations themselves; it also echoes and underscores the content, which focuses on three women—Sappho, Marguerite Porete, and Simone Weil—and the ways they found to cross the boundary of the self.

In all three cases, by crossing the boundary of the self, the boundary that both guarantees that self's integrity and separates it from the rest of the world, the self manages to exceed itself into an eccentricity of ecstasy. In the Sappho poem that opens the essay, Carson recognizes a description of "the condition called *ekstasis*, literally 'standing outside oneself'"; in the essay's second section, she finds that Porete's central doctrine culminates in "an ecstasy in which the soul is carried outside her own Being and leaves herself behind," and in the third, she notes that Weil "had a program for getting the self out of the way, which she called 'decreation.'" These women all longed to leave the private self behind in order to fuse with an undifferentiated world spirit that each defined differently; for Sappho, it was herself "greener than grass"; for Porete it was God as "overflowing and abundant Lover," and for Weil it was "God's light," which she took "for a Being." Despite differences of goal, they all saw the path to it in Weil's decreation, which aspires not so much to an *un*doing of the self as to an *out*doing of it, both literally and figuratively.

By escaping their internal lives, these women hoped to make themselves into objects in the external world, and thus be able to participate in that world with complete immediacy. All three, with different nuances, saw that to rid the self of the self is the only way to make oneself completely available to God. If we can ever be of any use to God, it can never be as ourselves—it can only be as objects freed from the internal gravity of personal history, and all three saw their work in the world as precisely this. It is spiritual work, and Carson extracts from their examples the definition of spiritual work as precisely this operation of getting the self to cross the boundary from interior to exterior. In doing so, they not only leave their inner selves, but they also lose their inner selves, for in leaving, they create a vacuum, which necessarily collapses in on itself, creating an exclusively exterior being—a surface that hides nothing and presents everything—constantly, entirely, and simultaneously.

Carson combs the writings of these three to reveal an unexpected ally in their spiritual process—jealousy. Jealousy has long been an ally of opera; it abets any number of plots—Othello, Salome, Carmen, Lucia, Norma, Pagliacci, Tosca, Rigoletto—but clearly, it must be working very differently in order to fuel the plot of spiritual work. First, Carson locates jealousy as the central opening figure in the Sappho poem, which describes a love triangle, and then traces the equally triangular relationship among "God, Marguerite, and Marguerite," noting that "Jealousy is a dance in which everyone moves." And in the third part, she recognizes that "Simone Weil wants to discover in the three-cornered figure of jealousy those lines of force that connect the soul to God." Here we see the rule of three rising again, and for the third time: three parts, three women, and the three-sided dynamic of spiritual liberation—and it is the dynamic that's important, but it must be directed; it must be prevented from simply going around in circles (or triangles), and the etymology of jealousy offers the way out.

One might object that etymological roots that have been forgotten or lost cannot have any contemporary effect, but I think that, actually, they're never lost—they remain deeply engrained, deeply participant, like a cultural DNA that keeps us connected to centuries of history through the evolution of the words that created it. We cannot remember this history entirely, but we retain it, and it remains active through the histories that haunt our words. And Carson tells us on the second page of the first part of her seven-part "decreation" that "The word [jealousy] comes from ancient Greek *zelos* meaning 'zeal' or 'hot pursuit,'" which is also an extreme evacuation of the self—when we pursue with zeal, we leave ourselves behind. We so deeply invest in the other that we manage, finally, to get beyond our own selves. This is the promise and the work of infatuation; it enables and even forces the self to exceed itself; it forces the ego to realize that life exists, thrives, beyond its own boundaries; in short, that life (as Gilles Deleuze said) is not a personal thing. Ironically, the complete and self-absorbed event that is infatuation is one of the quickest routes to jealousy, which is, in turn, one of the quickest and surest ways to catapult one outside oneself. According to Carson, Porete uses jealousy in exactly this way: "as a test of her ability to de-centre herself, to move out of the way."

But what has this got to do with opera? Opera works in exactly the same way. An opera has no inside. Its over-the-topness, its excessiveness, is a display of the rich interior of culture, spread out across a surface, so that that wealth becomes publically available. In fact, an opera performs the same sort of crossing that these three women are enacting, and it happens on every level through a thorough evacuation of the center and a consequent multiplication and elaboration of surfaces. The "hidden" depths that drive other forms of theater and literature are missing here; instead, it's not only the deus ex machina that reveals its inner workings; it's every aspect of opera; all meaning is exposed on the surface, and this begins with emotion. In an opera, there's no guessing about who feels what—it's all screamed (tunefully) at the top of the lungs, and that process of belting it out is a literal transformation of internal sensation into the outside. The breath that's been brought within is dramatically, even violently, expelled from the interior of the body and spread as widely as possible. This surfacing of emotion is followed up on every other level: vivid color, sweeping gestures, dramatic stories—movement, music— Wagner phrased it as an aim for a total art, by which he meant a fusion of every medium appealing to every sense and every emotion—with opera, *it's all out there*; opera goes "all out."

And yet this excessiveness is actually achieved through a poverty that is not dissimilar to the poverty that Carson identifies at the center of these women's projects, and that is, in itself, involved with surface. "*Love dares the self to leave itself behind, to enter into poverty*," writes Carson, and just when God's abundance overflows Porete, she declares, "I who am in the abyss of absolute poverty." Opera's poverty is active in its content: the plots are basic—convoluted, perhaps, but nonetheless, they are the basic tales of love, power, greed, sacrifice; their complications are the exterior ones of mistaken identities (confused surfaces) or missed opportunities, rather than the intricacies of hidden motives or complex psychologies; it does not make use of subterranean innuendo; it refuses the resonances of layered feeling and history. Similarly, the characters are not fully developed individuals with rich inner lives; they are instead place-holders for the staple human qualities of love, loyalty, jealousy, hatred, green, ambition, etc. Characters are often identified and symbolized by their costumes or physical attributes. Yet it's precisely this inner impoverishment that feeds the rich surface—as if everything that once was inside the person was now outside; the sets, too, are elaborate, as if the interior of the world had been turned without.

By setting her discussion of the radical self-externalization of these three women as an opera, Carson explains the wealthy surface that inner poverty can occasion. In the case of living people, such self-emptying doesn't create the rich sensual evidence, but it is there nonetheless. And the fact that Carson's opera also lacks the surface wealth points to that absence as an inverse presence on the surface of these women, a radical surface that has become the wealth of the whole world, and is available to it.

JOHANNA SKIBSRUD

"To Undo the Creature"
The Paradox of Writing in
Anne Carson's Decreation

In the title section of Anne Carson's *Decreation*, Carson explores the work of three female mystics: Sappho, the Greek poet from the seventh century BC, Marguerite Porete, a Christian mystic from the fourteenth century, and Simone Weil, the twentieth-century author of the concept of "decreation"—the process by which we might, as she writes, "undo the creature in us," in order to pass beyond the limits of the individual self and move closer to God.

It is the exploration of this "de-creative" effort, shared by all three women—to pass beyond the "creaturely," in order to achieve a spiritual state beyond any "intact intellect of the ordinary human kind"—that provides the key to Carson's collection. Though made up of thirteen discrete sections of verse and prose, *Decreation* as a whole functions as an investigation into what it means to be human in a very concrete sense. What are the limits of the human "creature" itself? Carson asks. Is it possible to confront those limits, or even move beyond them?

Almost immediately, the investigation flounders. The state of being sought by Sappho, Porete, and Weil beyond the limits of individual identity is necessarily, after all, also a state of being beyond any place from which one might "tell" of it. "To tell is a function of self," writes Carson, and it is this situation that creates "a big problem for the writer." More than a contradiction, "it is a paradox," she tells us. To illustrate this, she provides us with an excerpt from Porete's religious treatise, *The Mirror of Simple Souls*, for which she was burned at the stake for heresy in 1310:

> For whoever talks about God . . . must not doubt but know without doubt . . . that he has never felt the true kernel of divine Love which makes the soul absolutely dazzled without being aware of it. For this is the true purified kernel of divine Love

which is without creaturely matter and given by the Creator to a creature *and takes away absolutely the practice of telling.* (173)

But the paradox that creates the "problem" is also, very shortly, revealed as the solution. A few pages later, referring to Simone Weil's phrase, "Eternal beatitude is a state where to look is to eat," Carson points out that "the written page can also reify this paradox for us." A writer may tell what is near and far at once. In this way, Carson explains, "the writer's dream of distance becomes an epithet of God" (175).

It is not, therefore, that writing about being creates a paradox as Carson suggests, but that writing reveals the paradox of being as such: it is only because a creature *can* and *does* "tell" about an experience perceived to have been "given by the Creator to a creature [that] *takes away absolutely the practice of telling*" (173) that the paradox is revealed as existing at all. Writing in this way both introduces and resolves the "problem of writing" by creating the "dream of distance" through which the "untellable" can in fact be told. But it is always—as Carson encourages us to keep in mind—"a dream." To write is, as Carson says in the first section of *Decreation*, to enter into life through "the sleep-side";[1] it is this approach that affords the possibility of something "*incognito* at the heart" (Carson, 20) to be revealed.

If we accept the definition of the human proposed by Carl Linnaeus, the founder of modern taxonomy—a definition characterized not by any descriptive qualifications but instead by the imperative *nosce te ipsum,* know yourself[2]—what we accept is primarily that to be a human creature is to *be cognitive* of your own creatureliness. The "sleep side" that Carson describes as the native space of the writer allows, in contrast, the possibility of encounter with that which remains "incognito"—that which is, in other words, outside, beyond, or uncreaturely about our being. Writing provides not only a way of "telling" *of* that experience, it marks the juncture at which that which is "incognito" rises to the surface, offering the possibility of contact. Writing is not—in Carson's sense—a "telling" of that which escapes the limits of subjectivity (and therefore a fixed point from which to "tell" anything at all); it is the untellable itself, and the very act of "decreation."

Drawing on the work of Jacques Derrida and Massimo Cacciari, and specifically their interpretation of Kafka's legend "Before the Law," embedded within the text of "The Trial," Giorgio Agamben reflects similarly on the "paradox" of language and subjectivity through a reflection of "the form of law." In Kafka's legend a man from the country seeks entry into the law through a manned doorway. He is not permitted to enter even though he remains at the gate for many years, and tempts the doorkeeper with bribes. Finally, at the end of the man's life he asks why no one else has sought out the law in all of those years. The doorman tells him that no one else could ever have been admitted because the door was constructed only for him—"and I am now going to shut it," the doorman says. Both Derrida and Cacciari emphasize that this story shows that "the power of the Law lies precisely in the impossibility of entering into what is already open, of reaching the place where one already is."[3] For Agamben, Kafka's legend "presents the pure form in which law affirms itself with the greatest force precisely at the point in which it no longer prescribes anything. . . . The open door destined only for him includes him in excluding him and excludes him in including him. And this is precisely the summit and the root of every law" (50). This situation works, as Agamben goes on to point out, "in analogous fashion" to language itself:

> Language also holds man in its ban insofar as man, as a speaking being, has always already entered into language without noticing it. Everything that is presupposed for there to be language (in the forms of something nonlinguistic, something ineffable, etc.) is nothing other than a presupposition of language that is maintained as such in relation to language precisely insofar as it is excluded from language. (50)

Because language situates itself as a pure form of relation, it is as impossible to enter into relationship with it as it is to absolve oneself of that relationship. This does not mean, Agamben reminds us, that "the nonlinguistic is inaccessible to man but simply that man can never reach it in the form of a nonrelational and ineffable presupposition, since the nonlinguistic is only ever to be found in language itself" (50). The inherent risk of presenting the "telling" of ineffable experience as a paradox—a paradox that, as Carson declares, writing "reifies" (175)—is that "telling" is represented as subsidiary, or subsequent, to the ineffable itself; this is not so. The ineffable exists in the *poetic*[4] approach to that which is always withheld.

It is this aspect of the writing process that lends itself easily to a comparison with the situation of the jealous lover. In response to the mystic writings of Marguerite Porete, Carson writes,

> Jealousy is a dance in which everyone moves. It is a dance with a dialectical nature. For the jealous lover must balance two contradictory realities within her heart: on the one hand, that of herself at the centre of the universe and in command of her own will, offering love to her beloved; on the other, that of herself off the centre of the universe and in despite of her own will, watching her beloved love someone else. Naked collision of these two realities brings the lover to a sort of a breakdown. (165)

This sort of breakdown is one that all three mystics whose work Carson explores undergo. In Sappho it occurs as the speaker "dislodges" her self from herself: "I am and dead—or almost / I seem to me" (as quoted, 159). In both Porete and Weil it occurs as they seek, first psychically, and then physically, to distance themselves from any knowledge or awareness of themselves and their limitations *as* human. But prior to the "breakdown" we have the "naked collision" itself—and something else, too: the residual reverberation of movement and contact with that which is withheld. Porete articulates the uncertainty introduced into the experience of subjecthood through this contact by coining her own term: "le Loingprés," which Carson translates as "the FarNear." The word is not in any way "justified" by Porete, Carson tells us—Porete simply begins to employ it in chapter 58 of *The Mirror of Simple Souls*, as though its meaning "were self-evident" (176). In the moment that the soul encounters God, God ravishes the soul, allowing peace to flow into it "like a glorious food." It is "in his capacity as le Loingprés, the FarNear," Porete tells us, that God enacts this ravishing—powerfully enough to "annihilate" subjectivity entirely.

The seeming contradiction of the term "the FarNear" introduces into Porete's account of its effects yet another contradiction. "Where the Soul remains after the work of the Ravishing FarNear, which we call a spark in the manner of an aperture and fast close, *no one could believe*," writes Porete, "*nor would she have any truth who knew how to tell this*" (176). As Carson points out, Porete cannot help but incorporate into her own "telling" "a little ripple of disbelief—a sort of distortion in the glass—as if to remind us that this dream of distance is after all just a dream" (176).

But what Carson calls "disbelief" here is not so much a wavering of faith as an acknowledgment of the limits of "telling." Narrative is abandoned. Porete surrenders her individual voice to a higher and more resonant frequency—to the "collision" of her own reality, the "known," with that which will always remain "incognito," outside and beyond her, "in force without significance."[5] It is the collision of these "two realities" that results in the "annihilation" of individual identity for Porete. She no longer exists in contrast to that which remains beyond her personal experience, but simply *resounds* within it. That is, this simultaneously passive and active response is not a sounding "of" or "as" or "against" something, but a *re*-sounding: an echo of that which is *already*—prior to consciousness—understood, and which cannot, therefore, be measured from any fixed point of cognition, thus narrated according to space or time. The "annihilation" of these categories within the language or writing which seeks to "tell" of it, might, presumably, allow for the revelation of precisely that resonance beyond individual identity—which (understood in contrast to a narrated space of being-for or against, or in-contrast-to, of judgment or action) we might call *pure presence*.[6] This "annihilation" is utterly unachievable in language, however, thus posing for all three mystics Carson discusses the seemingly unsurpassable "problem of writing."

Still, the nihilistic drive persists, shared by all three mystics, and cannot be considered separately from their creative impulse to "tell." The seeming impossibility of presenting dislocated and impersonal experience through the always located, personal medium of language is what constitutes the possibility of telling at all. Without the distance afforded by language, there would be no way of transmitting the unknown, even if "problematically," through the known. It is the reliance on—indeed, *insistence* on—the significance of "telling" (even under pain of death for Porete) that attests to the significance not only of what the writing finally manages to "tell," but of what it does not—gesturing, always, as it does, to that which remains in force *without* significance, outside language, or "the law."

For Sappho, Porete, and Weil, just as for Carson, writing is that desire which is also a jealousy—a perpetual hovering at the door. It is a manner of creating—through a simultaneous inability to equate experience with meaning or retreat from that possibility—the "FarNear" space of the encounter, or "collision," between subjective experience and that which will always exceed it. Having been absolved of any narrative potential—any link, that is, to locality, identity, process, or action—writing understood in this sense has the potential "to undo the creature in us" through the collapse of the opposing terms of being itself (I, non-I; contact and distance; the given and the withheld). The revelation of this space is one to which writing is not, therefore secondary—understood merely as re-presentation, a "telling," after the fact—it is the decreative act itself.

Notes

1. In "Every Exit Is an Entrance" Carson suggests that the writing process offers us the possibility of entering into experience "from the sleep side." She recounts one of her earliest memories—a dream—where her childhood living room appeared to her objectively the same in every way, but was nonetheless experienced as strange. It was "sunk in its greenness, breathing its own order, answerable to no one, apparently penetrable everywhere and yet so perfectly disguised in all the propaganda of its own waking life as to become in a true sense something incognito at the heart of our sleeping house" (20).

2. Giorgio Agamben, *The Open: Man and Animal,* trans. Kevin Attell (Stanford: Stanford University Press), 25.

3. Giorgio Agamben, *Homo Sacer: Sovereign Power and Bare Life,* trans. Daniel Heller-Roazen (Stanford: Stanford University Press, 1998), 49.

4. This word should be understood in the context of the original Greek form of the word, *poiesis.* The Greeks differentiated "between poiesis (*poien,* "to pro-duce" in the sense of bringing into being) and praxis (*prattein,* "to do" in the sense of acting)." Giorgio Agamben, *The Man without Content,* trans. Georgia Albert (Stanford: Stanford University Press, 1999), 68.

5. Agamben, *Homo Sacer,* 51.

6. The Greeks considered the essence of a work of art the very fact that, within the space of the work itself, "something passed from nonbeing into being, thus opening a space of truth (ἀ-λήθεια) and building a world for man's dwelling on earth" (Agamben, The Man without Content, 70).

JULIE CARR

No Video
On Anne Carson

Invited to write an essay on Anne Carson's work, I balked.

I first read Carson when I was twenty-three: *Glass, Irony and God* had just been published. I read "The Glass Essay" and gave up. Gave up what? Gave up not loving, is what I want to write. That is very dramatic and in no way true. But so is "The Glass Essay" very dramatic and possibly not true. Carson's "I" sat on her living room floor conjuring images, "naked glimpses of [her] soul." I was a dancer—I knew something about the images the mind can make, since despite its athletics dance is 90% mind. We danced with and in the mind's hallucinatory blasts. My mother was having back problems. I told her to lie on the floor and think of her back spreading out like pancake batter in the pan. She'd been making us pancakes for two decades. But pancakes were not just "comfort food," they were a defining symbol of my affiliation—my affiliation with the female side. My mother used to say that my parents' divorce was, finally, on account of pancakes. Not feminism, not affairs, but a fundamental difference about pancakes. He made them thick, with yogurt mixed in. She made them thin, more like crepes. They didn't like each other's, and I liked hers. I was loyal, for I lived with her. Despite her episodic rage, despite various hard slaps and one sharp kick on my shin, I was loyal to her, to her love and also to her pancakes. Therefore when I said, "Imagine your back spreading out like pancake batter in the pan," I was offering more than a dancer's image. I was offering a sign of my loyalty, my affiliation with the female. My father's pancake batter did not spread out in the pan. It sat there, more or less stiff, and browned.

I read "The Glass Essay" for the first time and encountered Carson's "I," facing her mother across a kitchen table, or sitting on her living room floor, bereft of her lover, "Law," conjuring images. (Ladislaw from *Middlemarch* was my literary beloved at that time. His curly head, his lad-like vague artistic ambitions, attracted me like no other. But understand, it was not that I wanted him; I wanted to *be* him—*Ladislaw*, the boy that *is*, that must be, that gets to be, the bearer of the law. Not Dorothea Brooke with her prim morality, and certainly not her floosy sister. Like Mary-Anne Evans herself, I wanted to be the boy, the lad, the George, aloof and unperturbed, to "live in my lantern / Trimming subliminal flicker / Virginal" [Mina Loy, "Songs" 1]. "It's better to be a neuter," wrote Carson ["Stanzas, Sexes, Seductions," *Decreation* 72]). I found "Anne" in the midst of what she called her "spiritual melodrama" and I thought I knew what she was up to. I'd conjured images too, though in the studio, that land of fantastic terror and delight.

"When Law left I felt so bad I thought I would die. / This is not uncommon," I read, tasting that curious blend of pathos and sardonicism that marks so much of Carson's work. So, I could sweat and shrug at once. Good. I kept going, into *Eros* (1998), into *Men* (2000).

Much of "The Glass Essay" is concerned with memory—a problem for those who remember, much worse for those who do not. "Perhaps the hardest thing about losing a lover," she writes, "is / to watch the year repeat its days."

I can feel that other day running underneath this one
like an old videotape. (*Glass* 8)

It's a poison, this "other day" this previous April 11, this video under real life. Memory is pain, whether happy or sad. In "The Glass Essay," Carson's father has Alzheimer's disease. She describes becoming aware that he no longer knows who she is on the phone, though he tries hard to be friendly. That year my mother had back pain, but a decade later, she could not remember the words to "Itsy-Bitsy Spider" or how to count change. For a while I took pride in the fact that she still knew me, seemed "just fine" when talking on the phone. I bragged about how few words she forgot during our conversations, just as you might brag about how a baby smiles at you. My stepfather, knowing what I was after, said, "That's because speaking to you makes her happy." Maybe her pleasure in me could keep her—not just alive, but "solvent," I want to say "solvent."

Solvent: able to pay one's debts, able to dissolve other substances within one's self. The two meanings seem in some kind of contradiction—the first directs itself outward; the second draws in. A solvent mother would do both at once: give what she owes, offer a within to enter and become. The mother with dementia can do neither.

Memory is bitter and no-memory is sick.

"My robotic nausea" is a phrase that presented itself to me when I found myself pregnant for the seventh time in my twenty-five years of "solvency." "Robotic nausea" is also a good way to describe the sensation that arises on the way up to the fifth floor where my mother resides in a chair. Her hair has been cut with no concern for fashion, but her breath no longer stinks; they brush her teeth here, evidently. The fifth floor's where old women play with dolls if they can. And old men announce themselves prepared for lunch all day long. Memory is bitter and no-memory is robotic nausea.

Carson has been milling the bitterness of memory since I was twenty and probably much longer than that. I know almost nothing about her, but I know her mother died in 1997, no longer carefully chewing lettuce at the kitchen table while asking questions about the airport. No longer dangling her feet in some Canadian pond. Carson compares death to a crossed-out sentence—there and not there at once—like that video running under every calendar day. "To my mother, / love / of my life, I describe what I had for brunch," she writes some years after her mother is gone ("Lines," *Decreation* 5).

The scents of oranges and geraniums are my mother's scents. Before her mouth began to stink, she passed peeled oranges from the front seat to the back. Geraniums bloomed year-round in a yellow kitchen. That day running under this one. Bitter scent of orange and dirt.

Invited to write about Anne Carson's work, I balked. There was no way not to emulate. And no way not be sentimental. For though I would never write, as she wrote, "I am not a sentimental person," I am easily embarrassed, also easily *embarazada* (pregnant). What these two tendencies have to do with one another, I cannot say, but to broaden it, perhaps I am not very protected. "Solvent" comes from the Latin verb *solvere*, which means "to loosen, to unfasten." "Contact is crisis," she wrote ("Dirt and Desire," *Men* 150), a phrase I took as an epigraph for my first book. And so, concerned about my tendency to gush, I thought instead of writing about her writing, I'd write about the dances.

I'd seen "Bracko" and "Nox," her collaborations with dancer/choreographer Rashaun Mitchell at the Institute for Contemporary Art in Boston in the summer of 2011. My father and stepmother bought the tickets, but they didn't love the show. To them, and they didn't say this, but I knew, Carson was too cold, too distant, too intellectual in her delivery of the text. The contrast between her Canadian chill, her academic correctness and, in "Nox," Mitchell and fellow dancer Silas Riener's wild boyish abandon made little sense to them, or at least did not move them. For me it was different. Carson didn't have to be in any way "passionate." She didn't even have to be good. It was better, in fact, that she was somewhat tight, awkward, not really a performer, but a little like someone in my department arguing for curriculum revisions. This way I could watch her unintruded, in a kind of privacy. Everyone loved the boys: they dashed around, did sexy impossible moves, breathed hard, and really meant it. But I kept one eye on awkward Anne, pushing around her little podium on wheels, reading from her book. One likes, in admiring, a certain seclusion. It's better if the world does not participate. (The world, actually, does participate in admiring Anne Carson, but my parents were enough world for me—their quiet response was enough to amplify my enthusiasm.)

And so I thought I'd write about the dance. But in order to do that well (I'd taken a dance criticism class with Jennifer Dunning in college!), I needed a video, or I needed to see the dances again so I could at least take notes. I wrote to Anne. "We have no video and we are not doing it again," she wrote back. Then, "Good luck."

This was not all she wrote, but it was all that I remembered.

As she tells it, her father's teeth grew black in the nursing home.

Of course I do not know if I read Anne Carson first when I was twenty-three or twenty-eight, or some age between. The floor I see her sitting on, conjuring her visions, is the living room floor of my Brooklyn Heights apartment where I lived between the ages of thirty and thirty-four. But that means nothing, says nothing about truth. In that apartment I became pregnant four times. In those years, my mother was still OK, though my grandmother, her mother, died in March of the final year I lived there. At the funeral—a meager chilly affair, just the family and Rabbi Millner clutching our jackets in the tiny Maine graveyard, the little kids, Nina and Benjamin, running around the graves—my mother, having very little nice to say about her own mother, decided instead to list all her mother's descendants. This would be a way to honor her as the matriarch whose blood we shared. But my mother could not remember everyone's name. Worst of all, she forgot my brother's wife and daughter entirely, though they were standing (or playing) right there.

Later, she was mortified and apologized profusely. But this was not simply grief or the late-winter cold numbing her mind: this was the beginning of her dementia, and we all knew it.

Memory fails. Or freezes: I had my own terrible secret that weekend and "I wish I could forget" (Apollinaire, "Zone"). Asked if we wanted to say or read something at the gathering, none of us did. Memories of my grandmother: one talking doll ("dance-with-me" *robotic nausea*), her panicked calls to my mother, one then another abusive husband, her underwear on the outside of her pants: Bitter gist, here we go.

> Who can sleep when she—
> hundreds of miles away I feel that vast breath
> fan her restless decks.
> Cicatrice by cicatrice
> all the links
> rattle once.
> Here we go mother on the shipless ocean.
> Pity us, pity the ocean, here we go.

> —"Sleep Chains," *Decreation* 3

The video-less dance exists, then, as the following: A history, which, as Carson tells us in the opening pages of *Nox,* is always akin to elegy: "The word 'history' comes from an ancient Greek verb ιστωρειν meaning 'to ask.' . . . But the asking is not idle. It is when you ask about something that you realize you yourself have survived it, and so you must carry it, or fashion it into a thing that carries itself" (*Nox* 1.1).

And so: The wildest boy, the "Brother," runs behind the glass wall that forms the back of the stage. Beyond him, Boston Harbor, summer light low. He does not "run," he *tears*. Forward and back, forward and back, before ample boats. He is, we might think, "lost," but not dead.

The two men, I'll call them "Brother" and "Sister," wrapped in a crazy embrace on the floor. "Brother" is somehow both inside out and upside down in "Sister's" arms and legs. She holds him, or she *autopsies* him: "Autopsy is . . . a mode of authorial power . . . I wonder what the smell of nothing is. Smell of autopsy" (*Nox* 1.2).

"Brother" and "Sister" spread themselves against a wall. Walls are useful in dance, for they make of the body a form, not just an activity. They provide a sliding dimension, a surface for slamming. This wall-dance is not original. It is slightly amateurish. And this is why I like it and why I (think I) remember it. Here "Brother" and "Sister" are like kids making treasure maps in the linen closet. Not very original, and not "professional," but dear.

After, there is a Q and A in which I do not want to speak to Carson. I prefer to remain an enthusiast, fan, lover, aficionado, admirer; informal buff, bum, freak, nut, fiend, fanatic, addict, maniac. A follower, adherent, supporter, advocate, disciple, votary, member, stalwart, zealot, believer, worshiper. Not one who receives an answer. So I ask the boys things. Which they answer with lies.

Nox, as most people reading this already know, is an accordion book, which is to say, a staircase. Up and down is how you read, or can, if you lift it up out of the box, rather than folding it open. A vertical reading is like listening to a deaf person's hands. It requires a new perspective. But "up and down" is one way we've understood the movement of poetry for a very long time. Since Orpheus at least, we imagine the poet traveling "downward" to find material, bringing that material back "up." Blanchot: "Orpheus' work does not consist of securing [the work] by descending into the depths. His *work* is to bring it back into the daylight and in the daylight give it form" (Blanchot, *The Gaze of Orpheus* 99). One also imagines travelling "down" into memory.

But toward what?

History can be at once concrete and indecipherable. Historian can be a storydog that roams around Asia Minor collecting bits of muteness like burrs in its hide. Note that the word "mute" (from Latin *mutus* and Greek μύειν) is regarded by linguists as an onomatopoeic formation referring not to silence but to a certain fundamental opacity of human being. . . . To put this another way, there is something that facts lack. "Overtakelessness" is a word told me by a philosopher once: *das Unumgangliche*—that which cannot be got round. Cannot be avoided or seen to the back of. And about which one collects facts—it remains beyond them. (*Nox* 1.3)

Carson speaks these words as the men dance. That their dancing is beautiful is a thing that cannot be said; to say so makes it less true than if one were to remain silent. Why a dancer is beautiful is something I've never understood. After all, I don't find anything particularly beautiful about the "human form." Though oddly, as I recall the "fundamental opacity" of the dance, recall very few "facts," of this history, into me drops the word my mother used to express surprise: "heavens." Heavens.

To read the book is to experience it falling. Lift it up and it falls back down, turn the page and rest it on the table and you risk a tumbling, and the need to regather, to pack it away. This awkward reading/spilling is not unlike the effort to remember, the effort to describe two men running, dropping to the ground, catching each other at the back of the head. Who would ever want to be a dance critic? Who would ever want to be a historian?

Better to be a poet—whose failure to catch the uncatchable story is given.

—

The brother lies down. Next to
The ~~book sister mother~~.

—

No video

ANDER MONSON

X inside an X
—Anne Carson, *Nox*

Is it not astonishing, entry.

Dear reader of this *Nox*, this book cradled in a box, approximation
of an epitaph for Carson's brother, an accordion-folded text, a series
of collaged scraps, photographs, correspondence bits, and glosses of
translation. Barely typeset, its apparent undesignedness brings us
physical intimacy: reading we're aware of Carson's hands, even if it's
an artifice, as they pressed snippet *x* into place with staple or with
glue. That is, you're aware of Anne, you're interfacing Anne.

Canada is cold and filled with distance. I think of another Cana-
dian, Margaret Atwood, and her invention the Longpen, which al-
lows the writer to sign her books remotely for a reader, to meet her
via real-time video in a bookstore, to mime a pen nib pressed into
the title page and have the apparatus make the movements in your
stead a thousand miles away with ink, so as to mediate a momentary
intimacy with technology and grace the page with human sigil.

A book should be graced with human sigil. *Nox* is filled with it,
her brother's bits, collected, though none of Anne's handwriting is
in evidence. Reading *Nox* at night, there's snow outside like Can-
ada, a tableau of white surprise because we are here, Anne's ghost
hand, her dead brother, and I, in Tucson, Arizona, well away from

frozen home and my own brother (whether he is cold, whether he sees snow, whether he is alive, I cannot know). A flake lands on the ledge, is cold, considers holding form a moment, disappears.

What else disappears: your time, your drink, your consciousness: consider rate—distance over time—when reading *Nox*. This is what we hope for, to lose ourselves in stream and look up some hours later and note that the world has moved: the cat's crept closer, following the sun. We often move through books more quickly than is wise. Slow, and reading reminds us of what we mark with the action of a turning page: an index finger's synecdoche. The slight lopsidedness of the box is physical, its verso opening slightly larger than the recto, so as to nest when closed. Reading in the box, the accumulating stack pulls slightly down. A spread hangs, inflates a little, a body under a bedsheet, or just enough to suggest fullness. Is this awkward effect intentional? Is a question a question or just an opening for your consideration? Is it us opening and considering our opening (and considering our opining and where the thoughts go—out into the air or mine)?

Reading's an opening, a translation, imperfect fit of cloud of mind that disappears into or behind a word when we inscribe it: we might write *here* and mean any *here* at all: your *here* (and you're here now hearing this line resound—my awkward Rs that melt into Ws or Ls when I get lazy or undergo sudden dentistry—in this I am for a moment resurrected in your mouth or in the axis of your inner ear) or mine or Anne's or any in between. This is not even considering the distances between us. In some mythologies we need intermediaries to speak to the dead. In some mythologies we believe in books to guide our wanderings and those of the recently released.

A pause: night now and away from book, I'm playing *Scrabble* ripoff *Words with Friends* on my smartphone with my thumb. I am cherishing the *x*. Prototypical algebraic variable, collision of two consonants, internal pluralized (two Ecks combined, perhaps Johann Maier von Eck, who tried to fuse the beliefs of Martin Luther and Jan Hus, and his brother, back to back), it always spots the mark, dots the pox, chants the hex, suggests the sex. I hold on to it longer than I should. I disconnect myself from the post office waiting line and here exist instead as server light and information. Asynchronicity is what makes it work, that you can reach across (a crux is a crucifix only if it's affixed with body, blood, or the simulation of one or both; once a crucifix it cannot again become a cross, even if disassembled, even if the body has been excised. If plastic it may be disposed. If blessed and therefore sacramental, it should be returned to the earthly elements—water, earth, fire, or air; usually one chooses fire because it works the fastest, is the sexiest. If sacred it must be preserved entire or one sins) a state time zone a country the work of weeks and silences between friends (a less engaging game) to interface in this small way.

Books are intermediaries—asynchronous and slow. A box like this is where it all collects, if you let it, the leftovers of a person (as in a meal shared but not completed and then brought home and perhaps abandoned or fed to pets), what their index fingers touched and left behind, how they wrote what bits they wrote, how they crossed their tees, how they wore their shirts, how they slashed their exes through and cut them from their lives. Reading *Nox* is reckoning with the dead: her dead and your own, your death and mine. Or: read backward, a text like this reflowers phoenix-like, is not extinguished. Read backward your life, your brother's life, is less a tragedy; we might find meaning in its apogee and eventual descent.

Acknowledgment

This essay previously appeared in *Flaunt*, and will appear in *Letter to a Future Lover* (Graywolf, 2015).

ͻentences on *Nox*

> *This book is a box that holds a body (text) that unfolds, and these sentences assume the reader has fingered that box. This box does not try to contain the disappearance and death of the poet's brother, but marks disappearance and death as they spill. A mortuary monument, with the epitaph inscribed not on the outside but on the inside of the slab (where the events are held in darkness), "a σωμα that becomes a σημα, a body that is made into a sign." (*Economy of the Unlost 85, 73*)

We try to pry free the stone. (I open the book.)

I seek warmth, but feel the night chill.

An invocation, in the poet's (?) hand ("Michael/Michael/Michael") moves quickly to Latin. Latin is not a rebuff, but it is another secret. I don't understand, but I read it anyway. It is a poem by Catullus, about the death of his own brother. We are directed to "what is not there," looking away from what is presumably the subject (*Economy* 73).

This is a touchable book about an untouchable brother. And so we have a ladder between tactility and distance.

This book frequently falls to the floor, and takes on its ladder shape.

Lisa says, accordion as stairwell (the stairwell where the sister/ poet and bloodied brother huddle). That dark, of the hidden and hiding, the absconded and the lost. Of bright memory groping through cold time toward a face and a name.

Soon, recurring on the left, a string of exhaustive definitions of each word in Catullus's poem.

Each word of Catullus's poem takes on the metal of deflection. Each word, as it proliferates definition, leads us up or down the stairwell, to and away (mostly away) from the more recent poet's brother.

The body pushes us back, the bones (from the photos, one would say frequently broken), the words do.

We break into the tomb by fits and starts, first at the end of all possibilities of *multas* (adjective, *many*), when the poet writes, "*multa nox*, late in the night, perhaps too late." In these words, something shows up for the first time. It is not the brother; it is the poet. She lets us in on *night*, opening an emotive door via modification, because it is "perhaps too late."

Still, the poet resists us (reader) as the brother resists the poet ("Death makes us stingy," she writes).

What is the duration of a word? An image? A brother? A poem?⎤
What is the relationship between "monument" and "memory"?⎦

A monument, too, is resistant to intimacy, but it has a kind of durability memory does not.

There is no back to this folding book—what does this say about history?

"Autopsy is a term historians use for the 'eyewitnessing' of data or events by the historian [herself]," Carson tells us, and then comes to the tale of her brother's dog "eyewitnessing" the brother's corpse and thereby shedding not tears but rage. The smell of nothing, she tells us, is the smell of autopsy. So seeing, one sees nothing.

To this nothing there is also something. The nothing of night—full of it.

We are reminded of AC's investigations into all that happens to the old heroes in sleep—the part of epic where its humans temporarily lose consciousness yet action doesn't stop.

In *Economy of the Unlost*, she writes: "Remembering brings the absent into the present, connects what is lost to what is here. Remembering draws attention to lostness and is made possible by emotions of space that open backward into a void. Memory depends on void, as void depends on memory, to think it" (38).

In that book, speaking of facts fished up from memory, she speaks of "vibrating with their disappearance" (vii).

In that book, she says, "Once void is thought, it can be cancelled," but in this book/box, she allows the backside (the void) to remain unthought (38).

On the other side of *Nox* is *nox*, the night, a white darkness the words do not seek to illuminate but guess within.

On the front side, when the words will not clarify, image takes over.

With each extending definition spreading from the Latin the words move farther and farther from their mooring.

What is their mooring?

A human, with a history?

A human, without history?

What is lost, and what is hauled up from the dark? What is unlost or unlosable?

This tomb book shows us how we say around.

AC has written compellingly of the geometry of the gaze, the triangulation of looking, in Sappho's Fragment 31 ("Phainetal moi," "He seems to me equal to gods that man" 62, 63). Here, we have a concatenation of geometries: brother, mother, daughter; dead Roman poet, brother, living Canadian poet, brother. Between them is the veiling of night, obscuring the looking. Between the daughter and the mother, "no speaking [of the brother] is left" (63). On this subject, they are in the "deep speechlessness of night" (*mutam*).

In the room of the poem, the living poet "gropes for the light switch."

But I am also divided between the right side and left side, front side and back side of the body. Whose body is it, as I read, definitions to the left, recursive, where I am perhaps invited to go blind (to definitions, to words). To the other side of the story, other side of the brother, the tomb, the book. Occasionally, the definitions shift to the right, and we reside in the pure threading of it. "It" is the asking of history.

Nan says, rather than an archaeology (a digging into the past, with something to be found), or a hole with a bottom, this is a spreading. Gertrude Stein says the difference is spreading. Simultaneity (says Nan), but I would also ask, what is the opposite of simultaneity? Or, not exactly its opposite, but its thwarting.

How many times does *Nox* say night? What fabric is night to this poet?

This poet is "made sadder by the brother's night than by the brother himself."

"Of wine, honey, flowers, night, etc."

"Nothing is night's gift."

What fabric where we lose those we think we love.

Loss: of brother, of mother; but also of specificity, uncharacteristic of this poet: "*one of those trees* that turns all its leaves over, silver, in the wind" (italics mine). As if naming were momentarily rushing away from her.

The poet calls out into the space; the brother does not respond. As it turns out, he has changed his name.

As it turns out, "There is no stone." The mooring is the poet. Or rather, plural: poets. For AC pulls across from the other side (of history, the body, from the left side of the page) <u>not a response but another possible brother-body, a poet who also mourns a brother, as if we could make sibling a verb casting its shadow across time.</u>

What I love: the photo, just after *nequiquam*, with AC as a child looking just like Anne Carson. What shines forth in this night is the poets' ipseity (presumably from *"ipse ipsa ipsum* . . . the actual himself [herself, etc.] as opposed to persons more remotely connected"). Not so much (for this reader) in contrast to the otherness of brother, but as a backlight (that bright realm on the other side) that kindles the words from the void into what is sound and seen, "which comes through the poet like a light shed on darkening things" (*Economy* 42).

Note

Lisa is poet Lisa Donovan, and Nan is poet Nan Burton. Both were Ph.D. candidates at the time of the quoted conversation.

BIANCA STONE

Your Soul Is Blowing Apart
Antigonick *and the Influence*
of Collaborative Process

It is not a writer's process but finished product—published, stamped
with a price tag in our hands—that we judge. We judge the book
for its implications, comprehension, importance, humor, presump-
tuousness, believability, and ultimately whether or not we want to
keep it within reach or far from sight. And our judgment is imme-
diate. This public critique contrasts greatly with the humble soli-
tude of artistic process. The process of a collaborative work, with all
its continuously moving parts, provides a more complex view of the
private/public sphere. It was Horace who called for the inspection
of poetry (in its broadest terms) to be viewed as close as the inspec-
tion of painting. "Some works will captivate you when you stand
very close to them and others if you are at a greater distance. This
one prefers a darker vantage point, that one wants to be seen in the
light since it feels no terror before the penetrating judgment of the
critic."[1] Horace's assertion echoes the poet John Ashbery's aesthetic,
which, while never forgoing the traditional power of words and
images, does not hold to the "immutability of their functions."[2] In
collaboration, the *process* is its own artifact; a dance troupe, curating
a dance while constructing their stage, will later perform the "real"
piece. Without the strange and unique route, the final performance
would not exist.

   One cannot approach Anne Carson's work without realizing its
entire range as it reflects her concern with artistic process. The *objet
de arte* that is *Antigonick* (and *Nox*, for that matter) reveals an intri-
cate process of collaboration. Anne Carson and her partner, Robert
Currie, have been dedicated to cultivating the uses of collaboration
and hybrid genre for years. It is the literal collaboration of two
minds, but also the collaboration with another work of art (in the
case of *Antigonick*, Sophokles, as well as Beckett, Hegel, etc., whose
substance appear throughout; and me, as the artist-at-large). Carson

is less about borrowing or interpreting from her sources than she is about breaking and rebuilding the possibilities of her art. In this way her work is never set, but always moving. It is a collapsing of categories: poetry and visual art.

The visual aspect in *Antigonick* was honed and guided by Carson's artistic credo, and with Robert Currie's vision of structure in conjunction with randomization. My part in the collaboration was to exist within this, but to create individually, within my own process as well. In a sense, it's incorrect to say that I "illustrated" *Antigonick*, for the very reasons I've stated. My own work as a poet and visual artist has revolved around an interest in experimental comics; using illustration not as an explanatory addition to the text, but as an element of form.

What Carson's work seems to say is "there are many different ways for a line to function. As is true for the visual images." The visual aspects of *Antigonick* do not act as instructive representation of the text, just as her "translation" does not function as a translation to merely read Sophokles's Antigone again. Anne Carson's *text* (within her personal process of translation) is the gorgeous mastery that makes *Antigonick* so relevant today. Everything else in the book vibrates around that fact. Yet the collaborative efforts of this book—presented through the use of image, text, structure, and blank space—invite the reader to engage in process and product simultaneously.

When working with Anne Carson and Robert Currie we often discussed process versus product. In collaboration both are important facets to the experience. Process is normally a private act. But when collaborating, the process is continuous trial and error. One of the most delicate elements in a collaboration such as *Antigonick* is how to balance the power of a visual image with the power of a written one; how to ease an illustration into a text's sacred space—that's already plenty rich—so that both can remain vital, individual, yet also gorgeously united. It should feel as though the text couldn't live without the image (though of course it could). The use of images on vellum paper to overlay the text provided an ingenious method of having it both ways. The drawings and the text could be experienced separately *or* together. The end result is the reader creates a whole new translation each time she opens the book. My artwork in the book is a result of my own, personal communication with Anne Carson's translation, with the sprit of her interpretation at heart. The outcome is beyond what I could offer alone. As a single element to her vision, my hand is in the book but never pointing. While one could argue that the images offer no direct line to the text, in fact this isn't at all true. In the spirit of Carson's oeuvre and interest in "thinking together," the art is not in the book to reaffirm what is already in the text, but rather to communicate with it. And isn't this the essential glory of artistic partnership? A communication that makes something new, something that's never been felt before.

How does one create art and illustration for this kind of radical translation without ruining the translator's intonations, her specific choices? I wrestle with this still. I too believe in the immutability of words. I can draw an image as another element of poetic form because of that immutability, and because (again to conjure Horace) *Ut pictura poesis*. I can take liberties in illustrating, within the abstract and the lyrical written word, easily. But it would be an injustice to assume that more narrative lyrics cannot be explored in the same way; that their words are less moveable.

Sophokles's Antigone is not an abstract, lyrical poem. It is a story, complete with narrative and characters, all part of a larger mythology. Thus, the first impulse an artist has is to *draw* that narrative. Carson and Currie gently guided me away from the idea of characters toward landscape and object. I sat down amid my art supplies and books, and despaired at how to approach such a text visually. This led me back to Carson's previous works. *Nox*, for example, deals with fragmentary images and space on that page, and a unique integration of text and image. I looked toward Carson's illustrations (which she had previously shared with me) for inspiration. I am continuously struck by the fact that there is no pretension in Carson's work. Rather, a stark willingness to communicate emotionally with her subject, while keeping a detached distance. Thus the reader can create and bring together, privately. Carson's writing engages with the rhetoric of essay writing which allows for exploration of theme, but it is the poet in her that allows for imaginative spontaneity and the artist in her that constructs tone. It was this distinctive method of creating that allowed me the means to create from my own space the drawings in the book. It is also what I believe will invigorate poetry, translation, visual art (and not least bookmaking) now and in the future: to engage with a single thing on multiple levels. *Antigonick* is a multidimensional transformation of something old and something new. A true collaboration between artists, between text, image, blank space; tone and absence of tone; time, and timelessness; bookmaking and the *collapsing* of our *idea* of the book.

And why shouldn't it? For the very fact is that the printed book becomes more obsolete in the mainstream—just as poetry has been recently branded as "dead," as painting was when faced with the invention of the daguerreotype. It is the exploding, innovative minds such as Carson's that will reject those inevitabilities. What she continuously reminds me of is that we make our own cannon. That we love the themes of the established cannon that we feel strongly about; that we create our own visions of the future, and play them out, as organically and originally as we see fit. There is no alternative to genuine creativity and the moving forward of art. Yes, something might be dead. Something that is irrelevant to this that is thriving now. What matters is remembering to pause and examine the invention in your hands. To stand very close and then at a greater distance. The object—whirlwind of text and art and past and future—is an artifact of process and painting and poetry that must be, as all Carson's works, turned over in your hands, again and again.

Notes

1. *Ars Poetica*, in *Horace for Students of Literature: The "'Ars Poetica" and Its Tradition*, edited by O. B. Hardison Jr. and Leon Golden (Gainesville: University Press of Florida, 1995).

2. Jed Perl, "A Magically Alive Aesthetic," *Conjunctions* 49 (Fall 2007): 364–71.

ANDREW ZAWACKI

"Standing in / the Nick of Time"
Antigonick in Seven Short Takes

Seven gates / and in each gate a man / and in each man a death

1.

"Have you heard / this expression the nick of time," Eurydike asks aloud in Anne Carson's translation-adaptation of Sophocles. "What is a / nick / I asked my son."[1] It's ironic that Eurydike should solicit Haimon, for he's suddenly dead, and his death exemplifies the very nick she's inquiring about. The death of a child, before the parents die, is time out of whack. "Neither of us has been able to come to terms with the monstrous fact that children may die before their parents," Freud wrote to Binswanger.[2] Freud's daughter Sophie had died a few weeks earlier, "the first of our children," he reminded his mother, "we have to outlive."[3] Unable to endure such a nick in time, Eurydike kills herself, having compared herself to a Virginia Woolf character: "Like poor Mrs. Ramsay who died / in a bracket of To the Lighthouse." The literary anachronism articulates a temporal rift, and Eurydike speaks in third person, as if she'd already passed out of agency. "Exit Eurydike bleeding," she instructs, to which the stage directions object: "[Eurydike does not exit]." Dying in brackets is death without death—sublated in the Hegelian sense: canceled and maintained. Her husband Kreon, king of Thebes, undergoes similar freefall, lamenting, "O / my child too soon dead." Haimon's untimely death, compounded by his wife's suicide, has undone him: "O filth of death you crack me you / crack / me open you crack me open again." Freighted by Freud's "resignation of the survivor," Kreon is condemned to life, labeling himself "nick of time" and crying, "Take Kreon away he no more exists than someone / who does not exist."[4] He, too, has slid out of first person, such that "I / do not count your life alive," his messenger says, "a corpse is more alive." Kreon manifests a paralysis that Mallarmé identified upon losing his own son: "—now interruption / in the father—," he wrote, the punctuation dramatizing not just separation from Anatole but internal fracture as well.[5] "The loss of a child," Freud averred, is a "serious, narcissistic injury."[6] To be "in / the nick of time," as the Chorus portends, is the opposite of the vernacular expression of speed and reprieve. It means arriving too late to prevent what has happened too soon.

2.

For Eurydike and Kreon, the irreplaceable is a child, as it was for Freud: "we shall remain inconsolable and will never find a substitute," Freud confessed, nine years after his loss.[7] For Haimon it's a fiancée; he suicides when Antigone dies. For the play's heroine, the severest love is reserved for a brother, precisely because he is a nick in time—with their parents dead, Polyneikes can't be replaced: "but who can grow me a new brother."[8] Polyneikes is not merely Antigone's sibling, however, and indeed kinship relations across Sophocles's trilogy, because incestuous, are nicked as per the French *niquer*: to fuck, fuck up. "Father's daughter / daughter's brother sister's mother mother's son / his mother and his wife were one!" Ismene conjugates, reprising flatly, "Our family is / doubled tripled and dirty in every / direction." Oidipous is father to Antigone as well as to Ismene, Polyneikes, and Eteokles. But because Jokasta is not only Oidipous's wife but also his mother, he is equally his children's half-brother. Which means Antigone's brothers are likewise her nephews, while her mother and grandmother are one—yet the name Antigone might mean "in the place of the mother."[9] Shouldn't a father come "before" a brother, a mother "after" a grandmother? Antigone's lineage is ruled instead by unruly simultaneity. "The terms of kinship become irrevocably equivocal," Judith Butler argues, with Antigone representing "kinship's fatal aberration."[10] Exclaiming, "How sweet to lie upon my brother's body thigh to thigh," Antigone reveals Polyneikes as her lover. Since he's dead, her already disruptive desire for him can produce nothing: "I'm the last one left," she says in her final speech, "in a line of / kings." As arranged by Antigone, kinship suffers temporal nicks that hasten the end of normative inheritance. Etymologically her name has been construed as "anti-generation" and might bespeak a rejection of kinship, period.[11]

3.

Instability and incoherence within the symbolic structure governing the house of Laius is exacerbated by Oidipous's curse on his family. Antigone is "raw as her father," the Chorus observes, her voice often not her own, any more than her actions are free of a fate set for her in advance. "At our backs is a big anarchy," she reports in Carson's "TV Men: Antigone *(Scripts 1 and 2)*."[12] The present is nicked by another, spectral temporal pressure, and the demands on Antigone hail from conflicting sources: her father cursed his disloyal sons to slay each other, but her brother petitions Antigone's fidelity.[13] This interference in the transmission of the paternal word is further obscured, since the father is also a brother—whose word prevails? What time is Antigone "in"? Leveled against Polyneikes and Eteokles, the curse ricochets to disrupt Antigone's destiny, as her father's "words exert a force in time that exceeds the temporality of their enunciation." That Sophocles wrote the later play, *Antigone*, earlier than the earlier play, *Oedipus at Colonus*, is a figure for how "the forward movement of time is precisely what is inverted through the temporality of the curse." Moreover, in his radical rereading, Jacques Lacan observes that in Antigone's speeches Sophocles places the preposition μετά, normally located before the noun, "at the end of the line in an inverse position."[14] Hence a word signifying both jointure ("with") and disjunction ("after") emphasizes only the rupture, testifying to a "presence" that's "fierce" because that present is broken. Is the impossibility of regulating her clock what pushes Antigone to suicide? She hangs herself just as the Chorus tries to tell time: "An hour / an hour and a half / a year / a split second / a decade / this instant / a second / a split second / a now / a nick." How many competing times does that time contain—or prove unable to hold? The fatal fallout from the filial curse is felt before its words have even been uttered.

4.

Whereas Antigone's actions are governed by a prior malediction, Teiresias acts in accord with prophecy. The seer embodies this dual temporality through an androgyny that Antigone performs. Though Ismene intones that "we / are girls girls cannot force their way against / men," Antigone frequently assumes a masculine role. Indeed, Oidipous had referred to her as a man, likening his sons to women in turn, and by repeating Polyneikes's defiance she substitutes for him, while replacing Kreon as leader. "I'm the man here," insists the king, who won't take "wisdom from this stripling," but Haimon says his father sounds like "a boy dictator." Gender distinctions segue to issues of age: the Guard calls Antigone a "child," but her actions denote maturity beyond her uncle's. By the end, she has "taken the place of nearly every man in her family," as if the suffix -*nick* connoted theft.[15] These nicks in age and traditional gender roles are also at work in fraying orthodox martial binaries. "Enemy is always enemy / alive or dead," according to Kreon, whose arguments reprise Carl Schmitt's assertion, "The specific political distinction to which political actions and motives can be reduced is that between friend and enemy."[16] Antigone denies this logic of "patriot and traitor," however, by eroding the distinction between public and private. She loves her brother, outlaw to the state, asserting, "I am born of love not hatred," while threatening her sister, who exemplifies domesticity by refraining from an illegal act: "I'll have to hate you." In her adaptation *Thebans*, Liz Lochhead distills the tension between comrade and foe in Antigone's nearly homonymic pairing: "*my dearest   my direst enemy / my brother*."[17] And in Jean Anouilh's version, Creon admits having mixed up the brothers' corpses altogether: "I don't know which was which."[18]

5.

Replete with "confounded," indistinct states, "Time Passes" is a stylistically slow-mo caesura that nonetheless nicks Woolf's novel by accelerating the narrative.[19] This causes blur in Mrs. McNab's telescope, as she watches the old gentleman: "Some said he was dead; some said she was dead. Which was it?"[20] Death is no clearer cut in *Antigonick*. On one hand, Polyneikes has been killed. "This boy is dead," Teiresias reminds the king. But then he advises, "stop killing him": by trying to slaughter his nephew again, Kreon seeks to level what Lacan names the "second death," which paradoxically deprives the fallen soldier of his first.[21] On the other hand then, unburied, Polyneikes's spirit still wanders the earth—not alive, certainly, but nevertheless at large. "You've made a structural / mistake with life and death," Teiresias augurs, "you've put / the living underground and kept the dead up here / that is so wrong." This inverted arc is pivotal to the Laius family "archives of grief." Born crippled, Oidipous had been left for dead, but he was saved, surviving his extinction. His daughter mourns a child that will never be born.

6.

Guilty of burying her brother, Antigone is condemned to live burial: "I shall lie in the / bed of the river of death while I am still alive." Incommensurate with ordinary time, Kreon's structural error inflicts an ulterior temporality on Antigone, augmenting the nick afflicting her from the start: "I died long ago." Still breathing, she exists under postmortem conditions; deprived of any future, she hasn't yet ended on earth. Eurydike says Antigone has "the undead strapped to / her back," while in Brecht's adaptation she capsizes time, proclaiming, "I mourn for you, survivors."[22] Especially attentive to her "death that crosses over into the sphere of life, a life that moves in the realm of death," Lacan links Antigone's limit condition—poised at "the boundary of the still living corpse"—with a "phenomenon of the beautiful" emitted by the second death.[23] She's inhuman, for she traverses the perimeter of human being: the Guard reports accosting a "bird / in her childreftgravecry." Nor is Antigone's existential nick unknown to her. "I'm a strange new kind of / inbetween thing," she reasons, "not at home with the / dead / nor with the living." Placed within this "field of the Other," Antigone incarnates displacement and becomes the outside as such.[24] An ontological scandal, "the only one of mortals / to go down to death alive," she's a demigod—beautiful and terrifying, "in love with the impossible"—her entombment merely consecrating the death she's been living all along.

7.

Antigone and Ismene open this postmodern adaptation by paraphrasing the *Phenomenology of Spirit*. Beyond merely situating *Antigonick* within the play's critical reception, Carson writes that theoretical heritage into her text. Through this temporal reversal, whereby the tragedy anticipates its history, Carson clears a speculative space for quarreling with the terms of debate. In the *Phenomenology*, the female as exemplified by Antigone is relegated to converting a man's death from the abstract universality of natural extinction—the corpse, a thing—into the willed work of immanent community.[25] To place Hegel "before" Sophocles, by inscribing the *Phenomenology* in the classical drama, upturns the ground by which "woman," as Luce Iragary has critiqued Hegel, "does not take an active part in the development of history."[26] If Antigone's position is ironic, since she buries her brother without anyone witnessing for her, in Carson's outtake she's aware of that irony. "I was an organized person," she complains, "and this is / my reward I organized your deaths dear ones all / of you." Questioning the appraisals assigned to her, the Antigone of *Antigonick* suggests the possibility—or at least the glaring necessity—of alternative forms of community, premised not on self-fulfillment, let alone the female realization of male itineraries, but on the precariousness of mutual exposure, an estranging otherness of neighbor and kin that recommends respect over teleological project. Just as *Antigonick* imports modern references, so "a nick of classical Greek time becomes lodged in our own time," Butler argues in her review, "re-opening the question of rage, grief, and loss within another idiom."[27] Kreon diagnoses the genealogy of friendship in Western philosophy when he blurts with machismo, "When you / lay yourself under a pleasure female you / take an open wound into your house." Carson's antagonistic protagonist is that lesion in the received history, not least through her absence from that discourse. What happens when a sister is folded into fraternity "could be one of our most insistent questions," Derrida admits in *Politics of Friendship*, "even if, having done so too often elsewhere, we will here avoid convoking Antigone . . . to this history of brothers that has been told to us for thousands of years."[28] Maybe this is how we should read the typographical fact that the whole of *Antigonick* is bracketed: a story apart, outer edge to the official account. "A state of exception," Eurydike notes, "marks the / limit of the law." Antigone's exclusion is not without advantage. "If the woman does not even appear in the theory of the partisan," Derrida proposes, reading Schmitt, "such an invisibility, such a blindness, gives food for thought: what if the woman were the absolute partisan?"[29] That Carson's character Nick is mute may render his revisionary potential "all the more awesome," since it's from the clandestine margins he can trace the stage's dimensions, threatening to erase the distance from periphery to center. His work is an ongoing unworking. Opening with a directive for the sisters to "[Enter," *Antigonick* proceeds to a final bracket

that closes without, however, closing down: "Exeunt omnes except
Nick who continues / measuring]." The key word is "except."
Overriding the normative terminal mark, a mute temporal mutant
stays onstage, restless and recalcitrant, as formal convention collapses
beneath a phenomenon that cannot state its name.

Works Cited

Anouilh, Jean. *Antigone: A Tragedy.* Translated by Lewis Galantière. In *Five
Plays.* Volume 1. New York: Hill and Wang, 1958. 1–53.
Brecht, Bertolt. *Sophocles' "Antigone."* Translated by Judith Malina. New
York: Applause, 1990.
Butler, Judith. *Antigone's Claim: Kinship between Life and Death.* New York:
Columbia University Press, 2000.
Butler, Judith. "Can't Stop Screaming." In *Public Books.* September 5, 2012.
http://www.publicbooks.rg/fiction/cant-stop-screaming.
Carson, Anne. *Antigonick.* Illustrated by Bianca Stone, designed by Robert
Currie. New York: New Directions, 2012.
Carson, Anne. *Men in the Off Hours.* New York: Vintage / Random House,
2001.
Derrida, Jacques. *Politics of Friendship.* Translated by George Collins. New
York: Verso, 1997.
Freud, Sigmund. *Letters of Sigmund Freud.* Edited by Ernst L. Freud, trans-
lated by Tania and James Stern. New York: Basic, 1975.
Freud, Sigmund. *The Sigmund Freud–Ludwig Binswanger Correspondence,
1908–1938.* Edited by Gerhard Fichtner, translated by Arnold J. Pomer-
ans. New York: Other, 2003.
Hegel, G. W. F. *Phenomenology of Spirit.* Translated by A. V. Miller. Oxford:
Oxford University Press, 1977.
Irigaray, Luce. "The Eternal Irony of the Community." In *Feminist Readings
of "Antigone,"* edited by Fanny Söderbäck. Albany: SUNY Press, 2010.
99–110.
Lacan, Jacques. "The Essence of Tragedy: A Commentary on Sophocles'
Antigone." In *The Ethics of Psychoanalysis, 1959–1960: The Seminar of
Jacques Lacan, Book VII,* edited by Jacques-Alain Miller, translated by
Dennis Porter. New York: Routledge, 2008. 297–353.
Lochhead, Liz. *Thebans: Oedipus Jokasta Antigone.* London: Nick Hern;
Glasgow: Theatre Babel, 2003.
Mallarmé, Stéphane. *A Tomb for Anatole.* Translated by Paul Auster. New
York: New Directions, 2005.
Schmitt, Carl. *The Concept of the Political.* Translated by George Schwab.
Chicago: University of Chicago Press, 1996.
Woolf, Virginia. *To the Lighthouse.* Edited by Margaret Drabble. Oxford:
Oxford University Press, 1992.

Notes

1. Anne Carson, *Antigonick* (New York: New Directions, 2012), not paginated.

2. Sigmund Freud, *The Sigmund Freud–Ludwig Binswanger Correspondence, 1908–1938*, ed. Gerhard Fichtner, trans. Arnold J. Pomerans (New York: Other, 2003), 150.

3. Sigmund Freud, *Letters of Sigmund Freud*, ed. Ernst L. Freud, trans. Tania and James Stern (New York: Basic, 1975), 326.

4. Freud, *Letters*, 330.

5. Stéphane Mallarmé, *A Tomb for Anatole*, trans. Paul Auster (New York: New Directions, 2005), no. 56.

6. Freud, *Letters*, 328.

7. Freud, *Letters*, 386.

8. Carson mourned the death of her own brother in her previous volume *Nox*. As she'd written of her mother's death, in "Appendix to Ordinary Time," while examining cross-outs in Woolf's manuscripts: "by a simple stroke—all is lost, yet still there." Cf. Anne Carson, *Men in the Off Hours* (New York: Vintage / Random House, 2001), 166.

9. The suggestion is Robert Graves's. Cf. Judith Butler, *Antigone's Claim: Kinship between Life and Death* (New York: Columbia University Press, 2000), 87.

10. Butler, *Antigone's Claim*, 57, 15.

11. Butler, *Antigone's Claim*, 22, 88.

12. Carson, *Men in the Off Hours*, 101.

13. Butler, *Antigone's Claim*, 58, 60–61.

14. Jacques Lacan, "The Essence of Tragedy: A Commentary on Sophocles' *Antigone*," in *The Ethics of Psychoanalysis, 1959–1960: The Seminar of Jacques Lacan, Book VII*, ed. Jacques-Alain Miller, trans. Dennis Porter (New York: Routledge, 2008), 326.

15. Butler, *Antigone's Claim*, 11, 62.

16. Carl Schmitt, *The Concept of the Political*, trans. George Schwab (Chicago: University of Chicago Press, 1996), 26.

17. Liz Lochhead, *Thebans: Oedipus Jokasta Antigone* (London: Nick Hern; Glasgow: Theatre Babel, 2003), 57.

18. Jean Anouilh, *Antigone: A Tragedy*, trans. Lewis Galantière, in *Five Plays*, volume 1 (New York: Hill and Wang, 1958), 40–41.

19. Virginia Woolf, *To the Lighthouse*, ed. Margaret Drabble (Oxford: Oxford University Press, 1992), 171.

20. Woolf, *To the Lighthouse*, 190.

21. Lacan, "The Essence of Tragedy," 313.

22. Bertolt Brecht, *Sophocles' "Antigone,"* trans. Judith Malina (New York: Applause, 1990), 48.

23. Lacan, "The Essence of Tragedy," 306, 330, 320.

24. Lacan, "The Essence of Tragedy," 341.

25. G. W. F. Hegel, *Phenomenology of Spirit*, trans. A. V. Miller (Oxford: Oxford University Press, 1977), 272–73.

26. Luce Irigaray, "The Eternal Irony of the Community," in *Feminist Readings of "Antigone"*, ed. Fanny Söderbäck (Albany: SUNY Press, 2010), 108.

27. Judith Butler, "Can't Stop Screaming," in *Public Books* (September 5, 2012), http://www.publicbooks.rg/fiction/cant-stop-screaming.

28. Jacques Derrida, *Politics of Friendship*, trans. George Collins (London: Verso, 1997), viii–ix.

29. Derrida, *Politics of Friendship*, 156–57.

What's So Funny about *Antigonick*?

A search of "Antigone jokes" reveals no one- or two-liners about Sophocles's tragic heroine. Yet, with *Antigo Nick*, Anne Carson and Bianca Stone have made a comic book of her story. Stone's freely drawn cartoons lay lightly over, by way of vellum paper, Carson's fresh translation of Sophocles's tragedy, itself written in "Squeaky Chalk" comic font. The translation is complete, that is, it is a complete transformation. Including, as noted, the addition of images, or icons for the iconic, which must include a measure of iconoclasty (e.g., "Squeaky Chalk" comic font). So Sophocles's lines are interlarded with Carson's editorials and asides, often allusive, often ahistorical, sometimes on the down low: Hegel and Brecht rub noses Stooges-style, with Beckett and Woolf; Tetresius the Seer is accused of being an entrepreneur (it's a futures game); play is rhymed with "OK," which seems its predicate condition; there are lots of drawings of fish and horses, which will read Greek (Poseidon made the latter from the foam of the home of the former); plus drawings of a Chorus of today's folk with cinder blocks for heads, and a similarly populist disavowal of the misfortunes of fate. Nota bene, Lucy called Charlie Brown "blockhead," as I recall, and was famous for repeatedly whisking away the football he was about to kick, causing him to, without exception, fly up and fall on his back, all according to the hilarious laws of physics and cultural biography. Similarly, Carson references Woolf's Mrs. Ramsay as having been killed off in brackets (unspecified causes) just before citing Agamben's state of exception (unspecified cause), as that which "marks the limit of the law."[1] This is another punch line, for the limit of the law is that there is no limit, no specific cause-effect connection, because the law sets the limit as it sees fit. And as Carson and Stone illustrate, *this* is how tragedy becomes comedy. Not by way of reiteration, as Marx said (and Lucy demonstrated), but by way of animation. That is to say, by way of cartoon, which is the parenthetical art.

In 1809, August Wilhelm von Schlegel argued that the first property of Greek tragedy was universality, an elevation "above reality."

In this, Schlegel compared Greek tragedy to Greek sculpture as tragic figures similarly stand on an idealized universal base (pedestal), and present "an independent and definite whole" (figure), detached from contingency, historicity, and all that does not endure.[2] Beauty in proportion is the singular purpose of sculpture; Beauty in balance, its tragic argument. The Greek Chorus, for Schlegel, was "the ideal spectator," the objective affective prism through which the audience was trained to train its vision. A marbleized mind. By comparison, Hegel's Chorus was spectator as medium-moderator[3] (how very Greek in its moderations), and Lacan's was spectator as meta-emoter, "people who are moved" (how very Greek in its phallo-philias).[4] Via Stone's cartoons, the abstracted spectator is literally and literarily sketched in for Carson's comedy. Our emotive ideal is represented for us (which means as us) as a bunch of airy blockheads, a representation that is not oxymoronic. For it is a trait of our current today that metaphors are the things themselves and things themselves ring with their metaphors. We are all of us sobjects, things set in simultaneous situations. And in this sense, Aristotle is finally wrong about poetry trumping pictures insofar as there is little or no difference in our reading between them. Put another way, text = image = text as we encounter them, each to each, left to right, scanning them similarly on the same screen, or, in Carson's book, one read through and as the scrim of its twin. Like a sculpture, then, by Mallarmé, this new Chorus is frozen, not at the bottom of the deep blue abyss, but atop its Hegelian mountain. For if the eternal Fates are progressively dictatorial, our comedic fortunes are more statically dialectical.

Such that, after rejecting Ismene's offer to share the blame for their brother's burial, Antigone says: *I think a man knows nothing but his foot when he burns it in the hot fire*, lines traditionally attributed to the Chorus. To which Ismene responds: *Quoting Hegel again*. Antigone first answers, *Hegel says I'm wrong*, then notes she has *no ethical consciousness*. Here, this Antigone conjures Hegel's standard of "the true Spirit," because, according to Hegel, the properly ethical consciousness "knows what it has to do, and has already decided whether to belong to the divine or the human law."[5] But our Antigone is overmodest, for Hegel approved Antigone as the paradigm of ethical reflexivity—proof that the ethical can only be ethical in and as opposition—realized in an act lawful in itself, set in contradiction to a lesser order of law that is only legislated. (This is the difference between mimesis as mirror and as mere.) Moreover, given that law, according to Benjamin, is law only by virtue of its founding violence, there can be no lawful act that is nonviolent. (*See* any revolution, all religion.) To be ethical is to be guilty. And guilt, as any lawyer knows, requires the union of *mens rea* and *actus reus*—one must have a guilty *act* as well as a guilty *mind*. In this, Slavoj Žižek argues that Antigone embodies the contradiction between the abstract universal (the eternal law) and the concrete contingent (the particular act). The eternal law that one should respect the dead can be ethically tested only via the "concrete universality" of burying this particular dead. Žižek locates the ethical moment in Antigone's speech when she says the "unwritten and unchanging laws" she is appealing to are precisely fraternal.[6] In other words, Antigone acts not out of generic love, but of a love that is sui generis—because, as Jacques-Alain Miller puts it, "We love the one that harbours the response, or a response, to our question: 'Who am I?'"[7]

Taking up Schlegel post-Hegel, Alenka Zupančič's evocative essay "The 'Concrete Universal'"[8] argues that whereas tragedy is the dialectical movement from individual to universal, comedy moves from the universal to the individual. We can say that it is Antigone's participation in a pointless and idiosyncratic *act* that renders her *I* concrete—that is, we *are*, if only temporally. So Stone puts real heads on real shoulders in her Chorus after Antigone buries Polyneikes offstage, which is when "Antigone" becomes Antigone. Although it should be noted that our hyperrealist heroine also knows that this is (that there is an) offstage, cementing the comedy of her shtick. For the truly Hegelian comic character is the one who "doffs his mask," who sees himself as occupying a stage while he "acts" as if he is occupying a stage.[9] Note further that Kreon says earlier, *Actually, I prefer verbs*: Kreon also knows he "acts," and therefore he also acts entirely ethically, insofar as the rule of the law must be obeyed if there is to be a rule of Law. Like any lawyer, he knows the law.

In 1927, Freud called humor the "triumph of narcissism": through humor, the superego demonstrates that the ego cannot be pushed around by the outside world, and that traumas are "no more than occasions for it to gain pleasure."[10] In a 1959 discussion of *das Ding*, Lacan had a specific take on Harpo Marx's face: "is there anything that poses a question which is more present, more pressing, more absorbing, more disruptive, more nauseating, more calculated to thrust everything that takes place before us into the abyss or void . . . that face with its smile which leaves unclear as to whether it signifies the most extreme perversity or complete simplicity?"[11] The take is always a double-take, the face another doffed mask. In my 1959 Signet book of psychiatrist gags, *The Girl in the Freudian Slip*,[12] there is a cartoon of a biggish bald man, his arm conspiratorially circling the shoulders of a smaller bald man, who has a small mustache. The fact that the smaller man is an analyst is signified by the piece of paper in his hand; the fact that they are in an analyst's office signified by the ubiquitous daybed behind them. The larger[13] man says, from the side of his mouth: *Let me tell you something else, Doc—I enjoy being a little tin god.* A "tin god" is one who is either self-important, dictatorial, or who is erroneously regarded as holy or venerable. As with any good joke, the punch line holds: from time immemorial to time memorialized, we *enjoy* being little tin gods. (And for that matter, believe that this is the "else" we are telling.) Leaving Carson's question before us: which tin-type god is Kreon, and which, Antigone?

Antigo Nick starts with an argument about proper citation, which is an argument over authority: who is the proper author of Antigone's first line, *We begin in the dark and birth is the death of us.* Antigone says it was Hegel; Ismene says it sounds like Beckett. The point is not who said it—who cares?—the point is that it was said previously by someone of greater authority than Antigone. Like this essay, Antigone relies upon her authorities for her authority. She wants to do what she wants to do. (For here lies the "else" wherein lies her comedic register.) Like any lawyer, she wants precedent. Whereas Lacan posited Antigone as the one who never cedes her desire, it seems in Carson that desire is, in this sense, not for this or that, but for *that.* *That* being the something wanting, not for the something bigger, the Law beyond the law, as is usually suggested, but for something much smaller—the law beyond the Law beyond the law. The stupid and singular love that proves the loveliness of love itself. If we suspend our moral approbation of the contingent locus of Antigone's desire (to bury her brother) and look at it with a full sense of its perversion (for Lacan, the pervert is the one who claims to know the big Other, and act as a direct instrument of its divine will),[14] then Carson's *Antigo Nick* is the comedic story of a perversion. But the big joke here is that the big Other knows Antigone—that God is a pervert. Such that Kreon is in on the gag when he says: *No doubt the god of death will save her life.* Because the death drive, the drive toward the finite eternal in the face of the eternal finite, is the proper poet's favorite drive, the drive of what we call great art, and the drive of all cartoon characters in the face of all exploding cigars, all falling safes. So the joke is that the comic figure keeps going, that the *it* of it, as Beckett knows, *will* go on, even as it cannot go on. Put another way: "God forbid: for then how will God judge the world?" (Romans 3:6). Or, that was no lady, that was Antigone.

Schlegel noted that in Greek tragedy, the just and unjust may suffer equally—the larger social purpose served is that the spectator preserve a sense of balance in "the prospect of futurity." We like us a higher order. Comedy, it seems, agrees. Only the higher order we like is one where we dodge the bullet *cum* cream pie of our larger behaviors. Where Harpo is perfectly mirrored by Lucy, Viola *is* Sebastian, Fogel *is* McLovin', and just desserts are less just, more dessert. But Carson can't promise us anything. Toward the end, her Chorus says what sounds like the beginning of a lawyer joke: *How is a Greek Chorus like a lawyer*, but instead of the jab, there is only the plain wrap argument:

> *They're both in the business of searching for a precedent*
> *Finding an analogy*
> *Locating a prior example*
> *So as to be able to say*
> *This terrible thing we're witnessing now is*
> *Not unique you know it happened before*
> *Or something much like it*

Then, a few lines later, the real punch line:

> *Antiogne buried alive Friday afternoon*
> *Compare case histories 7, 17, and 49*

The final movement then, is from the general tragedy of Antigone's father, Oedipus, whose real complex was his desire to outwit the gods (itself inherited from his father), and was, in turn, turned into a generic symbol of such suffering, to the specific comedy of Antigone, who is not her father's daughter, who feigns to outwit no one and who will be, in turn, turned into the individual hero who properly honks at the law of the father—the *l'oie du père*. Put another way, here is a tragedy: an expectant couple is killed in a Brooklyn traffic accident on the way to the hospital to deliver their baby. The baby lives a day or two, then dies.[15] In the aftermath, a neighbor says, "But it's what God wants. Maybe the baby's death, and his parents', is not for nothing; God doesn't have to give us answers."[16]

Here is a joke: There are two kinds of lawyers—those who know the law and those who know the judge.

Notes

1. According to Agamben, the state of exception is the suspension of the law itself that acts as predicate for both binding and abandoning "the living being" to the law. Giorgio Agamben, *State of Exception*, trans. Kevin Attell (Chicago: University of Chicago Press, 2005), 1. Though Agamben (and perhaps Carson) focuses on the thesis that we are now in a permanent state of exception, I am more interested in the "living" qualifier here, as it raises the question whether the dead are ever subject to the law or its exceptions. In other words, dead is dead, and there lies Polyneikes's little joke on both Kreon and Antigone.

2. To be distinguished from epic, which presents as a bas-relief, a banner ongoing, forever fixed to its background. August Wilhelm von Schlegel. *Lectures on Dramatic Art and Literature* (1809), http://infomotions.com/ etexts/gutenberg/dirs/etext04/7ldal10.htm. In conversation, Lanny Jordan Jackson set me on this track by referencing a Trisha Donnelly lecture in which she compared Greek sculpture to Greek tragedy. Viewing Trisha Donnelly's recent "Artist's Choice" exhibition at the Museum of Modern Art, it would seem conceptual art/curation (and what is the difference) could be profitably compared to the trivium.

3. G. W. F. Hegel, *Phenomenology of Spirit*, trans. A. V. Miller (New York: Oxford University Press 1977), 584.

4. Jacques Lacan, *The Ethics of Psychoanalysis, 1959–1960*, trans. Dennis Porter (New York: Norton, 1997), 252.

5. Hegel, *Phenomenology of Spirit*, 280.

6. Slavoj Žižek, *Less Than Nothing: Hegel and the Shadow of Dialectical Materialism* (New York: Verso, 2012) 566–67. In *Antigone's Claim*, Judith Butler also identifies Antigone's telling deed as "an act in language" (10.) Calling Antigone's act "manly," Butler argues Antigone exposes the vulnerability of both kinship and the state, such that the universal is revealed as contingent. Judith Butler, *Antigone's Claim: Kinship between Life and Death* (New York: Columbia University Press, 2000). I would add in this sense, "contingency" serves as Butler's universalization of singularity (singularity as teleology). And move possibly on from there.

7. Jacques Alain Miller, "Jacques-Alain Miller: On Love," interview by Hanna Waar, *Lacan.com* http://www.lacan.com/symptom/?page_id=263, accessed June 22, 2013.

8. Alenka Zupančič, "The 'Concrete Universal,' and What Comedy Can Tell Us about It," in *Lacan: The Silent Partners*, ed. Slavoj Žižek (London: Verso, 2006), 171–97.

9. Hegel, *Phenomenology of Spirit*, 584. In comedy, "The individual knows himself in his individuality as the Absolute." Or, in Carson's Lacanian translation: Antigone: *Hegel says people want to see their lives on stage.* Lacanian

insofar as she points out the "want" that is the lack that constitutes the self to the self. Carson also drops a couple of Brecht references, underscoring the defamilarization that occurs when one sees oneself in real life performing an action as if in a play. Which, of course, Antigone is not in, given that Carson's work is a cartoon about a play rather than a play about a cartoon (as in my reading). Of course, Antigone herself believes she is in a play, keeping her Brechtian perspective intact.

10. Sigmund Freud, "On Humor," 1927, 162. http://www.scribd.com/doc/34515345/Sigmund-Freud-Humor-1927.

11. Lacan, *Ethics of Psychoanalysis*, 55.

12. The top third of the book's cover is a black box framing the author's name and the book's title as follows: WILLIAM F. BROWN author of BEAT BEAT BEAT THE GIRL IN THE FREUDIAN SLIP. In addition to the masturbatory connotations of Brown's previous work, it could be noted that a "beat" in screenwriting refers to any moment in the script that alters the protagonist's pursuit of his or her goal (desire).

13. It is not for nothing that the smaller man is the analyst and the larger man the analysand, presuming the cartoonist was not an analyst.

14. Slavoj Žižek, "The Fundamental Perversion: Lacan, Dostoyevsky, Boyeri," *Lacanian Ink 27*, http://www.lacan.com/lacinkXXVII6.htm.

15. Christine Hauser and Anemona Hartocollis, "Baby Whose Parents Died in Car Crash Also Dies," *New York Times*, March 3, 2013, http://www.nytimes.com/2013/03/05/nyregion/baby-whose-parents-were-killed-in-crash-also-dies.html?pagewanted=2&_r=0&hpw.

16. Colleen Long and Verena Dobnik, "Violent Past for Suspect in NY crash; Family Dies," Associated Press, March 5, 2013, http://enews.earthlink.net/article/top?guid=20130305/30cd7362-5c0e-4d11-a9b7-29fada87ce22.

LILY HOANG

From Geryon to G
Anne Carson's Red Doc> *and the Avatar*

To talk about Anne Carson is to talk about myth. After all, she's a classicist, and her books center around myths—recharging through translation, creating through creation—but *Red Doc>*, Carson's continuation of *Autobiography of Red (AoR)*, is a challenging of myth, taking the form and function and definition into the twenty-first century by virtualizing it. Whereas the narrative itself displays few concrete examples of electronic influence—as in *AoR*, the contemporary is a mere present, unassuming, not bothering—the characters are neither people nor gods: they are avatars, sublime and sublimated Internet identities, names without corporeal.

This is not an essay about intentionality. If anything, it is about Carson's unintentionality, the way technology modifies text—text here can refer to *Red Doc>* specifically but it also points to the body as text—how it permeates unobtrusively, its omnipresence and infiniteness, our greatest *progress* and the threat that shadows it.

To talk about Anne Carson is to talk about *AoR*, a book that broke fiction for me. By break, I mean: *fix*. I was eighteen, nineteen maybe. I wanted to be a writer, kind of. I had been writing poetry—bad poetry, of the slam variety, of the eighteen-year-old angsty-selfromanticized-crazy-selfmutilating-semisuicidal-reallyfuckingdeepvariety, I mean, legitly bad poetry—and then I decided I was going to be a fiction writer. My friend Michael lent me *AoR*. I liked Michael. He was smart and charming and handsome and impressive and a damn good writer and I wanted to impress him so I read the book. I wasn't expecting to like it. I planned to read enough to bullshit smart enough critiques so he would like me. [Note: This is all myth. Michael gave me the book and I wanted to impress him, true, but everything else belongs in the legacy of oral narrative that demands exaggeration as explanation, or: myth.] And so I began *AoR*, not knowing what to expect, he'd said something about volcanoes and red-winged monsters, which is something akin to distilling an entire human down to, say, lawn care and graying hair—insufficient. I read the book, and fiction doesn't do that. It should've come with a warning label: If you're expecting a novel, that's been 86ed off the menu, sorry. All those forms and connections, all that majestic sublime, all that magic and sexuality and liminality and tenderness. It's a love story, a bildungsroman, something that ought to be easy digestion but isn't.

To talk about *AoR* is to talk about intentionality. The jacket copy calls it "whimsical," as do many reviews. Maybe it's because I don't understand what *whimsy* means because *AoR* is hardly whimsical. Every piece, every move, every line break is vital. It is a book of manipulated forms, each page exists exactly as it should, as though there could be no other possibility. Yeah, so *AoR* changed my life—as a writer, a reader, it may have catalyzed mutations in my very personhood, or, at least, right there in the spine, just like Nabokov said great literature would do.

It isn't that *Red Doc>* didn't evoke the same feeling because it did: it slammed my spine into compression too, but the experience was different. I admit that I am more discerning—*ahem*: a snob—about books now, now that I've read, a lot, and part of my love for *AoR* is locked to how *groundbreaking* it was for me, an access into the potentiality of fiction, but whereas *AoR* is a punch in the gut to convex the spine, *Red Doc>* is a shouldered weight, squashing, straining, and I wish Geryon's wings would come lift me from the suffocation of a narrative so heavy with gorgeous artifice and obstinate suffering.

To talk about *Red Doc>* is to talk about myth. Myth: a word bloated with history and misuse, and so I turn to others for help.[1]

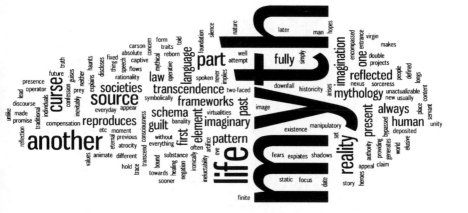

Only, who needs great thinkers and their great definitions? So I will take a nudge from Carson herself and bow to technology to generate a definition of myth in the language of the contemporary: the image.[2]

Technology generated the form of *Red Doc>*. Carson readily admits that a word-processing error formally renovated her page. That is, technology unintentionally modified the text. Unlike its predecessor, the bulk of the poems in *Red Doc>* are cramped into newspaper columns, occupying the page in strips—and here, you can imagine critics battling for the correct interpretation: she's making a political statement about the lack of transparency in media by imitating a newspaper, or, she's clearly queering the phallus. I'm being hyperbolic, obviously, but only because before I knew it was a computer glitch I tried to impose meaning on the form too. It's striking, almost aggressive, ink boxed and blocked against such glowing white, but no, all of it was just an accidental mouse click— Hint: Command + z would've fixed it!—and all of the sudden, the narrative itself changes because of form. Here is the contemporary, imposing itself on myth, reshaping it in the most literal way possible. Furthermore, Carson even let technology dictate the title—*Red Doc>*—which was the name her word processor defaulted to, although I imagine it probably looked like: Red.docx or Red.doc or red.doc or red.rtf etc.

Carson defines myth as something leading a double life,[3] and so it makes sense that the characters in *Red Doc>* wouldn't be replicas— *reproductions*—of Geryon and Herakles. Yes, time has passed, life has been lived, they have changed, sure, but Carson emphasizes the mythical double life by renaming them. Almost as if accounting for the real time lag between these two texts, the chorus—taking shape as Wife of Brain, the collective voice of Geryon's red cattle, specifically Io, his favorite—commands: "but / remember / the following faces / the red one (G) / you already know (what's he done to his hair) his old friend / Sad / But Great."[4] And so Geryon is no longer Geryon and Herakles is no longer Herakles, the act of renaming spotlit, the chorus charging us to both remember and forget those old characters.

Because that's exactly what they are: old characters.

Geryon and Herakles: they don't exist anymore.

In *AoR*, they were teenagers, coming into themselves, discovering and excited. In *Red Doc>*, they are middle-aged, distant, cautious, weary and wary and worn. This is—*sadly*—an expected route. As we age, naïveté loses its allure and we remove ourselves from potentially hurtful situations, or, at least that's what experience teaches us, but we don't go renaming ourselves, now do we? The act of renaming—not one's patronymic, which may change with marriage, but a given name, given names that Carson herself chose with nominative determinism, and their names alone dictate their fates and existences: Geryon the red-winged monster, Herakles who must steal the monster's herd as his tenth labor, they are enemies by destiny, perpetual *eros* even after the physical has been pleasured—has real significance. The act of renaming invents a new fate for these two characters. The act of renaming creates new characters.

But come on, now: what's the big deal? OK, so most of us don't go legally renaming ourselves, but this isn't about legality. Geryon didn't get his name changed on his driver's license or anything, and the military gave Herakles the name Sad But Great, Sad, for short. We do the same thing, more or less, when we create Internet avatars of ourselves.

A key component of myth is the sublime—in the Kantian sense of nature as vast and awe-inspiring and dangerous, Romantic nature as inexhaustible splendor, ready to be harnessed and industrialized, the risk of imminent peril thrilling in the face of all that wild, Carson's volcano in *AoR* and the cave in *Red Doc>*—and as we square ourselves into a mythology of the present, the sublime manifests itself in the digital, the virtual, the Internet. In the same way colonizers envisioned the New World as simultaneously dangerous and altruistic, a space with endless *potential*—potential here meaning potential to be exploited and controlled—and in the same way as early nineteenth-century Europeans imagined Niagara Falls as a precarious utopia, tiptoeing the line between menace and technological innovation, such is the sublime narrative surrounding our contemporary understanding of the Internet: it could be our utopia—consider its liminality, its immeasurability in space as a literal translation of utopia as no place—but here there be monsters and viruses and nightmares and power like we can't even imagine.

In *Red Doc>* the sublime is a two-headed monster—not unlike some depictions of Geryon. One is intentional and literal: G falls down a cave and his wings fail him, and then, from nowhere, bats rise and lift his weight, giving him momentum until his wings can flutter him to freedom. The other is unintentional and metaphorical: in the act of renaming, Carson makes avatars, new identities, which ignite a connection to the virtual, all artifice and double-identitied and recreation and re-creation.

Conceptually, the avatar is common now. We make new versions of ourselves all the time, it's easy. We can make ourselves into whatever we want, portray ourselves as anything we can imagine, and until there is an intersection between the virtual and the real, to the person on the other side of the screen, we are only our avatars. Inevitably, there is a rupture between the virtual self and the real self, and it's impossible for there not to be. Within electronic space, everything is different. Time loses its significance. Causality is forgotten. The virtual flattens us into likes and clicks, tagged pictures and character count. And I'm only talking about social networking, where there is supposed to be some verisimilitude to our actual selves. Once we move into role-playing games, the possibilities unrelent.

Red Doc> is a rewriting of *AoR*. The two books follow a similar plotline—in *AoR*, Geryon and Herakles go on a journey to sublime nature (the volcano) in *Red Doc>*, G and Sad go on a journey through sublime nature (the cave)—but plot aside, almost nothing is recognizable, even the recurring characters. It would be ridiculous to expect Geryon and Herakles to be exactly the same—they aren't the type to stay stagnant, especially not for decades!—but they aren't the same characters at all. Physically, G remains a red-winged herder and Sad is still handsome, but these are superficial markers and we are running low on ink.

The thing about avatars is that they're just fronts, projections of desire. They are the self, in caricature, in imagination, they offer us the opportunity to move through a world as someone else, or, at the very least, the self maximized. And yet, G and Sad deny themselves this optimism. Sad is holstered to his PTSD, searching for escape, pill after experimental pill, and G has abandoned his autobiography.

Unlike *AoR*, in *Red Doc>*, their journey is not propelled by *jouissance* and desire. They begin their odyssey without catalyst, without goal, they are simply driving away, into darkness.

Or: maybe they are on a quest to find Geryon and Herakles, those old monsters hidden somewhere beneath these new monsters, these new selves lost in the sublime of virtual avatar. G and Sad are lost—Will someone get these men a map!? Where's Siri to save the day?—and they are looking for their real selves, a physical journey to metaphor their internal journeys, but they can't go back,

revert, the facade of the avatar is all that remains, an electronic out-
line of what once existed.

Describing G's herd, Carson explains: "ankles like pines. Like /
queens like queens / dressed in pines. Musk / oxen are not in fact
oxen/ nor castrated bulls nor do / their glands produce musk. /
Much is misnomer in our / present way of grasping / the world."[5]
If the role of myth is to explain some facet of the unexplainable, to
offer comfort and safety to the frightening, *Red Doc>* exists as its
opposition, a world of grand misnomer. Homer describes Odysseus
as the man with a thousand faces—he is cunning, a mask for every
occasion—but behind each avatar, there was still the man, Odysseus,
eager to find his way back to Penelope. G and Sad, they're gone.
Step into their virtual sublime, there is no Geryon, there is no Her-
akles, their myths and legacies and identities deformed, emptied,
holographic.

Appendix: Myth, Defined

Ludwig Wittgenstein: A whole mythology is deposited in our
language.

Roland Barthes: Myth does not deny things, on the contrary, its
function is to talk about them; simply, it *purifies* them, it makes them
innocent, it gives them a natural and eternal justification, it gives
them a *clarity* which is not that of an explanation but that of a state-
ment of fact . . . Myths provide *euphoric clarity* by eliminating com-
plexities and complications.

Simone de Beauvoir: A myth always implies a subject who proj-
ects his hopes and fears towards a sky of transcendence . . . [Myth]
cannot be grasped or encompassed; it haunts the human conscious-
ness without ever appearing before it in a fixed form. . . . Woman is
at once Eve and the Virgin Mary. She is an idol, a servant, the source
of life, a power of darkness; she is the elemental silence of truth, she
is artifice, gossip, and falsehood; she is healing presence and sorcer-
ess; she is man's prey, his downfall, she is everything that he is not
and that he longs for, his negation and his *raison d'être.*

Vincent Mosco: Myths are stories that *animate* individuals and
societies by providing paths to transcendence that lift people out of
the banality of everyday life. They are an *entrance* into another reality,
a reality once characterized by the promise of the sublime.

Anne Carson: All myth is an enriched pattern, a two-faced proposition, allowing its operator to say one thing and mean another, to lead a double life.

Claude Lévi-Strauss: Myth *is* language: to be known, myth has to be told; it is a part of human speech. . . But what gives the myth an operative value is that the specific pattern described is everlasting; it explains the present and the past as well as the future.

Laura Cruz and Willem Frijhoff: Unlike the immortal heroes that they so often contain, myths can die, and they can also be reborn in new guises. In this sense, myths are rarely static but, ironically, their claim to eternal existence is part of their nature and their appeal.

C. A. Tamse: Symbolically, the myth discloses the substance of the past and of the present, making them appear as interrelated part of the same reality.

Theodor Adorno and Max Horkheimer: Mythical ineluctability is defined by the equivalence between the curse, the atrocity that expiates the curse, and the guilt that arises from the expiation and reproduces the curse. To date all law bears the trace of this schema. In myth, every element of the cycle makes compensation for the previous element and thereby helps to establish the nexus of guilt as law.

Thomas Mann: The myth is the foundation of life; it is the timeless schema, the pious formula into which life flows when it reproduces its traits out of the unconscious.

Markus Gabriel and Slavoj Žižek: Reflection is inevitably bound to a set of finite, discursive expressions of itself generating imaginary frameworks, mythologies. Those frameworks are usually not reflected and cannot be fully reflected: any attempt to achieve such a totalizing reflection simply generates another myth, a different imaginary, another image which will sooner or later hold us captive.

Jacques Derrida: There is no unity or absolute source of myth. The focus or the source of the myth is always shadows and virtualities which are elusive, unactualizable, and non-existent in the first place.

Roland Barthes: Myth is neither a lie nor a confession: it is an inflexion.

Albert Camus: Myths are made for the imagination to breathe life into them.

Camille Paglia: The moment there is imagination, there is myth.[6]

Works Cited

Adorno, Theodor, Mark Horkheimer, and Robert Hullot-Kentor. "Odysseus or Myth and Enlightenment." *New German Critique* 56 (1992): 122–23.

Barthes, Roland. *Mythologies*. Translated by Annette Lavers. New York: Farrar, Strauss & Giroux, 1972, 142.

Benjamin, Walter. "The Work of Art in the Age of Mechanical Reproduction." In *Illuminations*, edited by Hannah Arendt, translated by Harry Zohn. New York: Shocken Books, 1961.

Camus, Albert. *The Myth of Sisyphus and Other Essays*. Translated by Justin O'Brien. New York: Vintage, 1991, 119.

Carson, Anne. *Autobiography of Red*. New York: Vintage, 1996.

Carson, Anne. *Red Doc>* New York, Knopf, 2013.

Carson, Anne. *The Beauty of the Husband: A Fictional Essay in 29 Tangos*. New York: Random House, 2001, 33.

Cruz, Laura and Willem Frijhoff, eds. *Myth in History, History in Myth*. Boston: Brill, 2009, 6.

de Beauvoir, Simone. *The Second Sex*. Translated by Constance Borde and Sheila Malovany-Chevallier. New York: Vintage, 2011, 162–63.

Derrida, Jacques. *Writing and Difference*. Translated by Alan Bass. Chicago: University of Chicago Press, 1978.

Lévi-Strauss, Claude. "The Structural Study of Myth." *Journal of American Folklore* 68.270 (1955): 428–44.

Lugones, Maria. "On Complex Communication." *Hypatia* 21.3 (2006): 75–85.

Mann, Thomas. "Freud and the Future." *Daedalus* 88 No. 2 (1959): 374–78.

Markus, Gabriel, and Slavoj Žižek. *Mythology, Madness and Laughter*. New York: Continuum Books: 2009, 19.

McGreevy, Patrick. "Imagining Niagara Falls." *Annals of the Association of American Geographers* 77 (1987): 48–62.

Mosco, Vincent. *The Digital Sublime: Myth, Power, and Cyberspace*. Cambridge: MIT Press, 2004, 3.

Nabokov, Vladimir. *Lectures on Literature*. New York: Mariner Books, 2002.

Paglia, Camille. *Sexual Personae: Art and Decadence from Nefertiti to Emily Dickinson*. New York: Vintage, 1991, 39.

Tamse, C. A. "The Political Myth." In *Some Political Mythologies*, edited by J. S. Bromley and E. H. Kossmann. The Hague: Nijhoff, 1975, 15.

Turner, Victor. "Are There Universals of Performance in Myth, Ritual, and Drama?" In *By Means of Performance: Intercultural Studies of Theatre and Ritual*, edited by Richard Schechner and Willa Appel. Cambridge: Cambridge University Press, 1990, 8–19.

Wittgenstein, Ludwig. "Remarks on Frazer's Golden Bough." Translated by A. C. Miles and R. Rhees. Newark: Brynmill Press, 1979, 11.

Notes

1. See the appendix.
2. This wordle was created using the words from the appendix.
3. See the appendix.
4. Anne Carson, *Red Doc>* (New York: Knopf, 2013), 6.
5. Carson, *Red Doc>*, 23.
6. See the bibliography for full citations.

ELIZABETH ROBINSON

An Antipoem That
Condenses Everything
Anne Carson's Translations of the
Fragments of Sappho

Hugh Kenner wrote that the translator "does not translate words. The words have led [the translator] into the thing he [sic] translates."[1] Thus, the translator's task requires exquisite balance. She must forge intimacy with a text, entering into decisions that strive to make it transparent and relevant for new readers. In the midst of this, the translator is doing a work of self-erasure. Whose voice is speaking? The original draws the translator into an ever-receding text, for it is never possible to replicate it. Yet the translator is an agent who beguiles the primary text forward until both original and translation are remodeled in the interchange. As Kenner says, the translation will "embody a vision which is neither [the original author's] nor that of the translator."[2] That vision is a route into an authorless site. In the introduction to *If Not, Winter*, Anne Carson's translations of the fragments of Sappho, Carson addresses this dilemma: "I like to think that, the more I stand out of the way, the more Sappho shows through." She allows that hope of such transparency is an "amiable fantasy."[3]

Carson has insisted on desire as a central trope in the poetry of Sappho, as her work in *Eros the Bittersweet* demonstrates. She has similarly scrutinized desire as a crucial element of the spiritual transformation that she calls (borrowing from Simone Weil) decreation. In this mystical process, the desiring subject draws forth presence even as presence is obliterated in the moment desire fulfills itself. Simultaneous manifestation/saying and disappearance/unsaying reside right at the heart of translation. The original text was written at the behest of the author's yearning to be heard. A translator expresses corresponding desire, reconfiguring the text in a new language: she imagines a readership which the original author could not have conceived. Translation necessitates that the text exist as a function of desire: the apparently "true" original desires new relation to readers. To make this transpire, it must, paradoxically, disappear.

> for you beautiful ones my thought
> is not changeable

So promises Fragment 41,[4] but its very manifestation on the pages of this book is a hopeful and poignant untruth. The reader longs to be addressed as one of these "beautiful ones" even while realizing that, through time's erosion, the fragment (much less the translation), the poem, can make no such address. It consists of its very changeability. The question that drives translation, especially in Carson's renderings of Sappho—from whom we have, after all, *only* fragments—is how to understand the workings of desire. These translations show us how the operations of desire in Sappho (and in translation generally) engage desire as a practice of decreation.

Carson upholds this view in her note to Fragment 2, observing in the fragment's invocational hymn "an emptiness or distance that it is the function of the hymn to make by an act of attention . . . as if creation could be seen waiting for an event that is already perpetually *here*."[5] The fragment begins by implying an absent imperative ("Come"):

> here to me from Krete to this holy temple

It ends with an explicit imperative, "pour":

> In this place you Kypris taking up
> in gold cups delicately
> nectar mingled with festivities:
>   pour.[6]

Significantly, Carson states that the invocation of the goddess in the poem entails her absence (else there would be no reason to call her), yet the poem concludes not only with a sense of Aphrodite's presence, but with the delicious surfeit of the imperative "pour." In that moment of suspension, nectar pouring into the cup, the writer invokes "a God who arrives bringing her own absence with her."[7] Carson's note ends with a quotation from Simone Weil: "God can only be present in creation under the form of absence."[8] Eros is enacted lyrically and narratively in the play of absence and presence as modes of *transit*. It's an excellent metaphor for the act of translation. Translation is invocational, multivocal, and avocal all at once. Its eros comes from the oxymoron of sculpted abandon shaped by a translator who makes presence tangible through evanescence. Speaking of the spirituality of such mystics as Marguerite Porete and Simone Weil, Carson suggests also the translator's conundrum:

> the telling remains a bit of a wonder. Decreation is an undoing of the creature in us—that creature enclosed in self and defined by self. But to undo self one must move through self, to the very inside of its definition.[9]

In "Decreation," Carson discusses the "wrench in perception" which "forces the perceiver to a point where she has to disappear from herself in order to look."[10] In other words, translating at its best—an act of desire that genuinely honors the original—may not be a graceful transposition of meaning between languages. The translator's distinct voice infuses the translation, intertwining with the original author's distinct voice, raising the cranky question of meaning itself. If Marguerite Porete insists that one "cannot go towards God in love without bringing myself along,"[11] neither can the translator go toward her text in good faith without bringing herself along.

Fragment 96 helps underline the parallels between Sappho's eros of desire, the mysticism of decreation, and the act of translation. This fragment presents fascinating variations on how boundaries are merged or transgressed. Observe the lushly imagistic vision of paradise depicted in this extended quotation:

> But now she is conspicuous among Lydian women
> as sometimes at sunset
> the rosyfingered moon
>
> surpasses all the stars. And her light
> stretches over salt sea
> equally and flowerdeep fields.
>
> And the beautiful dew is poured out
> and roses bloom and frail
> chervil and flowering sweetclover. [12]

The vision is gorgeous, but contains a quietly startling moment. Sappho conjures the "rosyfingered moon," and Carson's note acknowledges "rosyfingered" as a favorite Homeric adjective. However, Homer used this descriptor as a marker of *dawn*, and Sappho surprises us by applying it to the *moon*. Further, Homer might make an extended simile such as this ("But now she is conspicuous among Lydian women / as sometimes at sunset / the rosyfingered moon // surpasses all the stars"), but Sappho takes the unusual approach of permitting the simile to blend with the overall texture and imagery of the poem so that "she" merges with her landscape. "Homer," Carson tells us, "is more concerned than Sappho to keep the borders of the two surfaces intact."[13]

That very edge effaces into larger union, a monism into which lover, believer, or translator can melt. A border has been sensuously breached. It will be breached more aggressively in lines 14–16:

> But she goes back and forth remembering
>   gentle Atthis and in longing
>   she bites her tender mind [14]

The passage opens with a lissome, undulatory quality, flowing in the fluid medium of memory. The memory is of *gentle* Atthis, and so the reader is shocked by line 16 when suddenly longing causes the protagonist to "bite her tender mind." The translation does not clarify a grammatical ambiguity: whose mind has been bitten? That of Atthis or of our rosyfingered lady? Carson retains that uncertainty. The poem has thus far presented an idyllic garden of imagery. Consequently, this mind, in its tenderness, has the quality of ripe fruit. Still, the moment when "she bites her tender mind" is nothing if not a wrench in perception! The idea gestures toward larger possibility: something to be bitten into is to be ingested, absorbed, decreated in the larger interests of memory and poem. The image is erotic, fierce, disturbing. Lover and beloved are indistinguishable in the desire into which they are transformed and subsumed. If the decreation into a rosyfingered moon is aesthetically pleasing, the decreation of the bitten mind is no less true: whether for lover or translator, the play of intimacy irrevocably alters identity. A stutter here shows the fragment unsaying itself even as it is articulated. That apophatic, self-erasing quality of translation is rendered as it bites the mind.

One final example demonstrates the playful give-and-take of Carson translations. What is pertinent here is that sometimes the contemporary reader has access to Sappho only via the minutest fragments. Other translations may publish a page that is printed with a single word; even in *If Not, Winter*, there are times when Carson decides to isolate a terse phrase alone on the page (e.g., Fragment 119, "cloth dripping").[15] It's curious, then, to note that in some instances, Carson will layer a number of fragments down the page, as with Fragments 173 through 177:[16]

173
a vine that grows up trees

174
channel

175
dawn

176
lyre lyre lyre

177
transparent dress

This array could be considered merely random. There is little that a translator need do to interpret them tonally, since all are asyntactic nouns (or, in fragment 173, a noun phrase). It's in the paratactic relationship of the fragments on the single page that Carson opens up possibilities that marginalize both Sappho and herself as speakers, where the apparently random list of words rises above its status as fragments and becomes, strangely, a series of synonyms for—what?—desire? transcendence? the ideal transparency of language? This is a fanciful exercise, but consider the possibilities: desire as a flourishing vine; desire as a channel, as a dawning of new passion or meaning, as a translucent garment that reveals the beloved's form.

Might translation also function in these ways? Embedded in this sequence, though, is a moment that gives pause. Fragment 176 presents, in the Greek, three variant spellings of the word "lyre." Surely this word, too, fits with the pattern that could be ascribed to the others: a vehicle for song; music as elixir of desire. It is distinct, though, in being the only word in the entire collection that is repeated. Not only is it rhythmically discrete, it resounds unmistakably with its English homonym, "liar liar liar." The text, if we agree to see an emergent pattern in it, almost absurdly undermines its own desiring aspiration by intimating falseness with a homonym. As in Fragment 96, where desire "bites the mind," this sequence enacts a twist in perception that reminds the reader (and, ostensibly the translator who worked through it) that no matter how ardent one's communion with the translation, it's never possible to achieve perfect "honesty," transparency, or mastery. Studying Marguerite Porete, Carson finds a conflict analogous to that with which the translator wrestles: a collision of longings "whose effect is to expose her very Being to its own scrutiny and to dislodge if from the centre of itself."[17]

Anne Carson's translations of Sappho are small miracles of vividness. They offer contemporary readers a fragile window onto a poet who lived hundreds of years before the Common Era. Presenting them to us, Carson engages a complex dance between presence and absence. The desire that Carson so keenly identifies in Sappho's work is transposed in her efforts as translator. Vanishing into the work, Carson demonstrates, is not merely a product of a quasi-erotic abandon. It is also a peculiarly spiritual event, for Carson shows us how language, in what she elsewhere calls the "drastic contract of the sublime,"[18] can help us to transact the merging of presences in a way impossible under more mundane circumstances. Like the mystic Marguerite Porete, Carson relinquishes her own center actively, not passively, so that she may function as a vehicle for another voice. In the end, we may borrow Longinus's praise for Sappho and apply it to Carson as translator: "Are you not amazed at how she researches all at once the soul the body the ears the tongue the eyes the skin all as if they had departed from her and belong to someone else?"[19]

Bibliography

Carson, Anne, *Decreation*. New York: Vintage Contemporaries, 2005.
Kenner, Hugh, editor. Introduction. *Ezra Pound: Translations*. Translated by Ezra Pound. New York: New Directions, 1963.
Sappho. *If Not, Winter: Fragments of Sappho*. translated by Anne Carson. New York: Vintage, 2002.

Notes

1. Kenner, *Translations of Ezra Pound*, 11.
2. Kenner, *Translations of Ezra Pound*, 12.
3. Carson, *If Not, Winter*, x.
4. Carson, *If Not, Winter*, 83.
5. Carson, *If Not, Winter*, 358.
6. Carson, *If Not, Winter*, 7.
7. Carson, *Decreation*, 179.
8. Carson, *Decreation*, 179.
9. Carson, *Decreation*, 179.
10. Carson, *Decreation*, 169.
11. Carson, *Decreation*, 169.
12. Carson, *If Not, Winter*, 191.
13. Carson, *If Not, Winter*, 372.
14. Carson, *If Not, Winter*, 191.
15. Carson, *If Not, Winter*, 243.
16. Carson, *If Not, Winter*, 349.
17. Carson, *Decreation*, 165.
18. Carson, *If Not, Winter*, 364.
19. Carson, *If Not, Winter*, 364.

JOHN MELILLO

Sappho and the "Papyrological Event"

To listen—to soundscapes, musics, languages—is to hear (at least) doubly: to hear the sound happening and to hear, at the same time, its relationship to other sounds. A translator places this simultaneity into sequence. She listens and repeats; she transforms what might otherwise be experienced by the listener as noisy incomprehension into the recognizable and meaning-producing sound shapes of speech, music, or poetry. In this sense, every translation has the quality of ventriloquoy: the translator becomes a medium, the dummy showing and telling while the body of the text remains silent and imperturbable, a cipher. "Greek," even.

Anne Carson differentiates her translation of the complete fragments of Sappho, *If Not, Winter* (2002), from the ventriloquism of previous Sappho translations not only through her spare constructions and precise syntax but, more radically, by folding the space between text, medium, and reader/listener into the very process of translating. For Carson, the task of translation—of "carrying over" sound, concept, and material from one place to another—not only produces "the echo of the original" but also gestures toward a dramatic, performative, and, ultimately, ecstatic space: the "papyrological event." This event—the "drama of trying to read a papyrus torn in half or riddled with holes or smaller than a postage stamp"— entails more than the *jouissance* of coming into contact with the archived object.[1] It also records a sensual temporality: a temporality framed by accessing and wandering in the archive, of "sequencing" the various other mediations and remediations that form the network of texts named "Sappho." Carson charges the fragments with a history of repeating, rewriting, and recording. The performance of the "papyrological event"—through Carson's visual, sonic, and philological gestures—leaves behind the projected lyric mask called "Sappho" in order to access the ways in which, behind the mask, voice emerges from the noise of history.

The drama of the papyrological event begins with a very simple visual-poetic device: the bracket. Using brackets to mimic the gaps, breaks and spatial organization of the various papyri that preserve Sappho's language, Carson hopes to "imply a free space of imaginal adventure."[2] These brackets are "an aesthetic gesture toward the papyrological event rather than an accurate record of it."[3] This aesthetic gesture marks and performs the erasures of history. Tears, holes, and gaps "riddle" these texts: and not only physically. They become riddles that ask to be solved and deciphered. In this way Carson produces a kind of textual erotics: not only in the pseudo-pornographic mimesis of actually touching the papyrus (Sappho's textual body) but also within a humming field of potential contact and content. Desire creates a soundscape in which "revenant" frequencies resound within every shard of information, every preserved and decaying sensory datum:

92

]
]
]
]
robe
and
colored with saffron
purple robe
cloaks
crowns
beautiful
]
purple
rugs
]
]

(181)

Even when the texts of these papyrological events manifest nothing more than the barest naming of things, as here in Fragment 92, the spatialized layout, the empty order of the brackets, and the action of pause, delay, and desire in the relationship between punctuation, word, and space form a syntax of decay and preservation that asks us to imagine the text as layered and polyvalent. Treated this way, these words do not simply enumerate regal and comfortable objects of decoration but take place within an expansive poetic field. Surrounded by their bracketed absences, the words move by a logic of aggregation. While the image of the bracket can call up the closed off or lost, Carson's brackets open up—literally, expand—the space of the fragment on the page. Our reading takes more time as the blank spaces of the page itself become part of the reading event. The silences are as significant as the sounds, and because of this, an aura of temporality, a sense of endurance through time, surrounds each word-sound. We are asked to freely imagine the impersonal historical and material forces that have sculpted these poems from the remains of history. And what remains is not the echo of an origin but rather a broken narrative of haphazard and contingent historical operations: sounding-out, repeating, writing, copying, documenting, printing, collating, translating . . . In short, the panoply of activities that create the warp and weft of the text's history. In Fragment 92, above, we move among "beautiful" woven things—cloaks, robes, and rugs. Carson asks us to imagine text as just such a thing: not merely a disembodied ideal but a rich *textile*—a concatenation of materials, mediums, and practices—a weaving together of divergent bodies, sounds, and concepts.

If each individual mark on the page conjures up, in this way, a vast sequence of historical time-scales, the words themselves, as organized sounds with rhythm and duration, mirror this chaotic prosody of historical process. Even in the most rebarbative fragments, meter matters. Just as the traditional function of meter is to sequence and measure time, the preserved blips and blops of mouth-sound work like some broken beat machine. But Carson also places those rhythms and sounds into a new listening context, a new ambience. To return to Carson's translation of Fragment 92, the contiguous dactyl and trochee in "colored with saffron," the trochaic "purple," and the isolated dactyl of "beautiful" give us a vague echo—within a field of monosyllables—of the hendecasyllabic line most associated with Sappho. This line, formed by the interplay of trochees and dactyls (/ u / u / u u / u / u, where "/" = long and "u" = short), shifts from urgency to languor, from energetic beginnings to paced interiors. In this fragment, like most, the sudden metrical continuities of rhythm seem to leap out of the sea of brackets and monosyllables surrounding them. They arise out of a void, as contingent as any other sound, and any potential recognition or organization remains a second-order chaos. That is to say, the poem is not an incomplete metrical form waiting to be dutifully "filled in" but rather a construction of fundamentally isolated particles—as if each word functioned as an individual sound event, combining and recombining endlessly to form new networks or constellations of sound. This is translation as John Cage or Morton Feldman: sound events happen in a dynamically static field rather than progressing by linear signification. Just as the text figures the material and historical apparatus that surrounds and forms it, it also figures words as sounds within a reverberating ambient space. They noisily mutter; they drone in a way that does not mark any particular timing. If, as the philosopher Maurice Merleau-Ponty claims in *Phenomenology of Perception*, "the world ceaselessly assails and beleaguers subjectivity as waves wash round a wreck on the shore," the sound of Carson's translation does not expand and contract with the inspired meters of lyrical expressivity but rather becomes the drone of wave upon wave as they wash over, in, and around the wrecked subject.[4]

Of course, the words still signify but that significance is tempered by a new relativity, as if Carson were not merely translating one language to another but excavating the geological obstinacy of sounds through the medium of poetry. Rather than simply making the ancient Greek familiar, Carson makes words like "robe" or "purple" or "and" alien to our ears. In this way, her translation does not "find itself in the center of the language forest but on the outside; it calls into it without entering."[5] To be outside language is not to remain trapped in an exteriority but rather to project force—call—into the array of language. This force can suddenly refigure the simplest transitions and concatenations: for instance, the chiasmatic echoing from "robe" to "purple robe" to "purple" in Fragment 92 delimits a kind of choral space around which and within which the other words adhere in their various and uneven forms. Repetitions and returns arrive without warning, not as individualized lines but as echoic hops, pauses, and bounces happening all at once. Carson transforms this body of work into an open and resonant chamber, calling and responding to void as voice and voice as void.

Voice, then, is not a question of "who is speaking" but rather the opening of a space to mark multiple processes of erasure: erasure of the translator (Carson herself claims this), erasure of the writer(s) (the anonymous stream of scribes, teachers, and mediators who construct Sappho), erasure of authority (the impossible attempt to present the author, the original word), erasure of the stuff of the text itself (its slow, geological decay), and finally, erasure of sound (in the wash of the world). These erasures and this decentered voice do not straightforwardly anthropomorphize the world, as in the classic rhetorical trope of apostrophe—what Jonathan Culler calls a "call in order to be calling"—but rather delay those anthropomorphizing effects through the historical or philological imagination.[6] Carson shows us a kind of antiphilology in which the process of forgetting actually remembers us to the dismemberment that constitutes voice. She asks us not to re-create a past voice but to "decreate" the very concept of voice, not to revel in an antiquarianism but to participate in the affecting play of the papyrological event.[7] These texts hum with this philological "meta-data," the ambience of their passing history and their being passed through history.

By grounding her translation within the historicity of loss, preservation, quotation, and repetition, Carson reframes a gendered epistemology in the interpretative and mediating work that simultaneously recorded and destroyed Sappho's legacy. In her essay "The Sound of Gender," Carson describes the Greek (and Western) understanding of women as incontinent and noisy:

> Woman is that creature who puts the inside on the outside. By projections and leakages of all kinds—somatic, vocal, emotional, sexual—females expose or expend what should be kept in.[8]

The misogynist fantasies Carson describes not only structure patriarchal interpretations of Sappho and lyric poetry in general as an overly emotional, expressive, inside-out display of self, but also point to the history of a gendered taxonomy and articulation at the root of Western culture. The grammarians who preserved, taught, and, ultimately, burned Sappho's poetry sought to articulate and order the world in and as language. That is, they worked to place one thing (certain mouth sounds, for instance) next to another thing in an indexical call-and-response that gave shape and meaning to the world. For them, as for us, language transforms amorphous stuff into objects, things into tools (even if those tools are merely grammatical rules or mathematical axioms). Language separates, categorizes, and filters the overflowing metamorphosis of the material world, a material world coded feminine in its very etymology: *mater*, mother. Carson's translation upsets and exposes the functioning of this ordering machine. Sappho stands not as an "expressive," inside-out subjectivity, material to be fixed and filtered, but rather as an outside-in noise: her residual presence acts as a force of disruption and possibility. She is a refusal of voice.

Such is the luxurious asceticism of Carson's translation: in refusing a singular voice, in encompassing erasure and productive multiplicity, in bracketing Sappho, she adds a vibrating hum of feeling to this language. This Sappho is not a nostalgic projection but rather an almost constructivist fabrication, a layering of strata, of unending and alternative histories, of new associations and distances. This textual body, touched by the papyrological event, takes on vast and intricate contours: an ambit marked by the deep times of text and sound, transmission and retransmission.

Bibliography

Benjamin, Walter. *Illuminations*. New York: Harcourt Brace Jovanovich, 1968.

Carson, Anne. *Decreation: Poetry, Essays, Opera*. New York: Random House, 2006.

Carson, Anne. *Glass, Irony, and God*. New York: New Directions, 1992.

Carson, Anne, trans. *If Not, Winter: Fragments of Sappho*. New York: Knopf, 2002.

Culler, Jonathan. *Literary Theory: A Very Short Introduction*. Oxford: Oxford University Press, 2002.

Merleau-Ponty, Maurice. *The Phenomenology of Perception*. Trans. Colin Smith. New York: Routledge, 2002.

Notes

1. Anne Carson, trans., *If Not, Winter: Fragments of Sappho* (New York: Knopf, 2002), xi.

2. Carson, *If Not, Winter*, ix.

3. Carson, *If Not, Winter*, xi.

4. Maurice Merleau-Ponty, *The Phenomenology of Perception*, trans. Colin Smith (New York: Routledge, 2002), 241.

5. Walter Benjamin, *Illuminations* (New York: Harcourt Brace Jovanovich, 1968), 76, quoted in Carson, *If Not, Winter*, xii.

6. Jonathan Culler, *Literary Theory: A Very Short Introduction* (Oxford: Oxford University Press, 2002), 78.

7. Anne Carson, *Decreation: Poetry, Essays, Opera* (New York, Random House, 2006).

8. Anne Carson, *Glass, Irony, and God* (New York: New Directions, 1992), 129.

bringing the House Down

Trojan Horses and Other Malware in Anne Carson's Grief Lessons: Four Plays by Euripides

Does grief lessen? Unlikely. Though Anne Carson presents first what she purports are the roots of tragedy—first rage, then grief—what she uncovers through the course of these four plays is the odd in the epic, that creepy fact of the funny amid the horror, that "trembling of laughter, terrible if it broke out."[1] That's the reason Herakles brings the house down *every time*, while you, the audience member, who has seen the play a hundred times, keep rooting around for the dramatic tool which might prevent him from the act.

Information is power: we know that in our digital age. In Theseus's case, in *Hippolytos*, it costs him his son. In Admetos's case, in *Alkestis*, it may or may not have brought his wife back to him from the land of the dead. Euripides himself is cagey about it (the resurrected woman does not speak) and Carson chooses to highlight that lack of clarity in both her introductory essay and the translation itself.

What people do and don't know about the lives of their companions and how they communicate or miscommunicate that information is one of the primary plots of Carson's Euripides. *Grief Lessons* haunts the house with the aftermath of messages gone astray, friends unfriended, and lurkers catfishing, not just to land a mate (who *is* that woman at the end of *Alkestis*?), but as in Hekabe's case, faking weakness to conceal strength.

Though in these plays *all* strength is faked. Carson points out the title character of *Herakles* is a "cliché";[2] having just arrived back from the land of the dead, he is unbeatable, "perfect." Not for long. Carson highlights in her essay the dividing moment in the middle of the play. She even suggests that once it happens, "You may think it's over and head for the door."[3] Then all hell breaks loose.

She calls more attention to the moment of division when she

talks about Admetos's partitioning of his house in the final play of the book, *Alkestis*, in order to accommodate Herakles's carousing during the funeral of his wife. But now we are looking into the future, which is a tricky thing and it is always good to remember that prophecy, in Carson's universe as well as in Euripides's, is vague and generally ill-advised.

Of course in a Greek tragedy the main characters are going through *motions* of a tragedy everyone watching *already* knows is coming. What's interesting then, to the audience, is how the chorus *processes information*.

Caught between the divine gods who make his fate and the chorus who *make it real* by uttering it—after all, if it's not on the Internet it didn't happen—Herakles, in what Carson identifies as a postmodern moment, turns his back on both. Having killed his entire family in bloodlust, he no longer believes the gods drove him to tragedy: "I don't believe gods commit adultery. I don't believe gods throw gods in chains. Never did believe it, never shall." He decides to go on with his life.

"We go in pity, we go in tears," moans the chorus at the close of the play.[4] What they've lost is not their friend, but their idea of the hero who could be blessed or even cursed by gods.

Echoing that closing phrase, Beckett's Vladimir asks, "Shall we go?" in the epigraph to Carson's preface to the next play, *Hekabe*. Beckett guides not only her structuring of the dialogue but also her perception of the bleakness of Euripides—"Why is Euripides so unpleasant?" she asks. "Certainly I am not the only person who thinks so."[5]

She goes on to quote Beckett on the question of tragedy: "Tragedy is not concerned with human justice. Tragedy is a statement of an expiation."[6] Hekabe, like Herakles, breaks down during the course of the play that bears her name. Unlike Herakles, she does not act in the madness but level-headedly goes straight for the kill. In contrast to the Greek masculine ideal who ends the play as a huddled mass, this Trojan woman begins the play broken and powerless but, as Carson says, soon "rises up, assembles herself one last time to action."[7]

It is not Hekabe's lack of traditionally "heroic" qualities or the weird structure of Euripides's plays that disturbs Carson; rather it is her Beckettian embrace of the fact that these plays, unlike the bulk of the Greek corpus, lack a "clear moral issue." Unlike *Iphigeneia* in Aeschylus or *Antigone* in Sophocles, whose deaths "change the stories in which they are set," the deaths in Euripides, to Carson, feel "muffled," or even to have "irrelevance" to the story at large.[8]

It's quite a claim, considering many of Euripides's women—Hekabe here, but in other plays Hermione, Medea, Agave and so on—are murderous if not actual murderers. If anything Hekabe seems neither to act based on the immediate revelation of Polyxena's death, nor that of Polydorus. Earlier in the play when Polyxena bids farewell in absentia to her brother Polydorus, Hekabe remarks, "If he lives. I am doubtful. My luck nowadays is not good."[9]

Her luck (unlike in *The Trojan Women* in which she loses a similar argument with Menelaus) is good enough that she is able to use her crafty tongue to sway Agamemnon into, at the very least, looking the other way while she plans her revenge. "Shit. No mortal exists who is free," she very reasonably points out to him. "Slaves to money or fortune or the city mob or the written laws—none use their own mind!"[10]

Regardless, there's no victory for Hekabe; she prevails in the trial at the play's conclusion, but cares not, and nor, in this case, does the chorus. Rather than deliver a final summation and coda to the play's lesson, they just slouch off stage muttering, "Now we taste the work of slaves. Hard is necessity."[11]

Neither Hekabe, Agamemnon, nor the chorus remark on the truly important event at the close of *Hekabe*—after Polymestor is denied justice for his children's murders and his blinding he begins to shout all he knows of the futures of the defendant and the judge, information revealed to him by others. He speaks of Hekabe's canine transformation, the betrayal and murder of Agamemnon, the killing of Kassandra—he spills it all out onto deaf ears while being dragged off stage by the Greek guards as Agamemnon shouts him down and Hekabe waves a dismissive hand. Carson explains away her nonchalance to her impending life as a dog thus: "Her suffering for the original sin of having been born is already off the human scale. Really there is nowhere for her to go but out of the species."[12]

Of course ignoring crucial information or misusing it is what Euripidean characters excel at, so it is no surprise when Theseus so badly misconstrues what is happening in his own house in the third play Carson translates, *Hippolytos*. In this case mere perception drives events more directly and powerfully than anything that actually happens.

What complicates matters here are three things: first, Hippolytos's own inability to reconcile a healthy spectrum of sexual expressions; second, the untranslatability of the Greek work *polle*, which Carson tries to explain as "muchness"—a quality of "access that cuts across certain lines of morality or moral sentiment we might prefer the gods to respect"; and finally the fact that Phaidra herself is "a tricky soul to capture, apparently" in that Euripides wrote two plays about her, the first no longer extant. Of it Carson says only nineteen short fragments and guesses that the first play "may have depicted an aggressive and lascivious Phaidra."[13]

Phaidra holds in between the two plays both sides of the sexuality that Hippolytos cannot grasp in either case. His inability to process this information renders him more relevant not as a human body but as a bit of programming. Aphrodite sets in motion a keystroke to delete the body while Artemis writes the code for the program into the wedding rituals.

And for her part, Phaidra, like most of the corpses that litter Euripidean stages, is more or less incidental prettiness.

Of course, all of this is happening in the house of Theseus, the man who appeared to offer Herakles safe harbor after that hero killed all of his own family in his god-driven madness in the first play of Carson's book. He, like Herakles, at a critical moment refuses divinity. "Without any test of oath or pledge or oracle, without trial, you'll cast me out?" cries Hippolytos upon being accused of violating Phaidra. "No need for divination!" replies Theseus. "Let the birds of omen fly over my head—be gone!"[14]

And then Hippolytos appeals to someone better than the gods: "O house! If only you could speak for me, bear witness!"[15] In the age of pure information, we want more than anything to *be* somewhere, to belong to a place and for that place to be *real*. It may be why it is so interesting for people to use their electronic devices to "check in" and post "status updates," to mark the times and places of their lives.

And though—typical in Euripides—it takes a slave and not a king to believe the boy, and a god to appear and clean up the mess, in the end, it is the gods who become irrelevant. First Hippolytos as a ghost gives his father an out to weasel out of guilt—"Yes I was deluded by gods," Theseus agrees in response to his son's opening gesture—and then he directly absolves him: "I free you from this murder."[16]

It's this kind of train wreck of the ideals of "justice" and "order" that were such foundational aspects of the earlier plays of Aeschylus and Sophocles that makes Euripides so "unpleasant" (in Carson's words) and she seems committed to exposing and highlighting that side of him.

The final play included here, *Alkestis*, was originally performed in place of a satyr play and it fulfills the same role in Carson's collection. Definitions blur and the main plot details seem to fluctuate. Admetos has made some kind of deal with Death to have his wife die in his place. No one is clear on the terms of the deal and when it happens Admetos seems blindsided by his grief, though Carson is quick to point out that he is making "free use of clichés of lament."[17] As if this situation itself isn't bizarre enough on its own, enter Herakles.

He brings with him the second reason to mistrust Anne Carson, whose craft and craftiness both mark these translations. Is one to understand this jocular, hard-partying Herakles meant to be understood as existing chronologically before the slaughter of his family in the opening play? Or has his madness utterly disappeared? What Carson intends matters because while she has opened her collection with the dissolution of Herakles, continued it with the crumbling of his guardian Theseus, and closes it with this completely surreal picture of the put-together and capable hero back in prime form (translating death into life is not for the weak of will)—the plays were indeed actually written and performed in antiquity in *reverse order*.

Dating Euripides is a tricky business, but it's generally accepted that *Alkestis* was performed in 438 BCE followed by *Hippolytos* in 428 BCE and *Hekabe* just a few years later, around 425–424 BCE. *Herakles* is harder to date, but it seems likely the play was written and performed much later, as early as 424 or, more likely, as late as 416 BCE. Kirk Ormand writes, "the later dates are based on a stylistic analysis of meter, and a tendency of Euripides to use certain metrical patterns with increasing frequency in later plays."[18]

Of course, by now Carson's audience, unlike Hippolytos, has learned how to understand all conditions—tragic and comic—as existing at once. Though the house itself is partitioned physically here, partitions in general—including that between Herakles's madness and sanity—are made, by Carson's placement of the plays, to seem completely arbitrary in the end.

In the end, it seems that Carson always wanted to write against expectation: to find the dry horror in the everyday, the nearly funny in the dreadful, using this "jarring comic and tragic effects against one another."[19] The key aspect of a tragedy for ancient audiences was always a rehearsal of an inevitable chain of events coming to pass, but in these plays by Euripides, the gods are tools, dumb as rocks, and it's really the wily who know how to navigate the chaotic overflow of information and sensation that is the human condition. Herakles seems completely casual in *Alkestis* about transcending death, as blasé as Hekabe is about her impending canine transformation.

After all, if information *isn't* power, then what *is*? As the chorus mumbles at the close of *Alkestis*, "What we imagined did not come to pass—God found a way to be surprising."[20] And that is always the real tragedy.

Notes

1. Anne Carson, *Grief Lessons* (New York: New York Review of Books, 2006), 249.
2. Carson, *Grief Lessons*, 13.
3. Carson, *Grief Lessons*, 14.
4. Carson, *Grief Lessons*, 84.
5. Carson, *Grief Lessons*, 89.
6. Beckett, *Proust*, qtd. in *Grief Lessons*, 89.
7. Carson, *Grief Lessons*, 90.
8. Carson, *Grief Lessons*, 92.
9. Carson, *Grief Lessons*, 119.
10. Carson, *Grief Lessons*, 138.
11. Carson, *Grief Lessons*, 159.
12. Carson, *Grief Lessons*, 90.
13. Carson, *Grief Lessons*, 167.
14. Carson, *Grief Lessons*, 223.
15. Carson, *Grief Lessons*, 224.
16. Carson, *Grief Lessons*, 239–41.
17. Carson, *Grief Lessons*, 248.
18. Email exchange between Kazim Ali and Kirk Ormand.
19. Carson, *Grief Lessons*, 247.
20. Carson, *Grief Lessons*, 306.

Lessons in Grief and Corruption
Anne Carson's Translations of Euripides

Anne Carson is a poet familiar with language rot and its tragic effects. In her long poem "The Glass Essay," she chronicles the grief of losing a lover and a parent by showing the way that language warps when lives and loves end. Take, for example, the narrator's father, snowed in by dementia, casting around in a language only he understands: "He is addressing strenuous remarks to someone in the air between us. He uses a language known only to himself, made of snarls and syllables and sudden wild appeals."[1] And in *The Beauty of the Husband*, Carson sings an ode to the corruption that steals into a lover's language and turns everything hot and sour from the start. After the narrator and her husband have sex "the real way" for the first time: "You're like Venice he said beautifully. . . . Neither of us had ever seen Venice."[2] His language is corrupted by beauty: it does not matter what he says so long as he says it beautifully.

It makes sense, then, that in *Grief Lessons* Carson would choose to translate Euripides, the ancient poet charged by his fellow Athenians with corrupting audiences through his use of language and story. Shortly after Euripides's death, Aristophanes staged a fictional competition in Hell between an older tragedian, Aischylos, and the newcomer, Euripides, for the throne of tragedy. Euripides's character boasts that he surpassed Aischylos in the art of writing tragedies "by staging everyday scenes, things we're used to, things that we live with, things that I wouldn't have got away with falsifying" (959–60).[3] According to Aristophanes's Aischylos, however, these "everyday scenes" and language are exactly what has corrupted the Athenians, turning them into "the civic shirkers, vulgarians, imps, and criminals they are now" (1014–15).[4]

Notice the connection between corruption and what is real, everyday, recognizable. There are two competing currents in poetry: one that embroiders a veil over the everyday, another that rips it away. Sometimes the same poem is implicated in both motions, embroidering and ripping, but often one current prevails. Euripides, and Carson with him, prefer ripping. So, when Euripides chooses to end the *Hekabe*, a play about how loss can turn you into a revenge animal, by turning the titular character into a dog, Carson is reminded of Beckett and his struggles with ripping the veil of language in his own writing: "More and more my own language seems to me as a veil, to be torn apart to approach the things (or nothings) behind it. . . . A time, let's hope, is coming when language will be best used when best abused."[5]

In her translations Carson sometimes abuses the elevated tragic idiom of the original in favor of the grossly modern, like when Hekabe grieves by saying, "Shit. No mortal exists who is free" (836–37).[6] Euripides didn't write "shit," but the expletive is true to Euripides's corrupting, sometimes shocking style, and is also true to Hekabe's character. With the startling juxtaposition of vulgarity and noble sentiment, Carson shows the way the broken queen's language decomposes until, at the end of the play, Hekabe "uses a language known only to [herself], made of snarls and syllables and sudden wild appeals."[7] Even before she becomes a revenge-dog, Hekabe supplicates the man who ruined her life, the general Agamemnon, by wishing for a bodily language to exhaust the Greek language, so rich in words for pain: "I want a voice put into my arms and hands and hair and feet by some magic of God, so they can all cling to you and cry out in supplication, cry out every word there is!" (807–11).[8] An abused language for an abused body.

When Euripides rips the veil away, sometimes there is something behind it: in the *Hekabe*, this screeching, murderous pain. But other times, he shows the "nothings" behind the veil of language, and the effect is just as devastating. In the *Herakles*, the hero returns from Hell to rescue his family from the tyrant Lykos, and is welcomed as "no less than Zeus the Savior" by his wife (504).[9] But as soon as the words exit her mouth, Euripides blasts open the emptiness of that word, "Savior." We hear Herakles walk offstage, go berserk, and kill his wife and sons, thinking they are the sons of his greatest enemy. Herakles spends the rest of his stage time struggling with the hollow echo of "Savior." Which is how Herakles became Sad But Great, among other things.

In *Alkestis*, too, the play that Carson chose to end her Euripides tetralogy, Euripides peels back the skin of words, like fraudulent peapods, to show the emptiness that has grown inside them. In this case, he uncovers the quotidian dishonesty of clichés of mourning by showing two normal people making an abnormal decision about death. Admetos is fated to die, but because of his friendship with the god Apollo, he is permitted to find another person to die in his place. The only person who offers is his wife, Alkestis, and Admetos foolishly accepts. Yet when she's drug out to die onstage, he mourns for her in formulaically desperate words: "Your dying is my dying" (246); "You take all joy of life away" (308); "When I die, we'll be together again" (324).[10] Remember Admetos's selfish request, and the litany of his mourning sounds more like empty shells.

Euripides's *Alkestis* is a deranged family drama, half comic, half tragic, a fitting cap to the other three plays that Carson translates in *Grief Lessons*. Each explores the various heart-eating ways that a family can fall apart, a concern in much of Carson's own poetry, whether it be a decaying marriage; the stubborn misunderstanding between mothers and daughters; abusive, distant, or lost siblings; the regret and heartbreak of waiting for a father's mind to slip all the way out. Tragedy allows us to grieve for the people most familiar to us through the safe distance provided by the strange costumes and dripping makeup of people we do not know at all.

I like Carson's translations of Euripides's plays because they remind me of one of the pleasures of reading ancient Greek: in the process of translation, you realize what is strange about your native language, which used to seem more natural to you than anything else in the world, more natural even than the shape of your fingers and toes. Carson creates this experience on the page, both in her poetry and in her translations; she gives the gift of sudden estrangement from the natural feel of English. In Carson's translation of *Herakles*, for example, the Chorus laments Herakles's mad killing of his sons by saying, "But you, O man of death, took your three sons together in the mad work" (998–1000).[11] Carson's phrase "mad work" condenses a phrase just as odd in Greek: λυσσάδι συγκατειργάσω μοίραι (1024).[12] She gets "work" from the rare compound verb συγκατεργάζομαι, which means, according to the *Greek-English Lexicon*, "help or assist anyone in achieving," but in this particular instance, according to the *Lexicon*, must mean "join in murdering."[13] How can a word that literally means "help or assist in achieving," as its root words suggest, stretch to mean "join in murdering" in this one instance? Carson captures this dissonance by stretching the English word "work" to mean "murder." Suddenly the innocuous word you thought you knew slices sharp and exits through the other side of awareness.

It takes a poet who knows how to rip the veil of language to achieve this beautiful estrangement. Historically, however, translation of classical texts has embroidered the veil, hiding the original beneath the poetry of another's language or voice, turning violent expressions more mundane, desexing. The 1935 Loeb Classical Library translation of the Greek romance *Daphnis and Chloe*, for example, translates the moment of the main character's defloration by an older woman not into English, but into Latin (see Book III, §§18–20).[14] Schoolboys long ago learned to skim for the Latin parts. Similarly, look up the word βινέω in the *Greek-English Lexicon*. You won't find English there at all.

Hippolytos, the most famous Euripidean play translated in *Grief Lessons*, was also an exercise in veiling. Euripides's first play about Phaidra, *Hippolytos Veiled*, shocked his fellow Athenians with its portrayal of a stepmother's greedy, shameless lust for her stepson. Rejected by his audience, Euripides decided to translate the play about Phaidra, to desex the sexiest of mythological heroines, veil her onstage, and show her ashamed of her own desire. Carson ventriloquizes Euripides's decision in her essay, included at the back of *Grief Lessons*, "Why I Wrote Two Plays about Phaidra, by Euripides." This is the ironic thing about veiling: sometimes it makes what is hidden more desirable. Skim for the Latin parts. Pine over the lost *Hippolytos Veiled*, Euripides's first attempt. Fall in love with the new Phaidra. Carson/Euripides writes in the essay about Phaidra, "Women learn to veil things. Who likes to look straight at real passion? Looks can kill. I would call 'feminine' this talent for veiling a truth in a truth."[15]

Veiling a truth in a truth—Greek in English, for example— could be a metaphor for translation. But Carson's English is part Greek already, part her own invention, as when she writes, in her translation of *Hekabe*, "Old women, old men, young brides torn from husbands. Dusts of Troy cover them" (335–37).[16] You might think that "dusts" translates a plural Greek noun because English prefers the collective singular, "dust." Euripides, however, wrote the singular κόνις, "dust." So it is to Carson's own invention that we owe this string of plural nouns: plural dusts to hide so many women, men, brides, and husbands. Other times a phrase sounds like Carson's own invention, as when the Chorus describes Polyxena's approaching death in *Hekabe* in vibrant colors: "Or you will have to watch her fall forward at the tomb and spray red blood from a blackbright hole as it opens her throat wide" (152–58).[17] The startling compound "blackbright" is a literal translation of Euripides's μελαναυγής, but it sounds as much like Carson as it does like Euripides. μελαναυγής, "blackbright," appears nowhere else in extant Greek (or English) poetry. Another word for Beckett's "abuse" is invention.

Tragedy is an unpleasant genre, and Euripides was the most unpleasant of the tragedians, to modify Aristotle's remark, because he dared to abuse the genre and the language he wrote in, to watch the rules rot, in order to capture something both true and beautiful about the world around him, and show how pliant Greek could be. Carson's Euripides is still able to shock—the spray of blood from a hole where black gleams. By refusing to retreat from this unpleasant beauty, Carson restores an aspect of Euripides's poetry often forgotten in polished translation. But she also calls attention to her own wild disruption of the English language, which will earn her a throne in Hell and a competition with the reigning Underworld king of tragedy, Euripides.

Works Cited

Aristophanes. *Frogs.* Translated by Jeffrey Henderson. Cambridge: Harvard University Press, 2002.

Carson, Anne. *The Beauty of the Husband: A Fictional Essay in 29 Tangos.* New York: Vintage Contemporaries, 2001.

Carson, Anne. "The Glass Essay." In *Glass, Irony and God.* New York: New Directions, 1995.

Carson, Anne. *Grief Lessons.* New York: New York Review of Books, 2006.

Diggle, James, ed. *Euripidis Fabulae.* Vol. 1. Oxford: Clarendon Press, 1984.

Liddell, H. G., and R. Scott, *Greek-English Lexicon.* 9th ed. Oxford: Clarendon Press, 1996.

Longus. *Daphnis and Chloe.* Translated by George Thornley, revised by J. M. Edmonds. Cambridge: Harvard University Press, 1935.

Notes

1. Anne Carson, "The Glass Essay," in *Glass, Irony and God* (New York: New Directions, 1995), 26.

2. Anne Carson, *The Beauty of the Husband: A Fictional Essay in 29 Tangos* (New York: Vintage Contemporaries, 2001), 11.

3. Aristophanes, *Frogs,* trans. Jeffrey Henderson (Cambridge: Harvard University Press, 2002), 155–57.

4. Aristophanes, *Frogs,* 163.

5. Quoted in Anne Carson, *Grief Lessons* (New York: New York Review of Books, 2006), 93.

6. Carson, *Grief Lessons*, 138.

7. Carson, "The Glass Essay," 26.

8. Carson, *Grief Lessons*, 137.

9. Carson, *Grief Lessons*, 39.

10. Carson, *Grief Lessons*, 265, 267.

11. Carson, *Grief Lessons*, 62.

12. Text of *Hekabe* edited by James Diggle, *Euripidis Fabulae*, vol. 1 (Oxford: Clarendon Press, 1984).

13. H. G. Liddell and R. Scott, *Greek-English Lexicon*, 9th ed., s.v. "συγκατεργάζομαι" (Oxford: Clarendon Press, 1996), 1664.

14. Longus, *Daphnis and Chloe*, trans. George Thornley, rev. J. M. Edmonds (Cambridge: Harvard University Press, 1935), 154–157.

15. Carson, *Grief Lessons*, 309.

16. Carson, *Grief Lessons*, 114.

17. Carson, *Grief Lessons*, 106.

ANGELA HUME

The "Dread Work" of Lyric
Anne Carson's An Oresteia

How can one tarry with the contested term *lyric* without also turning
in earnest to its earliest variations? Without opening one's ears to the
choral (sung) components of Greek tragedy, and also the strikingly
lyric, or—perhaps more often than not—*anti*lyric, "songs" of trage-
dy's female figures?[1] In my view—or, to my ear—it is Anne Carson's
translations that draw out these elements. In *An Oresteia* (2009), Car-
son offers her own definition of lyric—one that sounds forth not
through Apollo (traditionally associated with lyre music)[2] but through
the prophetic cries of Kassandra, Elektra, and the chorus.

In response to Elektra's unintelligible lament "E E AIAI . . .
PHEU," Carson's chorus responds: "*Don't make that sound.*"[3] Elektra,
devastated by news of her brother Orestes's death, utters cries so
terrible that the chorus implores her to stop.[4] It is the female voice
that reverberates through Carson's unorthodox *Oresteia*, which in-
cludes translations of Aiskhylos's *Agamemnon*, Sophokles's *Elektra*,
and Euripides's *Orestes*.[5] While it wasn't her idea to bring together
these plays by each of the three tragedians,[6] in the end Carson's
configuration illuminates the role of female utterance, resistance,
and refusal in the face of "law"—both the natural law of the family
and the emerging law of the community.[7] Residing at that limit
zone between life and death, lyric—a kind of "dread work"[8]—
registers, or prophesizes, the impossibility of any traditional projec-
tion of a future.

Aiskhylos's *Oresteia* has long been read as a political drama that
idealizes the transformation of "justice" from blood vengeance to a
democratic court of law;[9] the trilogy, however, is realized differently
by Carson, for whom female figures embody values subversive of
the emerging Athenian city-state. In her book *The Mourning Voice:
An Essay on Greek Tragedy*, the classicist Nicole Loraux argues that
female lamentation in tragedy complicates any reading of the genre
as serving a civic function, modeling instead a "politics of the

feminine"—an *anti*politics—that stands in stark contrast to the dominant paradigm of the polis.[10] On my reading, Carson (herself a classicist, too) underscores the role of "antipolitical" mourning (per Loraux) in *An Oresteia* while also offering an even more precise redefinition of lyric: that sound form which, in protest of democracy's value for *logos*, government, and measure, performs anarchic, antifutural, antihuman modes of being.[11] Moreover, lyric becomes *prophecy*, but one that knows it will not be heard. That is to say, lyric's prophecy is *failed* prophecy, but one that sounds forth in and through failure nonetheless.

Earlier I alluded to lyric's fraught history; because the term has carried different meaning at different points in time, the concept has eluded critics as they have attempted to pin it down.[12] Today classicists use the term to describe ancient poetry that was neither elegy nor *iambos* (narrative invective), and more generally to describe that poetry which was set to music.[13] Notably, the term lyric did not emerge until the second century BCE; it would not have been used by ancient lyric poets themselves, let alone the tragedians.[14] With this history in mind, and for the purpose of this essay, I use the term to refer somewhat generally to musical poetry and/or poetry set to music, including the chorus's sung passages. And because a number of tragedy's female figures refer to their own wailing as song—and, furthermore, because in antiquity these cries were sometimes also sung themselves[15]—I argue that we may read their sound forms, too (however unmusical), as lyric.[16] Carson's translations support this reading, highlighting instances of antilyric lyric.

In *An Oresteia*, lyric becomes intertwined not only with lamentation (per Loraux) but also with prophecy and antifuturity. While ostensibly opposed, prophecy and antifuturity are, on my reading, related in constitutive ways. In *Agamemnon*, Carson translates (Agamemnon's slave) Kassandra's initial utterance as "Woepollo!"—a repudiation of Apollo, the "god of [her] ruin," who has cursed her with the ability to see the future but "made [her] prophecy never believed."[17] Unlike in other translations, in which Kassandra's invocation is more of an appeal ("My Apollo!"[18]), in Carson's translation Kassandra defines herself *against* Apollo, the god of lyre music. Shortly after, this recalcitrant Kassandra will proclaim, "I will walk with my song torn open."[19] But before she does so, the chorus—unable to interpret her fragmented, screaming "song"—reproaches her, saying

You're mad—godstruck godswept
   godnonsensical
and you keep making that sound, it's not
   musical.
Like the nightingale who wails her lost
   child, you're inexhaustibly wild.
Sorrow this, sorrow that,
   sorrow this, sorrow that.[20]

Kassandra's "song" is senseless, unlyrical, feral, excessive. Here she is likened to the mythic figure Philomela, who is turned into a nightingale by the gods for murdering her rapist's infant son, Itys. Like Philomela, Kassandra is doomed to a life of interminable mourning. Carson's translation underscores the way "lyric" in Greek tragedy is so often constituted by its seeming opposite—broken song, lacking measure; a mournful song "torn open."

In *The Mourning Voice*, Loraux examines the phenomenon of lyric lamentation in compelling depth. Her reading of tragedy heeds what she calls the "lyric passages" of the chorus and women speakers.[21] She notes that *thrēnos*, or moaning, is often accompanied by invocations of music, bringing lamentation into close proximity with song and transforming lyric: in tragedy, lyric is realized anew as unmusical, or lyre-less.[22] Loraux cites the example of the chorus in *Agamemnon*, which, on Carson's translation, bemoans its unending desire for "signs of the future— / singing a prophetic song no one asked for."[23] The chorus continues:

Still at the edge of my heart the song of the
   Furies keeps nagging—
no one taught me this song and it has no
   music.[24]

Per Loraux: the chorus sings of its own unmusical song, casting lyric in a very different, very anti-Apollonian light.[25] What interests me most about Carson's translation, though, is not so much that lamentation is conflated with lyre-less song as the fact that unlyrical song understands itself as *prophecy*—one for which no one asked. In Carson, lyric is, very precisely, prophecy unsolicited, ultimately ignored. Importantly, here and elsewhere lyre-less song is the curse of the Furies—"ghastly goddesses" of vengeance (as Orestes will describe them in *Orestes*), female figures of prophetic vision but also antisociality and death.[26] Shortly after, Kassandra says, "I lose my screams they find me again! / The dread work of prophecy buckles me."[27] While Kassandra knows that her vocalizations register what will come to be, she also knows that no one can or will understand her. And so, lyric utterance: that "dread work" which knows the extent of its own incommunicability—the inevitability of its failure—crying out anyway. It is utterance that, left with no other choice, renounces *logos*, sounding persistently on. "I speak as one about to die," states Carson's Kassandra, moreover; "I want to sing my own dirge."[28] Lyric, as it is manifest here, resounds at the limit zone between life and death—prospective (speaking as one "about to die") and retrospective (singing one's own dirge) at once. From this liminal site, Kassandra—realizing the double bind that is the condition for and of her existence under "law"—proclaims defiantly, "I will walk with my song torn open."

I want to return to *Elektra*, which follows *Agamemnon* in Carson's trilogy. Recall that Carson translates the chorus's response to Elektra's indefatigable wailing as "Don't make that sound." H. D. F. Kitto, however, translates the line as "My daughter, do not weep," a softer appeal.[29] In contrast to Kitto, Carson evokes the exasperation of a chorus that can no longer bear the sound of Elektra's terrible voice. What makes Carson's chorus particularly uncomfortable is the anarchic nature of Elektra's cries. "You run yourself out / in a grief with no cure," the chorus argues.[30] "No time limit, no measure."[31] Lacking measure, Elektra's relentless mourning of Agamemnon (murdered by Klytaimestra) poses a threat to the order of the house, the power structure in place. "You breed enemies everywhere you touch. / But you must not / clash with the people in power," warns the chorus.[32] But Elektra knows that, under the regime of Klytaimestra and (Klytaimestra's lover) Aigisthos, there is no future for her; she lives an administered life: "my father's own killers: / they rule me. They dole out my life."[33] For this reason, Elektra argues, "self-control has no meaning. / Rules of reverence do not apply."[34] In the face of the oppressive law of her family, Elektra refuses a lawful existence, giving herself over, instead, to unrestrained vocal emission.

Importantly, Elektra herself likens her cries to song: "Never / will I leave off lamenting . . . Like the nightingale who lost her child."[35] And then:

Lament is a pattern cut and fitted around
    my mind—

like the bird who calls Itys! Itys! endlessly,
bird of grief.[36]

In Carson's translation of this lyric passage—lyric not only because
the speaker compares her lament to birdsong, but because the
words, according to some translations, in antiquity would have been
sung[37]—lamentation is tailored to the mind. Suited by grief, Elek-
tra's song, like Kassandra's, sounds forth from that limit zone be-
tween life and death, proclaiming that which it sees—"*I am at the
end. I exist no more,*" declares Elektra[38]—becoming prophecy, but
prophecy precisely in its compulsion to *refuse* what it sees. Under
Klytaimestra and Aigisthos, Elektra knows that for her there will be
"no children, / no marriage, / no light in my heart."[39] For these
reasons, she wishes for death: "Let me dwell where you are [father].
/ I am already nothing."[40] Convinced that her life is over, she says,
"*By dread things I am compelled . . . I know what I am. . . .There will
be no rest.*"[41] Here Carson's Elektra, like Kassandra, is overcome by
the "dread work of prophecy"—but a prophecy that amounts to
nothing, is "already nothing," snuffed out not only by those in
power but in and through her own refusal to realize a future.

Carson's *Orestes*, the final installment of her *Oresteia*, offers what
is perhaps the translator's darkest vision of lyric, one in which lyric
is a figure for a radical negativity or remainder—one that "sings"
from a place of madness. In the play a guilt-racked Orestes is pos-
sessed by the Furies (or Eumenides)—whose songs, recall, have no
music—and plagued by prophetic "visions" for which he did not
ask.[42] His cries, repetitive and mournful, tend toward lamentation:
"Oh. / Oh what. / Oh what am I do doing. What am I doing /
raving like this."[43] Others around him lament his condition as well.
The chorus cries,

AIAI!
O racing raging goddesses!
You dance a dance that is no dance
screaming
down the sky
in search of justice,
bowling down the sky in search of blood!
Eumenides! I pray you off, I pray you out!
Let Agamemnon's son
forget the lunacy
that drives him terribly about![44]

Here the chorus attributes the Furies' wrath to a lack of justice to be found anywhere. Throughout the play, the Furies haunt humans with their apocalyptic omens, their presence increasingly shrill as the contradictions of Carson's trilogy begin to crystallize. While natural law has failed to bring about justice ("Justice, on the one hand," says the chorus of the House of Atreus's natural (family) law; "Evil, on the other," replies Elektra, gesturing toward the inadequacy of the law's perpetual cycle of vengeance[45]),the emerging law of the community proves to be flawed, too, in that the citizens of Argos are as corrupt as their leaders, voting uncritically (suggests Orestes[46]) for the stoning of both Orestes and Elektra for the murder of Klytaimestra. Unlike in some translations of Aeschylus's *Eumenides*, in which Orestes is ultimately acquitted of murder charges by Athena and her court of "ablest citizens,"[47] or "finest men,"[48] in Carson's *Orestes*, the law of the community offers no promise of a fair trial. In the absence of any adequate law, Orestes and Elektra opt for a radical antihumanism, plotting the murder of Helen in addition to their own double suicide. "All we have is us," laments Orestes to Elektra, to which she responds, "All we have is impossible."[49]

For Carson, lyric, in protest of the impossible life under law, sounds what it sees—or, that (which) it *refuses* to see—despite knowing that its song will not be intelligible, let alone heard. Carson's dark vision of lyric as the "dread work of prophecy," or failed prophecy, throws into sharp relief the question of whether the administered life under "law" has ever been livable; the answer, she posits, is in the cries of she who sees, or refuses to see, and clashes, unaccompanied by any lyre.

Notes

1. Here already I gesture toward the work of Nicole Loraux, who explores the significance of lyre-less song in Greek tragedy. See Nicole Loraux, *The Mourning Voice: An Essay on Greek Tragedy*, trans. Elizabeth Trapnell Rawlings (Ithaca: Cornell University Press, 2002).

2. For more on Apollonian lyric, see Loraux, *The Mourning Voice*, 59–62.

3. Anne Carson, *An Oresteia* (New York: Faber and Faber, 2009), 131, my emphasis.

4. *Aiai* translates as a cry of sorrow, mourning as "pure vocal emission." See Loraux, *The Mourning Voice*, 35–36.

5. Representations of women's sound forms is a topic Carson has explored in depth. See Anne Carson, "The Gender of Sound," *Glass, Irony, and God* (New York: New Directions, 1992), 119–39.

6. The idea was Brian Kulick's. See Carson, "A Note from the Translator," *An Oresteia*, ix.

7. Notably, Hegel associated the natural law of the family (what he named "divine law") with women, and the law of the community, or "nation" (what he named "human law"), with men. On Hegel's reading, the two are always dialectically constituted; even so, "womankind" remains "the everlasting irony of the community," perverting that which is "universal" about the state. See G. W. F. Hegel, "The Ethical Order," *Phenomenology of Spirit*, trans. A. V. Miller (Oxford: Oxford University Press, 1977), 288.

8. Carson, *An Oresteia*, 55.

9. Peter Burian, introduction to *The Oresteia*, trans. Alan Shapiro and Peter Burian (Oxford: Oxford University Press, 2003), 5.

10. See Loraux, "Tragedy and the Antipolitical," *The Mourning Voice*, 26–41. Carson, too, discusses the subversive nature of women's "bad sound," pointing out that it was denounced by lawgivers in preclassical and classical Greece as "political disease" and was considered likely to incite "disorder" and "craziness" if not regulated. See Carson, "The Gender of Sound," 129–30.

11. At one point Loraux, too, points toward antifutural sentiments in Sophokles's *Elektra*: "[There] is no sequel to Sophocles' *Electra* . . . no future is included within it." Loraux, *The Mourning Voice*, 22.

12. See Virginia Jackson, "Lyric," *The Princeton Encyclopedia of Poetry and Poetics*, ed. Roland Greene and Stephen Cushman (Princeton: Princeton University Press, 2012), 826–34.

13. Felix Budelmann, *The Cambridge Companion to Greek Lyric* (Cambridge: Cambridge University Press, 2009), 2.

14. Ibid., 2–3.

15. See, for example, Sophocles's "Electra" in *Antigone, Oedipus the King, and Electra*, trans. H. D. F. Kitto (Oxford: Oxford University Press, 1962).

16. See Loraux for more on tragedy's conflation of *thrēnos* and lyre-less music. Loraux, *The Mourning Voice*, 61–62.

17. Ibid., 48, 55.

18. Aeschylus, *The Oresteia*, trans. Alan Shapiro and Peter Burian (Oxford: Oxford University Press, 2003), 81.

19. Carson, *An Oresteia*, 53.

20. Ibid., 52.

21. Loraux, *The Mourning Voice*, 54.

22. Ibid., 61.

23. Carson, *An Oresteia*, 44.

24. Ibid., 45.

25. Loraux, *The Mourning Voice*, 60.

26. Carson, *An Oresteia*, 220.

27. Ibid., 55.

28. Ibid., 60.

29. Sophocles, "Electra," trans. Kitto, 128.

30. Carson, *An Oresteia*, 94.

31. Ibid.

32. Ibid., 97.

33. Ibid., 100.
34. Ibid., 102.
35. Ibid., 92.
36. Ibid., 94.
37. Sophocles, "Electra," trans. Kitto, 107.
38. Ibid., 122, my emphasis.
39. Ibid., 95.
40. Ibid., 150.
41. Carson, *An Oresteia*, 98, my emphasis.
42. Ibid., 199.
43. Ibid., 194.
44. Ibid., 196.
45. Ibid., 191.
46. Ibid., 215.
47. Aeschylus, *The Oresteia,* trans. Shapiro and Burian, 167.
48. Aeschylus, *The Oresteia,* trans. Robert Fagles (New York: Penguin Books, 1977), 253.
49. Ibid., 195.

PETER STRECKFUS

Collaborating on *Decreation*
An Interview with Anne Carson

September 8, 2001, following the inaugural performance of Carson's opera *Decreation: Fight Cherries* at California College of Arts and Crafts (CCAC) in San Francisco, CA.

PETER STRECKFUS: **I want to first talk about the** *Decreation* **operas. I understand there are three, two of which have now been performed in one way or another. Could you talk about the relationship between the three?**

ANNE CARSON: They are organized around the concept of jealousy refracted in different ways. The first one is an ancient Greek myth. The middle one, an account of a medieval woman, a real historical figure who was a mystic in the thirteenth century and burned at the stake. The third one, *Fight Cherries*, concerns the philosopher Simone Weil and her parents.

PS: **I saw on the Internet the documentation of the second, the opera-installation** *The Mirror of Simple Souls*, **and I found it fascinating, especially in relation to having just seen** *Fight Cherries*. **I wonder if you could you tell me more about Marguerite Porete, the subject of the second opera.**

AC: Actually, there's little information about her life—we know her name and that she was tried under the Inquisition and put to death as a heretic in 1310. There's no information about where she came from, what her education was, what motivated her, or whom else she read in the mystical tradition. She's a completely mysterious figure. Her book, *The Mirror of Simple Souls*, was burned with her and suppressed. But imperfectly suppressed. Priests, fascinated by it, copied the book, appending an apologia, an explanation of how they thought the doctrines were not heretical, in case they themselves became liable to prosecution. So it was transmitted secretly, and as an anonymous work, from 1310 until 1946. Then somebody working with manuscripts in a French monastery found it and deduced it was the writing of Marguerite Porete. She flashes across the screen of history, disappears, and then reappears in 1946 as the author of this book. Nothing else, literally nothing else, is known of her.

PS: **How did you find the collaboration on** *The Mirror of Simple Souls*; **it was with your students, was it?**

AC: Fabulous. I didn't go to Michigan intending to do the opera. I just had the libretto in my backpack on the first day of school, and we were talking about the subject of the course, which was mysticism. I mentioned the libretto. We looked at it together, and they decided to do it as a class project. The school came up with $10,000 to help us. I gave the students the libretto, which has seven songs in it, and I assigned two people to each song. Each song became a room. The students built the rooms and developed installations for them. Another student, who wasn't in the class but found out about the opera, composed and recorded a score for all seven rooms. The score played in each room as the audience passed through.

PS: **Was this a class of artists?**

AC: Almost none of them had done art before. It was a class called "Humanities" in the English department. Most of them were either in the writing program or in the English program. One was from Classics. One was from Business. A few were from foreign languages. They simply took the libretto and did it. They had to learn how to build a room, for example. They just did it. I didn't consult with them from September until December.

We had a reception at the end of class but before the opening of the opera, to which their mothers and grandmothers came, and everyone made little speeches. They all said that what had made it a good experience for them was being trusted to do whatever they could do with the script. This astonished me: it wouldn't occur to me *not* to trust somebody who has an idea. But I guess in school generally you're not trusted. You're hovered over. In the end, the opera was an impressive thing. (Objectively!) More than four hundred people from the community came to see it.

PS: **Was the process the same for the third opera,** *Fight Cherries*, **which was put on here at CCAC? I sensed, as I've heard you speak about this opera, that collaboration was even more integral to this process. Is that so?**

AC: *Fight Cherries* was much more intense. The libretto and the music were written before, but we only rehearsed from August 27 till September 6. It was largely invented in rehearsal.

PS: **I find that remarkable, that it was put together in such a short time.**

AC: That's the value of stress. Theater is different than writing. For one thing, theater's expensive. You have to pay people to rehearse as well as to perform, so all the hours you spend fiddling around, working out the staging, money is going out. You need the collaborative thought processes to be simultaneous and to have momentum from the moment it starts to time the curtain goes up.

PS: **You've made statements about the distinctions between different genres of aesthetic writing in the past, and sometimes you've opposed that kind of writing to your academic writing. So those two distinctions seem to stand at some distance for you as a thinker. In this regard, was the collaborative effort essentially different for you from the experience of writing at your desk?**

AC: Not so different. When I started to write the libretto, I had already worked on an academic lecture about Simone Weil, Marguerite Porete, and Sappho. The analytic level was there. The libretto was the fumes coming off that analytic effort, the sort of intoxicating fumes left in the room by mashing up all the grapes of the academic part. So, not that different but more pleasant. Not a different part of my mind.

PS: **How about the creative work that went into the production of it as you were working with your collaborators?**

AC: That was quite different. I just stood back. During rehearsal, I'd be at the wall. I didn't feel crucial in any way. It's a different positioning of ego within action. And it's a different accountability. When you're writing a page, it's all you. You're responsible for everything that happens. In a rehearsal space, everyone's responsible, and that's liberating for a writer. For a director, it wouldn't be. Fortunately, I'm not a director.

PS: **Did you do much revision of the libretto during the process?**

AC: I added a whole section. The parental interludes were added to give the parents more to do and to separate the arias with something less grim.

PS: **I attended a session where you spoke with Ken Watt [the** director] and with Guillermo Galindo [the composer], and you said something about the negative space that the parental interludes gave the opera, that it gave the opera a quality that is hard to achieve in writing.

AC: There were two points I think I made there. One was about the parental interludes, and one was about the chorus. With regard to the chorus, I was saying that its function is to introduce the possibility of emptiness, because we don't exactly know what the chorus is. When that choral figure called The Void wanders through the action, he brings an empty space with him, and it's a space in which you, the audience, can think various things. It's not programmed for you as it is when the mother or father are up there saying typical mother or father remarks.

PS: "I'm a mother, and I am speaking as a mother."

AC: Right, and that's all quite predictable, and it's satisfying because it happens according to your prediction of what a mother would be like, but the chorus, The Void, is not that kind of character. The Void is indefinable. Mother and Father, on the other hand, provide a space of comfort or ordinary domestic dilemma, no wrestling with the void. What is the phrase I quoted from Gertrude Stein? . . . "ordinary pigeons and trees." That's from her opera. She says you have to have "ordinary pigeons and trees in a libretto."

PS: And the ordinary pigeons and trees would be the parents?

AC: Yes, those little things they do with chairs and whatnot.

PS: That gives the audience something to hold onto if lost.

AC: They give us a lot of nonsense about triangles and nonagons. It's a kind of emotional comfort.

PS: They also have very human, parental things to say outside the interludes.

AC: Yes, they do.

PS: You mentioned the triangles and nonagons. Could you explain their importance?

AC: Not my fault. Guillermo invented the nonagons; he explains them in terms of music theory. Every time he explains, it goes right past me. But I accept that it's important to him that, as musical, theoretical concepts, the nonagons didn't work and the triangles did. Leaving music theory aside, the triangle shape is important to the dynamic of the story: Simone is caught in a conventional family triangle with her parents. It's also an analogue of the relationship she longs hopelessly to have with God.

PS: **The triangle with God and Simone: who or what is the third angle in that one?**

AC: She says it's the world, creation, as she calls it. She often describes a frustration that she can't remove herself from the world so that the world can be in proper communion with God. She sees herself as an obstruction between these two entities, God and the world. I'm not sure exactly what "the world" is, but it's definitely another angle.

PS: **She also says she would like to see the world without her in it.**

AC: Yes.

PS: **In order to see the world, it seems that she also would be part of the world.**

AC: Her seeing her not there, yes. A paradox ineradicable for mystical thinking: the desire to use the self to get the self out of the way.

PS: **How did you feel about Simone Weil's life and how she died?**

AC: Ambivalent.

PS: **Is it a tragic life?**

AC: I don't think she saw it that way. Who gets to judge? In Greek tragedy the chorus does. That's one of their functions. I'm not sure that I would call her tragic. And I think her effect on people nowadays, people who read her writings, is very various.

PS: **I find her troubling when I read her.**

AC: She sets up a little whirlwind in your mind. You can't quite settle on what it is that's troubling or how to frame the question of the value of her existence. It keeps going round and round. It's a useful effect to have on people, to stop presumptions, to be troubling.

PS: **To be troubling, yes.**

AC: It's a saint's function, to be troubling.

PS: **I read an interview in which—speaking of troubling—you mentioned John Ashbery's writing. I didn't interpret your remarks as faulting Ashbery, but certainly there was an expression of being troubled about something in his writing. I was surprised by that remark. To be able to contain confusion in a way that has value and is redemptive, that seems to be a part of your work, although your**

work is very different from his. Could you say a little more about how his writing might trouble you?

AC: I think I was worried about not understanding. As you say, not understanding is an interesting state of mind, can be useful, and poetry is an instrument of producing this state of mind. But I guess with his writing—and he's a paradigm of this, not the only example—there's a puzzle presented that the author himself turns away from, which is not the same as a puzzle presented with both hands open. The difference isn't simply that in one place I can break the code and in the other I can't; it's something in his own attitude, the attitude that comes washing through as you read, something switched off. In mystical writing like Marguerite Porete's, every page presents this kind of puzzle, language trying to say something that doesn't come to you, that stays out of reach. Yet you have the sense that she's right there behind it looking at you, watching you strive. Somehow that's consoling. Ashbery withholds consolation.

PS: **I can sympathize with that in reading his work. When I read *A Wave*, I felt like I'd gotten a key into his writing. The key was to remember that he loves me. It sounds like the feeling you're missing.**

AC: Yes, I feel that missing.

PS: **And it's buried, but once I'd felt like I realized he loved me everything was . . .**

AC: Where did you derive that conviction?

PS: **From the way he speaks to the reader. I decided that whenever he says "you" it could be me, and he wants it to be that way. And he's often speaking with somebody with whom he's intimate and about whom he cares. I decided that was me.**

AC: So, it's your choice. Well, that's a strong choice to make. I think the "you" in poems from the beginning—Sappho may have invented this, the "you" as a construct placed in the poem for the reader to inhabit if they choose to—is a very useful mechanism, but you do have to make the choice to fill it. You have to collaborate.

PS: **You have to feel invited to also.**

AC: Yes, I guess I never have. I also read somewhere that he thinks of poetry, the text that he comes up with, as the same as the experience of being in a hotel room and hearing two people in the next room who are having an argument. They're not quite audible, you put your ear to the wall, you get bits of phrase. It seems a loveless scenario, but maybe not.

PS: **You give poetry such value when you articulate its effects on imagination. I'd like to thank you for that. I reread** Economy of the Unlost **recently—it was a very important book for me as a poet.**

AC: The ancients think that actions, all actions, are incomplete, not sufficiently real, until they are expressed in a poem or celebrated in some effort of song. It's a strange notion to us. For us literature is added on, a layer you can remove and still have life, but for the ancients, you can't have life without utterance. The action and the word are two sides of one flesh. I like to think of it as a circuit. [Gestures with hand.]

PS: **The sleeping eight, the sign for eternity?**

AC: Eternity, maybe. Eternity takes in mortal and immortal time, doesn't it? I've often thought that's what the ancients mean when they say poetry is immortal or makes you immortal, that it puts you in a circuit where mortal time connects with immortal time so that *now* is also *forever.* Or you feel it is.

PS: **We were speaking of love a moment ago. It's an important subject in your work, but I also sense that you love your subjects—perhaps as opposed to an author who feels primarily ironic about them. You've spoken elsewhere about your trouble with irony in contemporary literature. I wonder, when do you allow yourself irony, or do you, or is that even an issue for you?**

AC: I don't believe I think of it as an issue of permission. Irony is always part of the way I go at things, maybe a defense. Humor is generally a defense against exposure, but I've learned . . .

PS: **You relate the two, irony and humor, closely?**

AC: Yes. But there's something peculiar with irony going on nowadays—everything has to be ironic from the beginning. It leaves you nowhere to go next: irony is properly a gesture of closure or farewell. It's a shadow that falls as something leaves the room. I don't know what to do about this. There has to be a substance on which the shadow falls. That substance seems to elude us.

PS: **I also understand that you are collaborating on a book that has images in it with another artist?**

AC: Yes.

PS: **Did you say that you were getting perhaps bored with the idea of just working in books?**

AC: Possibly I did, yes.

PS: **You're not speaking then of being bored with poetry, or are you?**

AC: Not bored with making. I don't know that I've ever thought of myself as doing poetry, frankly. But I like to make things, and I think to make a page of words and stop is not often satisfying anymore. I have been lately making one-of-a-kind books, little ones, adding material with paste, paint, staples. Taking the page of words and unfolding it at angles.

PS: **Exploding it.**

AC: Exploding it. That is satisfying from time to time. I'm not sure I'm going to find the form I want. I don't believe it exists.

PS: **Could we come back to the distinction between your academic and aesthetic writing? You said before that you thought that you would never be able to combine the two as you did in** Eros the Bittersweet. **Do you still feel that way?**

AC: When I was writing that book, I was at the beginning of my academic career, teaching at Princeton, trying to get tenure, etc. etc. I bought into those distinctions then. But gradually, on the path of my thought I couldn't separate the strands of it all. So, I gave up on it. Yes, that's how that went.

Contributors

Kazim Ali's most recent book of poetry is *Sky Ward*; his most recent book of essays is *Orange Alert: Essays on Poetry, Art, and the Architecture of Silence* (University of Michigan Press).

Dan Beachy-Quick is a Monfort Professor at Colorado State University, where he teaches in the MFA Writing Program.

Bruce Beasley is a professor of English at Western Washington University and author of seven collections of poems, most recently *Theophobia* (BOA Editions, 2012) and *The Corpse Flower: New and Selected Poems* (University of Washington Press, 2007). He has won fellowships from the National Endowment for the Arts and the Artist Trust and three Pushcart Prizes.

Julie Carr is the author of six books of poetry, including *Think Tank, 100 Notes on Violence, Sarah—Of Fragments and Lines*, and *RAG. Surface Tension: Ruptural Time and the Poetics of Desire in Late Victorian Poetry*, was published in 2013. She teaches at the University of Colorado in Boulder and is the co-publisher of Counterpath Press.

Martin Corless-Smith is a poet, painter and sometime critic. His most recent essay subjects include Robert Herrick, W. G. Sebald, and Thomas Traherne. A book of poems, *Bitter Green*, is forthcoming from Fence Books in 2015.

Jennifer K. Dick is the author of *Circuits* (Corrupt Press, 2013), *Enclosures* (BlazeVox eBook, 2007), and *Fluorescence* (University of Georgia Press, 2004). Jennifer teaches American Literature and Civilization at the Université of Haute Alsace in Mulhouse, France, cocurates the Ivy Writers reading series in Paris and the Ecrire Art mini-residency at La Kunsthalle Mulhouse, and is a poetry editor for *Versal* out of Amsterdam.

Hannah Ensor is from Ann Arbor, Michigan. She is the Events Coordinator at the University of Arizona Poetry Center, a member of the board of directors of Casa Libre en la Solana, an assistant poetry editor for *DIAGRAM,* and a co-editor of textsound.org. With Laura Wetherington and Jill Darling, she co-wrote a chapbook called *at the intersection of 3* (dancing girl press, 2014)

Jessica Fisher's first book, *Frail-Craft,* won the 2006 Yale Younger Poets Prize, and her second, *Inmost,* received the 2011 Nightboat Poetry Prize. She was awarded the 2012–2013 Rome Prize in Literature and is currently an assistant professor at Williams College.

Graham Foust works at the University of Denver and is the author of several books of poems, including *Necessary Stranger* and *To Anacreon in Heaven and Other Poems.* With Samuel Frederick, he has translated three books by the late German poet Ernst Meister.

Richard Greenfield is the author of *Tracer* (Omnidawn, 2009) and *A Carnage in the Lovetrees* (University of California Press, 2003), which was named a Book Sense Top University Press pick. He is professor of creative writing at New Mexico State University and is coeditor of Apostrophe Books.

Lily Hoang is the author of four books. She teaches in the MFA program at New Mexico State University.

Harmony Holiday is a writer/archivist/choreographer/antique-futurist living in New York. Her first book *Negro League Baseball,* was published by Fence Books in 2011 and received the Motherwell Prize. Her following book, *Go Find Your Father / A Famous Blues* is forthcoming. She is the founder of Afrosonics, a growing archive of rare jazz and poetry LPs that will be held at Columbia University's Wiener Music Library.

Angela Hume is the author of *The Middle* (Omnidawn, 2013) and *Second Story of Your Body* (Portable Press at Yo-Yo Labs, 2011). Her critical work appears in *ISLE: Interdisciplinary Studies in Literature and Environment, Evental Aesthetics,* and *Jacket2.* Currently she is writing a dissertation on lyric, dialectic, and ecology at the University of California, Davis.

Christine Hume is the author of three books, most recently *Shot* (Counterpath, 2010), and three chapbooks, *Lullaby: Speculations on the First Active Sense* (Ugly Duckling Presse, 2008), *Ventifacts* (Omnidawn, 2012), and *Hum* (Dikembe, 2013). She teaches in the interdisciplinary creative writing program at Eastern Michigan University.

Karla Kelsey is author of three books of poetry: *Knowledge, Forms, the Aviary* and *Iteration Nets*, both published by Ahsahta Press, and *A Conjoined Book*, forthcoming from Omnidawn Press. She edits and contributes to Fence Books' *Constant Critic* poetry book review website and has had essays on poetics published in literary journals and anthologies. With Aaron McCollough she coedits SplitLevel Texts, a small press that publishes books of contemporary innovative poetry and prose.

Virginia Konchan's poems have appeared in *Best New Poets*, *The Believer*, *New Yorker*, and *New Republic*, and her criticism in *Boston Review*, *Quarterly Conversation*, *Barzakh Magazine*, and elsewhere. Cofounder of *Matter*, a literary journal of political poetry and commentary, she lives in Chicago.

Timothy Liu is the author of ten books of poems, two of which are forthcoming: *Don't Go Back to Sleep* (Saturnalia Books, 2014) and *Let It Ride* (Station Hill Press, 2015). He lives with his husband in Manhattan.

Douglas A. Martin is the author most recently of an autobiographical novel, *Once You Go Back*. His other books include *Branwell*, a novel of the Brontë brother; *They Change the Subject*, a collection of stories; and *Your Body Figured*, a lyric narrative. He is also the author of volumes of poetry, including *In the Time of Assignments* and *The Haiku Year* (coauthored with friends). He holds a PhD in English from the Graduate Center of the City University of New York.

J. Michael Martinez's first book received the Walt Whitman Award from the Academy of American Poets; his second is forthcoming from the University of Arizona Press.

Kristi Maxwell's books of poetry include *That Our Eyes Be Rigged* (Saturnalia Books, 2014) and *PLAN/K* (Gold Wake Press, 2014). Her critical work includes an essay entitled "From No Bodies to Some Bodies: A Reading of Jenny Boully's *The Body* and *[one love affair]**," forthcoming in *Textual Practice*.

John Melillo is an Assistant Professor in the English Department at the University of Arizona. He researches the relationship between noise, listening, and affect through literary and musical history. John also makes music, most recently in the pop/noise project Algae & Tentacles.

Ander Monson is the author of six books, including the forth-coming book in a box, *Letter to a Future Lover* (nonfiction, Graywolf, 2015), a website, a decoder wheel, two chapbooks, and other paraphernalia. He edits the magazine *DIAGRAM* (thediagram. com) and the New Michigan Press.

Vanessa Place is a conceptual artist, poet, critic, criminal defense lawyer, and codirector of Les Figues Press.

Andrea Rexilius is the author of *Half of What They Carried Flew Away* (Letter Machine, 2012) and *To Be Human Is to Be a Conversation* (Rescue Press, 2011). She teaches graduate and undergraduate writing, literature, and small press editing courses at Naropa University's Jack Kerouac School of Disembodied Poetics, where she is also Coordinator of the Summer Writing Program.

Elizabeth Robinson is the author of many collections of poetry, most recently *Blue Heron* (Center for Literary Publishing) and *Counterpart* (Ahsahta). A new hybrid book of essay/memoir/poetry, *On Ghosts*, is just out from Solid Objects.

Eleni Sikelianos is the author of the scrapbook-essay *You Animal Machine (The Golden Greek),* among other books.

Bianca Stone is the author of several poetry chapbooks and an ongoing poetry-comic series from Factory Hollow Press. She is the illustrator of *Antigonick*, a collaboration with Anne Carson and her first full-length collection of poetry *Someone Else's Wedding Vows* is forthcoming from Tin House / Octopus Books. She lives in Brooklyn where she runs the small press Monk Books, with poet Ben Pease.

Johanna Skibsrud's most recent book is the novel *Quartet for the End of Time* (W. W. Norton, 2014). She teaches English literature at the University of Arizona.

Peter Streckfus is the author of *Errings*, winner of Fordham University Press's 2013 Poets Out Loud Editor's Prize, and *The Cuckoo*, which won the Yale Series of Younger Poets competition in 2003. He is the 2013–14 Rome Prize Fellow in Literature and on the faculty of the Creative Writing Program at George Mason University.

Cole Swensen is the author of fourteen books of poetry and a volume of critical essays. Recipient of a Guggenheim Fellowship and other awards, such as the Iowa Poetry Prize and the National Poetry Series, she is also a translator and the founding editor of La Presse Poetry.

A former NEA Fellow, **Brian Teare** is the recipient of poetry fellowships from the MacDowell Colony, the Headlands Center for the Arts, and the American Antiquarian Society. He is the author of four books—*The Room Where I Was Born*, *Sight Map*, the Lambda Award–winning *Pleasure*, and *Companion Grasses*. He's also published seven chapbooks, most recently *Helplessness*, *[black sun crown]*, and *Sore Eros*. An Assistant Professor at Temple University, he lives in Philadelphia, where he makes books by hand for his micropress, Albion Books.

Erika L. Weiberg is a PhD student in Classics at the University of North Carolina at Chapel Hill, where she is completing a dissertation on wives of returning veterans in Greek tragedy. Her research and writing interests include Greek poetry, rhetoric and narrative, and translation.

Joshua Marie Wilkinson is the author of several books of poetry, and he has edited five anthologies of poetry, essays, and conversation. He lives in Tucson, where he runs a journal called *The Volta* and directs a small press called Letter Machine Editions. He is an assistant professor at the University of Arizona.

Andrew Zawacki is the author of the poetry books *Videotape, Petals of Zero Petals of One, Anabranch,* and *By Reason of Breakings.* A former fellow of the Slovenian Writers' Association, he edited *Afterwards: Slovenian Writing 1945–1995* and co-translated Aleš Debeljak's *Without Anesthesia.* His translation of Sébastien Smirou is *My Lorenzo.*